A Star
Is Reborn

GAYNOR & GARLAND & STREISAND & GAGA
THE MOST FILMED HOLLYWOOD STORY OF
LOVE FOUND AND LOST

A Star Is Reborn

ROBERT HOFLER

CITADEL PRESS
Kensington Publishing Corp.
kensingtonbooks.com

CITADEL PRESS BOOKS are published by

Kensington Publishing Corp.
900 Third Avenue
New York, NY 10022

All Kensington titles, imprints, and distributed lines are available at special quantity discounts for bulk purchases for sales promotions, premiums, fundraising, educational, or institutional use. Special book excerpts or customized printings can also be created to fit specific needs. For details, write or phone the office of the Kensington sales manager: Kensington Publishing Corp., 900 Third Avenue, New York, NY 10022, attn Sales Department; phone 1-800-221-2647.

10 9 8 7 6 5 4 3 2 1

First Citadel hardcover printing: February 2026

Printed in the United States of America

ISBN: 978-0-8065-4438-0

ISBN: 978-0-8065-4440-3 (e-book)

Library of Congress Control Number: 2025945766

The authorized representative in the EU for product safety and compliance is eucomply OU, Parnu mnt 139b-14, Apt 123, Tallinn, Berlin 11317; hello@eucompliancepartner.com

To the memory of Stephen M. Silverman

Introduction

Once Upon a Time in Hollywood

The hard facts that birthed all the movies titled *A Star Is Born* played out in real life with far more drama and damnation than the fiction up there on the screen.

Whether the movie couple is Lady Gaga and Bradley Cooper or Barbra Streisand and Kris Kristofferson or Judy Garland and James Mason or Janet Gaynor and Fredric March or Constance Bennett and Lowell Sherman, none of them ever captures the toxic mix of public glamour and domestic terror that were the real-life marriages of the famous couples who inspired Hollywood's most filmed story of love found and man destroyed. When it comes to remakes, only *King Kong* rivals *A Star Is Born* in the category of narratives born at the movies. Among love stories, *Romeo and Juliet* came from the theater over 400 years ago; among horror classics, *Dracula* and *Frankenstein* began as nineteenth-century novels. *A Star Is Born* remains, by far, Hollywood's favorite homegrown source material.

It was the silent film star Colleen Moore and her turbulent seven-year marriage to John McCormick that established the prototype of the successful older man who falls in love with a younger woman and single-handedly turns her into a movie star, only to see his own fame and power plummet just as hers ascends with inverse alacrity. In the 1920s, McCormick earned a salary of $100,000 a year as a top film executive—until he succumbed to chronic alcoholism, making substance abuse a hallmark of all the *A Star Is Born* movies. Equally dark, McCormick's marriage to Moore put into dramatic display how, when two careers in show business move in opposite directions, it is the woman who must subjugate her own name and identity to protect his name and legacy, even in death. The final and most famous line from the first two films titled *A Star Is Born* makes it clear: "Hello, everybody! This is Mrs. Norman Maine."

The makers of the 1976 and 2018 versions of *A Star Is Born* jiggered that line but never completely abandoned its sentiment and ethos, because the element of female sacrifice is central to the story, no matter how much Barbra Streisand ballyhooed that each film in the series offers a "stronger" female character. Her statement is far from true. None of the five female characters is ever more vulnerable, damaged, and unsure of herself than Judy Garland's Esther Blodgett (a.k.a. Vicki Lester), and none is more confident, resilient, and aware of the fleeting vapors of fame than Constance Bennett's Mary Evans in the 1932 film that started it all, *What Price Hollywood?*, directed by George Cukor, who also brought the Garland remake to the screen.

Cukor once described Bennett as having "a kind of romantic, F.-Scott-Fitzgerald look about her. It was the look of the 1930s—or perhaps the 1930s looked like her." It was one more example of life and art reflecting each other in Hollywood's dark hall of projectors.

"She was like some silvery comet who streaked through life with daring speed," actress Joan Bennett said of her older, richer, blonder, and much tougher sister. During the making of *What Price Hollywood?* at RKO Pictures, agent Myron Selznick got Constance Bennett a pay upgrade to $30,000 a week for her new contract at a rival studio, Warner Brothers. That deal made her the highest-paid person, male or female, in Hollywood. She supplemented that income by being, in her own words, "the best femme poker player in the country."

The actress could afford spending a quarter million dollars on clothes, whether or not she ever did. When newspaper critics charged her with such extreme extravagance during the depths of the Depression, Bennett told fellow movie star Marion Davies, "I couldn't spend that kind of money in ten years if I used ermine for toilet paper."

William Randolph Hearst's paramour could sympathize. Davies and Hearst also got hit with accusations of profligate spending while the masses lined up at soup kitchens. When it came to glittering party venues for Hollywood's elite, only Hearst's San Simeon castle up the California coast could rival Bennett's twenty-two-room estate in Holmby Hills, the exclusive neighborhood that formed the Platinum Triangle with Bel-Air and Beverly Hills. The manse was so grand that when Bennett wanted it surrounded by a veritable forest, she didn't wait for the trees to grow. She planted fully mature elms and oaks.

It didn't look good for a businessman like Hearst to spend that kind of money on champagne and caviar, much less trees. It was absolutely forbidden for a woman like Bennett to throw it around, especially at a time when 25 percent of Americans were out of work. Legendary film critic Pauline Kael once lamented that even Bette Davis, the strongest of all film actresses, had to kneel at the altar of male superiority in the final reel, whether she was playing a fiery Southern debutante in *Jezebel* or a fiery Broadway diva in *All About Eve*. Bennett delivered her greatest acting in the final reel of *What Price Hollywood?* when her fiery movie star character reunites submissively with her estranged and very wealthy husband. It's great acting because Bennett never did such a thing, and that included attaching the title of "Mrs." to her husband's name, even when that man was husband number three: Henry de La Falaise, Marquis de La Coudraye.

George Cukor liked the actress immensely. "Connie Bennett was intelligent, tough, realistic," said her favorite director.

Many men in America felt differently. While Cukor's and Bennett's movie *What Price Hollywood?* took up residence in movie theaters around the country, Franklin Delano Roosevelt traveled America to defeat Herbert Hoover to become the thirty-second president of the United States. In campaign speech after campaign speech, Roosevelt spoke of "the forgotten man at the bottom of the economic pyramid." More than a few reactionary voters believed that newly liberated women like Constance Bennett played a major role in taking away those jobs from men.

Women having to subjugate themselves even further to the opposite sex would be the greatest appeal of turning *What Price Hollywood?* into *A Star Is Born* only five years later. In the battle of the sexes, the winner is never more evident than when its female heroine, Vicki Lester, says, "Hello, everybody! This is Mrs. Norman Maine." Bennett's Mary Evans may remarry her ex-husband after the movie ends, but she never lets him dominate her by taking his name, even in death. Only "Frankly, my dear, I don't give a damn" from *Gone with the Wind*, released two years later, comes close to making the pecking order of the two sexes more distinct. The one line is lifted from a best-selling novel, the other completely original to the movies.

The ritual where the woman casts off her last name and takes her husband's is as old as the institution of marriage itself. Hollywood in 1927 gave it a novel twist. Only the year before had the *Exhibitor's Herald* held its annual poll of over 2,500 theater owners, and they voted a brunette pixie named Colleen Moore the number one box office attraction in the country. Bigger than Pickford; bigger than Fairbanks; bigger than Chaplin; bigger than Valentino, who had the publicity advantage of having expired from a ruptured gastric ulcer only a few months earlier, Moore repeated this popularity feat with movie exhibitors the following year—none of which prevented her from burying her celebrity under the precarious bushel of her producer-husband's job at their home studio, First National Pictures. She did it to rescue his floundering career in Hollywood.

"This is Mrs. John McCormick," the actress said by way of introduction. That cross-country phone conversation put another, much deeper fissure in the Continental Divide. The timing was crucial. Moore phoned Richard Rowland in the studio's New York office only days, maybe hours, before he could bring down the axe on her husband. "I just called to say hello," she added.

Not a stupid man, Rowland knew instinctively that "just" wasn't the half of it. He got the full message: The movie boss had every reason to fire McCormick, an increasingly incompetent drunk in his job as head of production. Moore made it clear with her phone call that if McCormick were fired, she, Hollywood's top box office attraction two years running, would not renew her contract with First National.

The Moore-McCormick union had not been a happy marriage from the get-go, the first major sign of discontent being his inability to consummate their union in a timely fashion. "It's our wedding night . . . and I am drunk," he told his brand-new wife before promptly slipping into a deep, vodka-induced coma. It's the kind of intimate detail that made the male character's alcoholism and substance abuse his tragic flaw in all the *A Star Is Born* films. Failure to perform, if not impotence itself, haunts the male character as early as the first reel of *What Price Hollywood?*. Famed film director Max Carey, played by Lowell Sherman, wakes up in his bed alone, and his date, Mary Evans, wakes up alone downstairs on his living room couch. In the film, the two have met only the night before, when, in a Cinderella moment of drunken pique, he invites the young waitress, who has served him drinks but not much food at the Brown Derby, to be his date within the hour at Grauman's Chinese Theatre for the dazzling premiere of his newest movie opus.

What Colleen Moore and John McCormick are to *What Price Hollywood?* is what Frank Fay and Barbara Stanwyck are to the first *A Star Is Born* film, which went into production only one year after the Fays' nasty divorce in 1935. Both women were stars, and both men were enormously successful until alcoholism upended their respective careers. It is possible Moore and Stanwyck would have become stars without the help of their respective first husbands. The central fact of *What Price Hollywood?* and the four films titled *A Star Is Born* is that both McCormick and Fay played their parts, and Hollywood's screenwriters were there to turn those two husbands' influence, major or minor, into an alternate celluloid legend that reeked of the truth.

In 1930, Fay was the star, not Stanwyck. A big name in vaudeville and on Broadway, he signed a contract with Columbia Pictures that year and tried to get Harry Cohn to sign his actress-wife too. Fay nearly turned his offer into a bribe. "You take up the option and I'll not only pay her salary, I'll pay half the production cost," he told the studio head. Fay hadn't always been so considerate, having forced his two previous wives to give up their careers in show business. However, like Mary Evans in *What Price Holly-*

wood? and Vicki Lester in the first *A Star Is Born*, Stanwyck was a very determined young woman.

A similar dynamic played out between McCormick and Moore, even before they got married. In his job at First National Pictures, he propelled her to the top echelon of movie stars when he lobbied hard for his fiancée to be the movies' first flapper in 1923. Flitting around somewhere between vamp and virgin, the flapper sprang like Venus from a Woolworth's dime-store catalog in Samuel Hopkins Adams's best-selling novel, *Flaming Youth*, a work so incendiary that Adams, a muckraking but respected journalist who helped get the Pure Food and Drug Act passed in 1906, published the book under the purple nom de plume Warner Fabian.

Even decades later, *Playboy* magazine remembered the star of *Flaming Youth*: "This slapdash disregard for convention symbolized the kind of girl whose spirit was free and who was willing to kick up her spiked heels in the uninhibited pursuit of pleasure. Colleen Moore helped give a name to a new generation in 1923. She made *Flaming Youth*. Overnight she was a flaming star."

The movies might not also have discovered Stanwyck without Fay pushing his third wife, seventeen years his junior. She reluctantly gave up her promising career on Broadway to migrate with him to Hollywood. Fay, despite earning over $17,000 a week on stage, thought there might be more money to be made in the movies. In the beginning, he lobbied to get Stanwyck a contract at Columbia Pictures. His little nudge turned into a rocket thrust when her films quickly eclipsed his in both popularity and quality, not to mention the sheer number of them. Stanwyck cranked out five films in 1931 and an equal number the following year, most of them major box office hits.

One of Stanwyck's early directors described her special magic on-screen. "When she turns it on, everything else stops," opined Frank Capra, who directed her in no fewer than four films in the early 1930s: *Forbidden*, *The Bitter Tea of General Yen*, *Ladies of Leisure*, and *The Miracle Woman*.

Amid such hectic screen activity, Stanwyck abruptly declared "screen retirement," according to *The Hollywood Reporter*, when she "failed to put in an appearance" on *Forbidden*. Trouble at home with a jealous husband rendered her booming career nearly impossible as his movies failed to perform at the box office. (Or was the actress wrangling for more than $2,000 a week at Columbia Pictures?) By 1933, Fay saw no features movies in release and found himself already back on the vaudeville stage, where his increasingly lackluster comedy routine, now seriously dimmed by his chronic drinking and frequent absences, needed the added attraction of his famous movie star wife. Stanwyck dutifully played straight man on stage to his no-longer-alpha comic. Their lopsided fame nearly created an earthquake of bad press in Hollywood. Louella Parsons took quick note, and on the subject of how Fay took advantage of Stanwyck, the gossip wrote in her *Los Angeles Examiner* column:

> *This town of supreme sophistication and hardboiled philosophy has been busy analyzing the Barbara Stanwyck case. A scattered few think it just sweet that Barbara is willing to give up a flourishing career for her husband. The more thoughtful, practical souls are frankly worried over the future of the little red-haired girl who is so content to bask in the shadow of Frank Fay's fame. . . . From all I gather, it is Barbara who is making all the sacrifices.*

As lousy alcoholic husbands go, Frank Fay gave John McCormick a good name. Ralph Bellamy, Stanwyck's costar in *Forbidden*, called her husband "a very unpopular guy—he worked at it." According to the American Vaudeville Museum, Fay was "dismissive and unpleasant, and he was disliked by most of his contemporaries."

Even in the worst moments of their marriage, and there were more bad than good, Stanwyck never failed to credit her husband. "Everything I know of etiquette, books and art and people and the world around me was nothing until Fay came along," she said, "and I would have been nothing a great deal longer if he had never come along." She also borrowed from the Colleen Moore playbook. "I am Mrs. Frank Fay first and Barbara Stanwyck second," she often said, even though her own name opened more doors, and faster. It's a factoid that worked its way into the first *A Star Is Born* film, directed by the actress's close friend William A. Wellman, who also co-wrote the original screenplay when the film was still being titled *It Happened in Hollywood*.

Over the years, the *A Star Is Born* franchise has depended on regular injections of real-life soap opera to keep it current. Beyond the world of Hollywood that informed the first two films, released in 1937 and 1954, the rock and roll deaths of Janis Joplin, Jimi Hendrix, and Jim Morrison in the early 1970s continue to echo in Kris Kristofferson's underrated performance in the 1976 remake. A more violent death of a rocker made its way into the 2018 version of *A Star Is Born*. Bradley Cooper, its director and star, had originally intended the male lead character to take his life by drowning, the means of self-destruction used in the first two *A Star Is Born* films. Then, during filming, Cooper changed it to death by hanging when Chris Cornell committed suicide on May 18, 2017. The grunge star hanged himself in a Detroit hotel room only hours after performing at the city's Fox Theatre.

The Judy Garland and Barbra Streisand versions of *A*

Star Is Born brought other dynamics into play, ones that took place behind the scenes. In a reversal of the female star being born from the rib of her male lover, professional gambler and B-picture movie producer Sid Luft used his wife's comeback vehicle to produce his first (and only) major motion picture, *A Star Is Born*, starring Garland in 1954. Two decades later, Beverly Hills hairdresser Jon Peters used his famous girlfriend's enormous box office clout to produce his first major motion picture, *A Star Is Born*, starring Streisand in 1976.

Both films, rather than duplicating the star-is-born legend, took a world-famous actress-singer and reinvented her for consumption by their respective movie audiences: Garland played her most dramatic role onscreen after she attempted suicide, endured electroshock treatments, and spent four years off the screen, and as for Streisand, she was finally not "playing Ray Stark's mother-in-law" yet again, as Peters so ruefully described her Fanny Brice impersonations in *Funny Girl* and *Funny Lady*, which tanked at the box office in 1975.

Finally, in 2018, Lady Gaga became the first actress to use the vehicle as a real star-is-born film debut, and while Bradley Cooper never brought the nothing-but-the-warts portrayal of his real-life counterparts John McCormick and Frank Fay to the screen, to his credit, he closely matched the unsentimental portrayal of a faded and floundering talent that Lowell Sherman delivered with his soused, destitute, and ultimately self-destructive star-maker in *What Price Hollywood?*.

Part One

"I'm Mrs. Norman Maine."

Chapter 1

In his seminal biography on producer David O. Selznick, *Showman*, critic David Thomson called *What Price Hollywood?* "the toughest, the funniest, and the most interesting" of all those Hollywood-themed movies.

The director of that 1932 film gave full credit to Selznick for its success. "Largely through David's influence, we didn't kid the basic idea of Hollywood," George Cukor said. "Most of the Hollywood pictures make it a kind of crazy, kooky place, but to David it was absolutely real; he believed in it."

Not by coincidence, Selznick also went on to produce the first *A Star Is Born* film, in 1937, and much of what is "absolutely real" about it came from the very knowledgeable people whom this wunderkind filmmaker hired to write that screenplay, as well as its parent film, *What Price Hollywood?* Selznick's cadre of writers included Dorothy Parker, Budd Schulberg, Adela Rogers St. Johns, and William A. Wellman, all of whom witnessed firsthand the cataclysmic and often tragic consequences of Hollywood's transition from silent to sound films.

Wellman considered Barbara Stanwyck a close friend, having already directed three of her films before receiving the assignment both to write and direct *A Star Is Born*. Colleen Moore and writer Adela Rogers St. Johns were more than close; they repeatedly spoke of each other as best friends. The actress dedicated her memoir, *Silent Star*, to Rogers St. Johns, calling the journalist "my friend and mentor since my first days in Hollywood." The writer returned the favor and showed real dedication by never putting her byline on a profile of the movie star (until long after Moore had retired). It was quite a sacrifice, because Rogers St. Johns relished in being called "the Mother Confessor of Hollywood," thanks to all the silver-screen sob stories she put into print at *The Saturday Evening Post*, *Photoplay*, and other national magazines.

Profiles with real names were one thing, a movie roman à clef quite another, and Rogers St. Johns, then working in the story department at RKO Pictures for $1,000 a week, convinced boss David O. Selznick that her short story, "The Truth about Hollywood," possessed enough real facts commingling with her ripe and melodramatic fiction to make a great movie.

Selznick briefly considered using the title of Rogers St. Johns's short story for the movie, as well as the far more lurid *The World, the Flesh, and the Movies*. He ultimately settled on *What Price Hollywood?* Selznick insisted the film be "authentic," a word that Bradley Cooper turned into a mantra during the production of his 2018 remake. In fact, *What Price Hollywood?* is more than authentic. It's downright scabrous in its portrait of the corrosive effects of stardom not only on the individual but also the American culture at large. In his Selznick biography, Thomson praises the film but derides the "sentimentality" of the first *A Star Is Born* movie, his major criticism being the burned-out male star named Norman Maine who commits suicide to save his wife's burgeoning career, which is the story of all the *Star* movies. *What Price Hollywood?* avoids any accusations of sentimentality from Thomson because it tells the same story but with an important difference: the once-famous film director Max Carey takes his own life, but instead of it being an act of self-sacrifice, which Thomson found phony, the suicide by gunshot erupts as a major tabloid spectacle that nearly destroys the successful film career of his protégée, actress Mary Evans, played by Constance Bennett.

Rogers St. Johns knew this basic story by heart, having essentially refashioned it from her 1923 *Good Housekeeping* short story, "A Hollywood Love Story." As she told it, stars weren't born. "It is a long and difficult process to make a star," Rogers St. Johns wrote. The studio chief in her short story has but one goal: "For five years, everything in Dave Palacky's great business had been subordinate to the making of Irene Wakefield. The youngest grip on the lot knew that."

Two years later, Rogers St. Johns turned that same scenario into her first novel, *The Skyrocket*, about an actress who defies the edicts of the diabolical studio chief, now named William Dvorak, who takes complete credit for making her a movie star. The actress, now named Sharon Kimm, commits the mortal sin of falling in love with her handsome leading man instead of Dvorak. Despite its elements of soap opera, *The Skyrocket* expresses a modern view of the career woman, especially when Sharon Kimm tells her actor-lover, "Don't spoil it all. I promised [studio president] Mr. Dvorak I would not get married. It would ruin everything for me. . . . You wouldn't ask me to sacrifice this wonderful thing that's happened to me, that most girls would give their souls for? . . . I'm going to be a great star!"

The Hollywood bona fides of the young Adela Rogers

could not have been stronger. She was born there, graduated from Hollywood High on the corner of Highland Avenue and Sunset Boulevard, and married Ivan St. Johns, her editor-boss at the legendary fan magazine *Photoplay*, in 1914. That was the glitz. Underneath, she knew the grist of the town's seamy underbelly since her father was the celebrated (and chronically alcoholic) trial defense lawyer Earl Rogers, who handled seventy-seven murder cases in Los Angeles and lost only three. With such a spectacular track record, fiction writers like Erle Stanley Gardner took notice, using Rogers as his prototype for the Perry Mason character in over eighty pulp novels.

For writers all over America, that was the wonderful thing about the little town called Hollywood. The facts kept bubbling up like sludge in the La Brea Tar Pits to create wonderfully noxious stories that practically wrote themselves. The only thing writers had to do was change names and call the story their own. One of those toilers in the Hollywood swamp was the man who would go on to write *What Makes Sammy Run?* and *On the Waterfront*. Like Rogers St. Johns, Budd Schulberg also grew up in Hollywood and cut his screenwriter teeth on the first *A Star Is Born* movie. His path often crossed that of Adela and her famous trial-lawyer dad, and he wrote about them, revealing that "she had been raised in knowledge of what the real world of homicide and grand larceny was all about. Accordingly, when she wrapped her stories in tinsel and fan magazine gush, she knew what she was prettying."

Rogers St. Johns accomplished just that with "A Hollywood Love Story" and *The Skyrocket*. Who cared that the novel had been made into a silent film starring Peggy Hopkins Joyce, less famous as an actress than as the divorcée of a few multimillionaires? From those many rich ex-husbands, Hopkins acquired enough alimony money to purchase the Portuguese Diamond, among other expensive trinkets that inspired both Cole Porter and Irving Berlin to write songs about her. Despite such a gloriously tawdry backstory, the movie version of *The Skyrocket* tanked at the box office, and nothing escapes the memory faster in Hollywood than a movie that loses money. Rogers St. Johns, always industrious, took her original triangle of an actress, an actor, and a jealous producer from "A Hollywood Story" and *The Skyrocket* and dumped it into a chaser with the unfortunate and recently dissolved marriage of her best friend, Colleen Moore.

That movie treatment—after a raft of other writers (Jane Murfin, along with Rogers St. Johns, received an Oscar nomination for best original story) worked it into a screenplay—became *What Price Hollywood?* Selznick put it into production in 1931, his first year at RKO, where, within his remarkably short tenure there (a mere eighteen months), he also managed to crank out such hits as Katharine Hepburn's debut vehicle, *A Bill of Divorcement*, and the only A-list film original to the movies that has ever come close to being remade more than *A Star Is Born*, Merian C. Cooper's horror masterpiece *King Kong*.

There were enough major departures from Moore's disastrous marriage to John McCormick in the screenplay to avoid a lawsuit or, more important, damage the actress's friendship with Rogers St. Johns. Most significant, the young Brown Derby waitress named Mary Evans who is discovered by the film director Max Carey is not the man she loves and marries in *What Price Hollywood?* Mary's romance with a millionaire polo player named Lonny Borden, played by Neil Hamilton, is the film's secondary plot, and the two storylines cross only when Max becomes resentful of Lonny's influence over Mary on the set of the last movie they make together. That two-man battle over the attention of a famous woman plays out in a newspaper gossip column titled "You Ask Me." In one of those blind items, it is announced, "What movie director is burned up over the marriage of his favorite star to an Eastern millionaire?" In another, the column's anonymous writer asks, "What director who discovered a famous blond star had a little argument with her brand-new husband when he visited the set?"

Where Rogers St. Johns's story borrows from the Moore-McCormick marriage is the husband's determination to make his wife a star, and, later, his erosion from alcohol as her career takes off and his implodes. Back in the early 1920s, Moore's career, after getting its start with no less a talent than D. W. Griffith, maker of *The Birth of a Nation*, had begun to languish in a series of dreary costume epics at First National Pictures. When McCormick fell in love with Moore, he showed his affection by radically goosing her stalled career. Rogers St. Johns reported, "From the time they met, John's campaign to help Colleen achieve stardom was persistent and brilliant."

McCormick saw *Flaming Youth* as the way to jolt Moore's career. For her part, Moore also showed more gumption in real life than her screen doppelgängers, most notably Judy Garland and Lady Gaga. Knowing just how much McCormick wanted to marry her, Moore told him in no uncertain terms, "Get that part for me for a wedding present, or else." He did as told, and *Flaming Youth* turned out to be as spectacularly momentous as any of the break-through films or rock concerts depicted in the four films titled *A Star Is Born*.

As Rogers St. Johns described it, "The Modern Girl as we know her was born into the twentieth century the night *Flaming Youth*, starring Colleen Moore, opened in 1923 to madly cheering audiences. No girl had ever appeared on the screen with straight hair, bangs, and boyish figure."

In some ways, the flapper wasn't all that removed visually from the stage performance that inspired Colleen

Moore (née Kathleen Morrison) to be an actress in the first place. As a child, she had seen Maude Adams in *Peter Pan*—and out the school door went little Kathleen's ambition to teach little kids to read and write.

Moore put her overnight success as a new sex symbol in uncommonly self-deprecating terms. "Any plain Jane could become a flapper," she wrote, describing her new radical look as "a Japanese girl's haircut." A pair of scissors made all the difference. "I felt as if I'd been emancipated."

She managed to express some gratitude to McCormick's influence, if not to the man himself. "Never had I been so happy in a movie role before. I loved every scene," she reported. "After six years of treacle, it's heaven to be given a little spice."

Rogers St. Johns gave a lot more credit to her best friend's husband. She even went so far as to mention him by name. "John continued to handle all Colleen's contracts, selected her stories, supervised her publicity, personally produced her pictures," Rogers St. Johns wrote.

McCormick also had his own fan club in the Hollywood press. For his "Movie Chat" column in *Olean Times*, Dan Thomas wrote, "John McCormick . . . is famous for three reasons: first, because he has given a 'break' to more beginners than almost any other man in the picture industry; second, because he is one of filmland's leading executives; and third, because his wife is the more than charming Colleen Moore."

McCormick handled his wife's career much better than he handled their marriage—in the beginning. Eventually, his drinking, temper, and insatiable ego took its toll on her career as well. The first sign of his decline came when, attending one of Moore's movie premieres, he accepted her fans' adulation as if intended for him. That penchant for soaking up his wife's applause became so infamous in Hollywood circles that it surfaced in the first *A Star Is Born* when Fredric March's Norman Maine accepts the ovation intended for the orchestra conductor at the mammoth Hollywood Bowl. His female date chastises him, "Sit down, you dope! That's for the orchestra leader."

More egregiously harmful to his wife's career was Mc-Cormick's deliberate negligence regarding January 11, 1927. Hollywood's greatest stars and executives gathered that night at the Ambassador Hotel in Los Angeles to create an organization that came to be the Academy of Motion Picture Arts and Sciences. Moore, the most popular star in the industry, received an invitation, of course. Mc-Cormick handled all her business matters, unfortunately, and purposefully failed to show her that invitation. As the actress's biographer Jeff Codori reported, "It was Colleen who was the big shot of the pair. John did not want to face the most powerful Hollywood personalities under those circumstances."

Rogers St. Johns fashioned that real-life episode into a scene where Mary Evans in *What Price Hollywood?* wins an award but the thrill vaporizes when she receives news that Max Carey, now out of work, has been arrested for writing bad checks. He needs her to bail him out of jail.

It's a moment that all the *A Star Is Born* films dramatize far more acutely—first by Fredric March accidentally slapping Janet Gaynor at the Oscars, then James Mason doing the same to Judy Garland, then Kris Kristofferson rudely and drunkenly interrupting Barbra Streisand's acceptance speech at the Grammys, and then the ultimate humiliation, Lady Gaga having to pull her Gucci gown in front of Bradley Cooper on the Grammy stage as he urinates in his beige trousers.

Movie audiences were not ready to see a marriage as scabrous as Moore and McCormick's on the screen in 1932. (They had to wait until 1966 when Elizabeth Taylor and Richard Burton starred in the film version of *Who's*

Afraid of Virginia Woolf?.) *What Price Hollywood?* pickled the rancid nature of the Moore-McCormick relationship but gave its toxicity to Mary Evans and Max Carey's doomed friendship and working relationship. Her falling in love with and marrying playboy Lonny Borden keeps the movie's romance untarnished—except for the many speed bumps of her all-consuming movie career on that marriage.

Unlike the rapid decline of the fictional Max Carey, John McCormick put up a fierce battle to keep his chronic alcoholism under wraps and remain a vital force in Hollywood. As his fortunes began to sink there, McCormick brazenly used his wife's enormous fame to leave First National and sign with Warner Brothers. He was only half successful in that ploy. McCormick negotiated with Jack Warner for Moore to sign a contract at $15,000 a week. In the end, McCormick rejected the deal because the contract did not include his services. Warner wanted nothing to do with the incompetent drunk.

Like Max Carey in *What Price Hollywood?*, McCormick never stopped obsessing over the woman he believed he made a star. In her memoir, Moore gave her husband shades of both Norma Desmond and spouse-turned-butler Max von Mayerling from *Sunset Boulevard*. "He ran my films over and over again, obsessed with the idea that Colleen Moore was his creation, telling me I would be nothing without him," Moore wrote. "Colleen Moore was only a part of my life. She was all of his."

McCormick's life did not end in suicide; he did not kill himself like the director in *What Price Hollywood?* or all the male lead characters in the *A Star Is Born* films. That melodramatic detail, however, did lurk around the bedroom door at the Moore-McCormick homestead. It took no imagination for Rogers St. Johns to turn McCormick's threat to kill himself into a plot point in her short story

"The Truth About Hollywood." As McCormick once told Moore, "I almost shot myself this morning when I realized what I'd do to you." Moore recalled, "He pulled a gun out of his pocket and showed it to me." In *What Price Hollywood?*, when the film director can no longer find work, he kills himself by gunshot, a self-inflicted death that would be changed in subsequent movies to drowning (*A Star Is Born*, 1937 and 1954), car accident (*A Star Is Born*, 1976), and hanging (*A Star Is Born*, 2018).

Hollywood is the kind of town that always keeps giving. Rogers St. Johns didn't have to look far to find an example of a famous filmmaker's violent death ruining not one but two stars' careers. On the night of February 2, 1922, director William Desmond Taylor was murdered by gunshot in his house in the affluent Westlake neighborhood in Los Angeles. The last known person to see him alive was his girlfriend, actress Mabel Normand, who dined with him that evening before returning to her own home across town. Taylor had been cooperating with federal prosecutors to help convict drug dealers supplying cocaine to Normand. As if that weren't lurid enough, love letters to Taylor were found on the premises, written not by Normand but the teenager Mary Miles Minter, being groomed by Paramount Pictures to be the next Mary Pickford. The careers of neither Normand nor Minter could survive the deluge of bad publicity that buried the two women when the details of Taylor's murder, which has never been solved, made headlines across the country.

Sometimes facts provide the basis for the fiction, and sometimes the facts only embellish the fiction after it has already been committed to celluloid. On June 2, 1932, a mere three months after the release of *What Price Hollywood?*, the movie-executive husband of Hollywood's biggest sex symbol committed suicide by gunshot. Decades later, Metro-Goldwyn-Mayer (MGM) writer and film producer Samuel Marx wrote a highly speculative exposé regarding the violent death of Paul Bern. Marx believed that Jean Harlow's brand-new husband did not take his own life, as was commonly rumored. Marx theorized that Bern had been murdered by his common-law wife, Dorothy Millette, who, within days of Bern's death, took her own life by jumping from a ferry boat into the Sacramento River. Or, as Marx suggested, had Bern's "ghost wife" been pushed into the water by studio-hired hit men looking to cover up their blonde bombshell star's messy domestic life?

If it sounds farfetched to credit MGM for being stocked with hit men, it should be noted that when Bern's household staff found his dead body, those same maids and butlers didn't call the police. They called MGM, employees of which scoured the Bern home, doing whatever it is lawyers, publicists, and other high-placed apparatchiks do when they come upon a murder scene they want to sanitize. Had Bern committed suicide because he failed to consummate his marriage to Harlow? Or had Bern killed himself to spare Harlow the bad publicity of his being a bigamist? A suicide note found on the premises left the debate open to question. Written to his "Dearest Dear," Bern confessed, "Unfortunately this is the only way to make good the frightful wrong I have done you and to wipe out my abject humiliation. I love you, Paul." A postscript added, "You understand that last night was only a comedy."

At MGM, Louis B. Mayer freaked. Fearing bad publicity, he asked Tallulah Bankhead to replace Harlow in *Red Dust*, then in production with Clark Gable. Tallulah had other ideas. "To damn the radiant Jean for the misfortune of another would be one of the shabbiest acts of all time," Bankhead wrote. "I told Mr. Mayer as much."

In the end, the public didn't care if the "comedy" were his impotence or Millette's sudden appearance at the cou-

ple's home on that fateful "last night." Only one thing
mattered: Bern had sacrificed himself to spare his wife the
shame of a sex scandal. It's yet another case of a much
older man using his influence to help make a young woman
a star and then taking his life when his transgressions
threatened her celebrity. At the time of his death, the forty-
two-year-old Bern worked as assistant to Irving Thalberg,
the boy wonder of MGM, and Bern left behind a twenty-
one-year-old widow, Jean Harlow, more popular than ever
when *Red Dust* became her most successful film to date.

Although David Thomson objects to the "sentimentality" of the suicide that's crucial to the survival of the
woman's career in all the *A Star Is Born* movies, Paul Bern
can be seen as the missing link between those four titles
and *What Price Hollywood?* By taking his own life, Bern
ties the suicide to the romance, and yes, it is very "senti-
mental," as Thomson put it in his *Showman* biography.
But since when does a little schmaltz ever cause moviegoers to stay away in droves?

Chapter 2

William A. Wellman claimed that the fictional suicide in *A Star Is Born* came from a real Hollywood tragedy, one that starred a silent film actor who could no longer find work after the advent of sound.

John Bowers appeared in nearly a hundred movies in a little over a decade before he found himself reduced to accepting a few uncredited bit parts in Zane Grey Westerns directed by his friend Henry Hathaway. Upon hearing that Hathaway was at work on *Souls at Sea*, a big-budget film starring Gary Cooper at the height of his fame, Bowers tried to visit his director-friend on location on the island of Santa Catalina. Cheap little Westerns were one thing, a big Gary Cooper movie quite another, and when Bowers discovered that Hathaway had already fully cast the film epic, he promptly drowned himself in the Pacific Ocean. His body was found days later and miles away on the beaches of Santa Monica, on November 17, 1936.

Wellman remembered the actor, whom he said "had a bad voice, a John Gilbert–bad voice, and when he went into talk [before the cameras], they said he was through [in the movies]." Skipping over the seven years between the advent of sound and the actor's suicide, Wellman employed even more dramatic condensation to describe the drowning. As he told the story, "Bowers just took his shoes off and his bathrobe and swam out into the ocean—committed suicide." Actually, Bowers took the time to rent a boat first. The actor often said he wanted to "sail into the setting sun," and that's just what he did one last time.

Wellman never gave himself enough credit for his own abilities as a creator of fiction. He had already turned in a polished draft of *It Happened in Hollywood* that summer to David O. Selznick, a few months *before* the Bowers suicide. Together with Robert Carson, Wellman had only been working for a year on the screenplay at another studio, MGM, where "they didn't like it at all," Wellman recalled.

Myron Selznick, an agent who handled most of the big talent in Hollywood, negotiated for Wellman and Carson to leave MGM and move a few blocks east to his younger brother's new studio, Selznick International in Culver City. "He was the greatest agent of them all," Wellman said of the older, nastier, and more inebriated Selznick brother.

Unfortunately, David O. Selznick was no more receptive to the two screenwriters' Hollywood romantic tragedy than was Louis B. Mayer. According to Wellman, Selznick told him, "No, Bill, I don't like it. I'm sorry."

Instead of tearing up the script, Wellman went to Selznick's wife, who, in the small town that is Hollywood, was the daughter of Louis B. Mayer. He told her the story of his script, "and she went crazy about it," Wellman claimed.

Irene Mayer Selznick, for her part, told another story. She insisted that Wellman "never told me a story in his whole life. We had nothing in common. He was a terror." She insisted that her husband's second Hollywood movie had everything to do with her, not Wellman. The birth of *A Star Is Born* came about "because I nagged and nagged and nagged. . . . Out of the nagging came a lot of stories," she reported.

In her opinion, her husband's first film about the movies "wasn't right." George Cukor agreed with Irene on that point. He had fought to keep *What Price Hollywood?* focused on the actress Mary Evans and her Svengali director Max Carey, but Selznick wanted the romance between Mary and her husband, Lonny, to carry equal weight. Only later did Selznick come to regret that decision, hence the need to "get it right" with *A Star Is Born*. His wife's nagging may have played its part, but no amount of grousing produces a script—and neither does writing a ton of memos. Selznick thought himself a writer, and while his obsession with cranking out memos is legendary (a fraction of the thousands he "wrote" fill a 640-page posthumously published book, *Memo from David O. Selznick*), many of them were dictated. He never possessed the requisite patience, thanks in part to his addiction to Benzedrine, to sit down and write an eighty-page script. He was unquestionably a genius when it came to throwing out ideas, however.

"*A Star Is Born* is much more my story than Wellman's or Carson's," Selznick said. "I refused to take credit on it simply as a matter of policy. Certainly, Wellman contributed a great deal, but then any director does that on any story. The actual original idea, the storyline, and the vast majority of the story ideas of the scenes themselves are my own."

But a few were not, and an outline or a few dozen ideas jotted down in a memo are not a screenplay, and Wellman and Carson needed to flesh out all of Selznick's ideas. For his part, Wellman said the story of a marriage that goes bad as soon as the wife's career eclipses that of her husband had been based "on things that happened in Hollywood," not what Selznick told him. Some of those "things" happened to his good friend Barbara Stanwyck, and some of those "things" happened to Wellman himself. In the finished 1937 film, when Norman Maine is jailed for drunk driving and is asked if he's the famous movie star, the judge immediately chastises him, "You've come pretty low, haven't you? There isn't a man here who's had the advantages you've had."

Wellman insisted, "Word for word, that happened to me. And all these things were things from memory."

It took more creativity to jump from Wellman's own Oscar humiliation to Vicki Lester being slapped by Norman Maine at the awards ceremony. The director relished coming up with that scene, because he had never forgiven the Academy members for failing to nominate him for best director for his World War I epic, *Wings*. As if that weren't scarring enough, the newly formed Academy also failed to invite him to that celebration on August 1, 1927, at the Hollywood Roosevelt Hotel, when *Wings* became the first film ever to win the best picture award.

One major scene in the first *A Star Is Born* came directly from Selznick, via one of his favorite directors, who was also the man who directed *What Price Hollywood?*

In 1935, when George Cukor began production chores on directing *Camille* with Greta Garbo, he envisioned John Barrymore in the featured role of Baron de Varville, the wealthy patron who financially supports the courtesan Marguerite Gautier before and after her affair with the much younger Armand Duval. At the time, Barrymore attempted to deal with his chronic drinking problem by checking himself into a sanatorium in Culver City. Cukor recalled, "It was an old frame house that called itself a rest home." Visiting his recuperating friend, the director walked into a dark reception area. "The back of it was the dining room, and I noticed something that always strikes me as very shabby and sad: They hadn't taken away the table-cloths, and you knew that they never changed them," he recalled.

When Barrymore finally appeared to greet his visitor, he came accompanied by a large man named Kelly. Cukor had directed Barrymore only four years earlier in *Dinner at Eight*. In that classic film, the actor delivered one of his finest performances, playing an alcoholic and down-on-his-luck stage actor who won't accept a supporting role in a play to help rejuvenate his career in the theater. That plot line was prelude to what happened in that rest home in Culver City. There, Barrymore asked his male nurse, "Can we sit here, Kelly? Nobody's going to come through and disturb us by pretending he's Napoleon."

After Cukor made his pitch, Barrymore rejected the offer to appear in *Camille*. He had no interest in playing a colorless supporting role. He had recently played Mercu-tio in Cukor's *Romeo and Juliet*, starring Norma Shearer and Leslie Howard as two very mature-looking teenage lovers, she being thirty-three years old, he being forty-two. Even though the best friend character is killed halfway through the picture, Mercutio is a splashy role and one written by Shakespeare, the actor's favorite author. Under the careful watch of Kelly, Barrymore spoke grandly to Cukor of his playing lead roles in significant films, roles that never materialized. Before he died of cirrhosis of the liver in 1942 at age sixty, Barrymore went back to playing lead roles but in B-pictures like *Bulldog Drummond's Peril*.

In most respects, the fictitious Norman Maine in all his incarnations is never as caustic as the real Barrymore, who called the movie industry a "goddamned sinkhole of cul-ture."

Cukor told his Barrymore-in-the-sanatorium story to Selznick and Wellman during their preproduction on *A Star Is Born*. "They liked the scene so much, they included it in the picture," Cukor said. In the movie, studio head Oliver Niles, played by Adolphe Menjou, offers a supporting role to Fredric March's Norman Maine, who, out of pride, rejects it. During this visit to the sanatorium, a male nurse nicknamed Cuddles, played by Pat Flaherty, refuses to leave the two men alone in the reception area. The nurse in *A Star Is Born* is every bit as protective of his charge as Kelly was of Barrymore.

Selznick had offered *A Star Is Born* to Cukor, but not wanting to repeat himself, and thinking the project too close in subject matter to *What Price Hollywood?*, the producer's favorite director declined. But, as Cukor observed in the 1950s, "Then, years later, I found myself redoing it." In the 1954 version of *A Star Is Born*, the dialogue is almost verbatim from the 1937 screenplay, right down to Norman Maine calling his male nurse Cuddles, an uncredited role played by a professional wrestler named Henry Kulky.

The sanatorium scene is just one of many Selznick claimed he gave to Wellman and Carson. He also claimed he gave the two screenwriters the picture's arc. He wrote to them, "Suggest looking at what we did in *What Price Hollywood?* with the Bennett character and her husband. We must be awfully careful that the fall of the [male] star won't seem to have started with his marriage. We should plant his faults very early and try getting over the idea that Esther feels she can help him if they are married."

Wellman and Carson excised the polo-playing husband character from *What Price Hollywood?* and, instead, had the female character fall in love with the alcoholic film director, whom they turned into a major movie star. Norman Maine's attraction to Esther Blodgett is love at first sight, a romance so kinetic that the male character could be interpreted as an instant stalker. Again, the two writers borrowed from real life, using John McCormick's quick infatuation with Colleen Moore, when those two met on the dance floor in 1922. According to the actress, he told her after one waltz, "I'm in love with you. When will you marry me?"

Moore took a step or two back. "Call me up in the cold gray dawn and tell me that," she replied.

Only five hours into the following day, McCormick phoned to say, "It's the cold gray dawn, and I love you. When are you going to marry me?"

That kind of only-in-the-movies romantic passion became a feature of all the movies titled *A Star Is Born*, right up to Bradley Cooper's Jackson falling in love with Lady Gaga's Ally in a drag bar after his removal of just one plastic eyebrow from her face.

In Selznick's memo to Wellman and Carson, he also strongly advised, "More important, after the death of her husband, we should keep the idea that she is through, she won't go on, the producer pleads with her to no avail, but then at the very end, we can have some sort of tremendous lift with the grandmother telling her that there are a few people in the world made for more important things— giving her a pep talk on her career and stardom, etc."

Wellman and Carson, not Selznick, came up with "the grandmother" character, and it is Grandma Letti who pushes Esther to leave their small town in North Dakota to go to Hollywood. The old woman's pep talks don't end there. At the end of the movie, Grandma Letti, played by character actress May Robson, encourages the renamed Vicki Lester not to give up her successful career. Again, it's Adela Rogers St. Johns's best friend who provided the prototype with her own grandmother, a well-known colorful old dame about town in the 1920s.

In 1915, when D. W. Griffith offered the fifteen-year-old girl a contract, Colleen Moore's move from Tampa, Florida, to Hollywood had been facilitated by Mrs. Mary Moylan Kelly of Kilkenny, Ireland. At the time, the old woman told her daughter and son-in-law, "Let me go with my granddaughter and no harm will come to her." It would also be Grandma Kelly who objected when Mack Sennett offered the teenage Colleen a contract. "You'll not be a bathing beauty so long as I am with you," Grandma warned her starstruck granddaughter. "If you have to parade around with only half your clothes on to be an actress, I'll be taking you home tomorrow."

One element that Wellman and Carson brought to their script has been repeated in all the remakes of *A Star Is Born*, with few changes. They wrote Norman Maine's refrain to Esther, "Do you mind if I take just one more look?" In each of the four *A Star Is Born* films, a slight variation on the line is repeated at least twice.

"The device is one that Wellman uses often," his biographer Frank T. Thompson wrote. Other repeated lines that the director-writer made hallmarks of his films are "All set?" in *Wings* (1927) and "I promise you!" in *Beau Geste* (1939). Wellman didn't write either of those screenplays, but as Selznick put it, "Certainly Wellman contributed a great deal, but then any director does that on any story."

The line "just one more look" also reflects what Sidney Howard accomplished with his screenplay for *Dodsworth*, arguably the best film released in 1936, the year in which Wellman and Carson worked on their final drafts of *It Happened in Hollywood*. In that William Wyler classic, Walter Huston's automobile mogul repeatedly tells his philandering wife, played by Ruth Chatterton, "Did I remember to tell you today how much I adore you?"

And there is other inspiration for "Do you mind if I take just one more look?" In *What Price Hollywood?*, there are

Max Carey's last words to Mary before he commits suicide: "I just wanted to hear you speak again."

Since Selznick wanted a more unabashedly romantic movie, Wellman and Carson took a comic moment from *What Price Hollywood?* and turned it deadly serious in *A Star Is Born*. When Mary and Lonny marry in *What Price Hollywood?*, they are mobbed by fans outside the church. The vulgar studio boss Julius Saxe, played by Gregory Ratoff, looks to make the most of the event. Rather than obey wedding tradition, he orders her, "Mary, throw the flowers to your fans!" She obliges, only to see the long-stemmed white lilies torn into bits as the crowd fights over the flowers. When the newlyweds try to descend the church steps, those same ravenous fans rip the wedding veil from her head, and in retreat, the bride must be carried back into the church and safety. The groom, not accustomed to such Hollywood pandemonium, is shocked. Julius Saxe, however, remains true to his crass form to bathe in the publicity. "Wasn't that a marvelous wedding?" he asks. "We broke all the house records for this judge! It was terrific! I wish my mother was here!"

That grim but comic moment is turned into a complete horror show in *A Star Is Born*. When Vicki Lester descends the church steps after Norman Maine's funeral, fans mob her, screaming, "Let us see your face!" When a woman snatches away her black veil, Vicki screams in shock mixed with disgust.

Again, it is a fictional scene that first surfaced in real life. When MGM mogul Irving Thalberg died at age thirty-seven, his funeral was held two days later on September 16, 1936, at the Wilshire Boulevard Temple, the oldest Jewish congregation in Los Angeles. Seven thousand spectators gathered to witness an event that featured not only Thalberg's movie star widow, Norma Shearer, but also such A-list ushers as Clark Gable, Fredric March, and playwright Moss Hart, who would go on to write the first re-make of *A Star Is Born*. Even more vulgar than the wedding in *What Price Hollywood?*, the Thalberg funeral sported invitations reading, ADMISSION BY THIS CARD ONLY and a rabbi who considered himself a film critic. In his eulogy, Rabbi Magnin plugged the last movie Shearer and Thalberg made together at MGM, telling the assembled mourners, "The love of Norma Shearer and Irving Thalberg was a love greater than that in the greatest motion picture I have ever seen, *Romeo and Juliet*."

When Shearer walked down the steps of the synagogue on the arm of Louis B. Mayer, the thousands of people gathered there swarmed around the famous widow. One woman in the crowd wanted a better look at Shearer's face and proceeded to grab the black veil from her head.

Chapter 3

Then there was the film's title. David O. Selznick harbored all sorts of qualms about calling the movie *It Happened in Hollywood*. The title brought to mind his previous film *What Price Hollywood?* and RKO Pictures had already made minor legal noises about charging Selznick International with copyright infringement, an accusation that went no further than a few angry letters. More troublesome, Selznick felt the title *It Happened in Hollywood* conveyed an "exposé quality" that would tarnish it in the eyes of the movie-going public. He looked to make an "important, sophisticated" movie. There was also the problem that films with the word "Hollywood" in their title weren't doing well at the box office anymore. In a memo to William A. Wellman, Robert Carson, and others, Selznick wrote, "Our feeling is that Hollywood has become identified with cheap titles of cheap pictures, and this is more true today than ever because *Hollywood Boulevard* has been an outstanding failure as a Paramount quickie, and also because of *Hollywood Hotel*, which Warners are making as a musical and which will probably be released before our picture."

Equally significant, Selznick had endured the recent unpleasant experience of addressing a movie exhibitors convention in Los Angeles. He made the mistake of asking for a show of hands regarding a picture about the movie industry. "Did anyone want to see a movie about Hollywood?" he asked.

Nobody bothered to raise his hand.

Undeterred, Selznick toyed with an inauspicious title, *The Stars Below*, but in the end he much preferred *A Star Is Born* when suggested by the millionaire publisher of the *New York Herald Tribune* who just happened to sit on the board of Selznick International. Despite his East Coast newspaper pedigree, John Hay Whitney knew all about Hollywood. He invested in Technicolor when the new technology was only being used for short films, and he put up $870,000 to help start Selznick's new studio. His movie largesse didn't stop there. When Selznick wanted to buy the options to a couple of best-selling novels, Whitney ponied up a great deal of the money to purchase the movie rights to Daphne du Maurier's *Rebecca* and Margaret Mitchell's *Gone with the Wind*. Thanks to his print background, the publishing mogul also had a way with words and, all on his own, came up with the title *A Star Is Born*. Those four words never appeared in any versions of Wellman and Carson's screenplay *It Happened in Hollywood*.

Excited about the new title, Selznick asked his legal department to do a search to see if any movies or books had already used *A Star Is Born*. As it happened, P. G. Wodehouse recently published a short story with that very title in *American Magazine*. Simultaneously in 1933, the famed humorist published an expanded version of the same story in the British publication *Strand*, where it appeared under the somewhat less catchy "The Rise of Minna Nordstrom." To the relief of everyone at Selznick International, the Wodehouse story—whatever it was being called—bore little resemblance to the plot of the gestating *It Happened in Hollywood* and the soon-to-be retitled *A Star Is Born*.

Wodehouse wrote something as far afield from a romantic tragedy as possible and still be set in Hollywood. His was an absurdist tale about a young woman named Minna Nordstrom, who, with dreams of becoming a movie star, seeks employment as a maid so she can blackmail several of her employers, all of whom just happen to be movie moguls. She threatens to expose the serving of alcoholic beverages in their respective homes during Prohibition. Minna is so successful in her devious exploits that the moguls are forced to band together, merge their studios, give her a contract, rename her Vera Prebble, and relentlessly promote her movies. And so, a star is born.

Selznick knew Wodehouse, who had been writing screenplays for MGM in the early 1930s. "I doubt he will give us any trouble," Selznick reported. Nonetheless, he wanted to get the writer's approval to use *A Star Is Born* even though titles are not subject to copyright laws.

Selznick, indeed, knew Wodehouse very well. The writer gave his unqualified blessing and asked only that he be sent "two tickets to the movie's first preview." Even that insignificant payment proved unnecessary. Since 1934, Wodehouse had been living in France for tax reasons and harbored no intention of returning to America, even to see a movie with his winsome short story title attached to it.

A Star Is Born may be the best movie title ever, one that has the advantage of being not only original to the movies but also a complete sentence. The title offers a strong beginning (someone who is talented but unknown). It suggests a strong second act (someone becomes a big success). Best of all, the ending is completely up in the air (what happens to this person?).

The new title led to an immediate addition to the screenplay's dialogue: When Norman Maine and Vicki Lester sneak out of the theater after her first film is previewed to great acclaim, he tells her, "A star is born." The couple then runs off into the night. The addition of that line and the film's new title first appeared in the script authored by Dorothy Parker, Alan Campbell, and Robert Carson on October 16, 1936. And for the first time, Wellman's name did not appear among those screenwriter credits on the script.

Selznick believed the script needed some "punching up," the reason he brought on Parker and Campbell. The couple, who were recently married, had written a few screenplays together, sometimes uncredited, she being far more famous than he. An original member of the Algonquin Round Table (often nicknamed the Vicious Circle), Parker frequently contributed to *The New Yorker*, where her scabrous short stories and poems solidified her reputation as a wicked wit, who, rather than taking prisoners, lacerated them in print. Campbell, on the other hand, remained an erstwhile actor who struck out in the movies and looked to make the switch to working behind the cameras. It was a big leap facilitated by marrying Parker in 1934. In the beginning, she earned $1,000 a week to his $250 a week. It was never a typical marriage. Parker took pleasure in describing her first husband as being "queer as a billy goat."

Whatever the state of the marriage, the couple's working relationship produced one-liners that would have delighted friends Robert Benchley and Harold Ross at the Algonquin Round Table. Selznick, however, was not Robert Benchley, a best-selling humorist whose career began at the *Harvard Lampoon*, nor was he anything like Harold Ross, who founded and edited *The New Yorker*. What delighted Benchley and Ross sometimes horrified Selznick, whose audience extended far west of Riverside Drive in Manhattan. The filmmaker kept some of Parker and Campbell's wit. The final screenplay's most acerbic dialogue belongs to them, most significantly the scenes with publicist Matt Libby, played by Lionel Stander. If there's a villain in *A Star Is Born*, it is Libby, who hates Norman Maine, the unruly movie star who won't submit to any press maneuvers to improve his image before the moviegoing public. Even after Maine commits suicide by romantically walking into the Pacific Ocean at sunset, Libby celebrates by having a drink at his local bar. When news of the tragedy breaks over the radio, the studio publicist tells the bartender, "First drink of water [Norman Maine] had in twenty years . . . Pardon, how do you wire congratulations to the Pacific Ocean?"

It's pure Parker.

But sometimes she and Campbell punched too hard for what Selznick wanted to achieve, especially regarding the film's central love story. The couple wrote the following scene to go right before Norman's arrest for intoxication. They didn't even bother to type it up. The scene is handwritten and shows Norman accusing Vicki of telling people that he feels sorry for himself. Norman launches into an uncontrolled rant: "You've said it all over town. You've got ev'rybody sayin' 'Poor little girl. She has to do all the work. Because he's through.' That's what you've done."

In the scene, Parker and Campbell allow Vicki to show real anger after being verbally attacked by her husband. "What I've done!" the character screams. "Don't you blame me for that! You've done it to yourself! Because you're weak. Because every time things go wrong with you, you get drunk so you don't have to face them. That's what you've always done. Look at you now! So drunk you don't know what you're doing—and you blame me."

Parker and Campbell wrote directions for Norman to

"stare stupidly at her" but to say nothing. Vicki asks him, "Well, why don't you say something? Why don't you answer me? Answer me! Answer me!" She then slaps Norman repeatedly, "again and again," as the directions indicate. When he doesn't reply, "staring at her humbly," Vicki stops, "aghast at what she has done, all her anger gone. She throws her arms around him." She goes on to beg for his forgiveness.

The scene, which was never filmed, comes close to what Colleen Moore described in her memoir regarding her own frequent tirades against John McCormick. "I hate you, you weak, dumb idiot," she told him. "You're ruining my life and destroying your own career. How long do you think it will be before the New York office hears about your [alcoholic] disappearances. I can't save your job for you forever." However, Moore, unlike the fictitious Vicki Lester, never apologized for her outburst.

Another scene written by Parker and Campbell also got cut, even though Selznick dictated it to them. Most of the *A Star Is Born* films have been more than a little tone-deaf regarding issues of race. In the first remake, Judy Garland's Vicki Lester takes a lampshade from her living room, and to entertain James Mason's unemployed Norman Maine, she pretends to be Chinese in that film's extended "Someone at Last" number. Even Garland's daughter Lorna Luft complains about the scene in her book *A Star Is Born: Judy Garland and the Film that Got Away*, calling it "racially insensitive." In that remake, the song "Lose That Long Face" was originally planned to be sung in blackface by Garland before wiser minds prevailed, and she ended up playing a young street urchin, complete with painted freckles, to deliver the song.

The 1976 remake also has its insensitivities. On stage and in the recording studio, Barbra Streisand's Esther Hoffman is joined by two backup vocalists. The film forgets to name these Black women who perform in the group Esther calls "the Oreos." When the three of them sing together, it recalls that most unusual nightclub scene in Josef von Sternberg's 1931 film *Blonde Venus* where Marlene Dietrich, surrounded by Black chorus girls in full warrior armor, emerges from a gorilla outfit to don a blond Afro and sing "Hot Voodoo." The difference is, von Sternberg is purposefully offering up a comic scene that defines the word "camp." The Oreos are meant to be taken seriously.

For the 1937 *A Star Is Born*, Selznick wanted Parker and Campbell to write a scene in which Norman and Vicki, newly married, try to avoid the press by putting on blackface. They take refuge in a greasy-spoon restaurant where they are served at the counter by an "Aunt Jemima type" character. Although this waitress "eyes them suspiciously," the couple's disguise is only discovered when Norman accidentally wipes off some of the black makeup from his sweaty face.

As Parker and Campbell toiled away, Selznick asked for the contributions of an even more experienced screenwriter to look at the script. John Lee Mahin, among many uncredited efforts, had already achieved significant fame as Clark Gable's and director Victor Fleming's favorite screenwriter, having written such huge hits as *Red Dust*, *Bombshell*, and *Treasure Island*. Selznick worried that *A Star Is Born* was becoming half comedy, half tragedy and didn't know what direction to take the film. Mahin insisted the screenplay must emphasize the tragedy "since it ends in suicide." Mahin's contributions brought an even darker edge to the Norman Maine character.

In Wellman and Carson's original screenplay, Norman Maine is not only an alcoholic but also a chronic gambler. Again, they borrowed from events in the town they knew best: Hollywood titans like Paramount Pictures's B. P. Schulberg thought nothing of throwing away $22,000 in a single poker game. Mahin softened that addiction by having Norman lose only $12,000 at the gambling table in a single evening, much to Esther Blodgett's horror. In one scene, a croupier looks down at his watch, then remarks under his breath, "I wish for one night the sucker would smarten up and go home. I'd like to see how my wife looks in the dark." The Mahin scene, which he signed, was filmed but cut.

Mahin's influence survived elsewhere. He wrote another scene, also signed, that not only made it into the 1937 film but also appears in slightly altered versions in the 1954 and 1976 remakes: Norman Maine, alone at home and unemployed, receives telephone calls from industry insiders who want to speak to his suddenly famous wife, not him. He finds himself involuntarily turned into her secretary. In one conversation, a newspaper columnist asks if Norman can get him an interview "with your wife. I wish you'd fix it for me." He also receives a package from a delivery man, who tells him, "Sign here, Mr. Lester."

When Mahin also didn't give Selznick exactly what he wanted, the producer brought on two writers who were anything but experienced. However, one of them possessed another kind of pedigree. The twenty-two-year-old Budd Schulberg, if not the twenty-one-year-old Ring Lardner Jr., knew Hollywood far better than any of the other writers already at work on the screenplay, William A. Wellman included. Even at his delicate age, Schulberg had witnessed firsthand at home the tragic arc of *A Star Is Born*. When his top-dog father, B. P. Schulberg, lost his job as head of production at a major studio—he coined the slogan "If it's a Paramount picture, it's the best show in town"—Budd watched as his mother, Adeline Jaffe Schulberg, turned herself into one of the most successful agents in town. But first, Ad had to divorce B. P. for having an affair with movie star Sylvia Sidney.

The young Schulberg recalled his parents' big split. "I heard Mother saying, 'I've decided not to depend on Father—for anything,'" he wrote. "'In all these years, he has practically nothing to show for the millions he's earned . . . I don't think he's got a thousand dollars saved—he lives in that dream world of his . . . So, I've decided to go into the agency business.'" The only thing Ad Schulberg left out of this condemnation of her philandering husband were the two other things that made him a precursor to the Norman Maine character: Schulberg was also a chronic drunk and gambler.

The tragic arc of B. P. Schulberg's career mirrored that of Norman Maine's, making the son of the former Paramount Pictures boss a perfect choice to work on the screenplay for *A Star Is Born*. Having lived the movie's story, Budd Schulberg recalled, "I always think of New Year's Day in 1930 when our house was full of people uncorking champagne, [and then] ten years later, after my father had left Paramount, when no one ever called." B. P. was "out of work, on the outside looking in at that stained glass window, and advertising for a job—any job."

Meanwhile, Ad Schulberg only prospered after the divorce. As her illustrious partner in the agency business explained her phenomenal rise, "She was really Hollywood's first lady," said Charles K. Feldman, who went on to produce *A Streetcar Named Desire* and other major films. "In different times, she would have run a major studio."

B. P. and Ad Schulberg's radical contrast in fortunes taught their oldest son a hard lesson about life. "Nothing fails in America like success. And everything that's true about America is doubly, triply true of Hollywood," said Budd Schulberg, the self-proclaimed prince of Hollywood. He carried not only the tragic example of his father's quick demise but also a number of people who had worked for B. P. in the 1920s. They were these once-famous stars and directors who found themselves suddenly and completely forgotten after the advent of sound. Many of them took their own lives.

There was Art Acord, "one of the hundreds of marquee names caught in the switches. He went galloping off into the sunset of total obscurity. . . . Art found himself overcome by a world he thought he had conquered. The off-screen fade-out was suicide," Schulberg reported.

Another tragic figure was Karl Dane. With the end of silent pictures, "Suddenly he wasn't a five-thousand-dollar-a-week talking actor; he was an unemployed ex-actor with a guttural Scandinavian accent. There seemed nothing else to do except put a revolver to his head."

Directors were also vulnerable. Schulberg remembered Tom Forman as "one of Father's favorite directors from those sunny days at the Selig Zoo, [who] grabbed the same one-way ticket when he was declared 'Not Okay for Sound' in a new age of cinematic progress that had turned its back on Tom's silent Preferred Pictures."

Before the Paramount axe fell on his father, the young Schulberg enjoyed spending his Sundays in Malibu and Beverly Hills, hanging out with Hollywood royalty, including David O. Selznick, his future boss.

"That Sunday at Malibu, I was bailed out of my moral dilemma by a timely visit from Dave Selznick. He and Irene—live, loyal friends in those days—had stopped by for tennis, brunch, and local gossip," Schulberg remembered. "When David, ever-curious, ever-working, asked me what I was doing, I told him a story I was outlining."

The nascent screenplay tells the story of a Black cook who lives on a Bel-Air estate where her young son and the white owner's son of the same age are best friends. Despite the close relationship between the two boys, the cook warns her son, "Stay in your own backyard." But the cook's son refuses to listen.

Selznick liked Schulberg's screenplay *Stay in Your Own Backyard* but became distracted with his already in-the-works productions of *A Bill of Divorcement*, *King Kong*, and *What Price Hollywood?*. The screenplay never went before the cameras, but it did land Schulberg a job as a reader in the story department when the movie mogul later opened his own studio, Selznick International.

On the other side of the United States, Ring Lardner Jr. led an equally privileged life. He spent weekends on Long Island, where he and his father, the famed sports columnist Ring Lardner, often visited the home of his *New York World* editor Herbert Swope. It was quite the house. Swope hosted high-profile literati gatherings there, and the estate stood so big and grand that people believed F. Scott Fitzgerald used it to model Daisy Buchanan's East Egg home in *The Great Gatsby*. The young Ring Lardner met and befriended Dorothy Parker at one of those parties. While that connection would be useful later when Parker insisted that Schulberg and Lardner Jr. receive a screenwriter credit on *A Star Is Born*, it was Swope himself who made the introduction that led Selznick to hire the young Ring to be his publicist.

Meanwhile, Schulberg toiled away in the story department, where his job, as he recalled, "involved reading one novel a day and writing a twenty-page synopsis sketching in characters and situations."

Even before their respective tenures at Selznick International, the two young men had already met under most unusual circumstances. Both Schulberg and Lardner attended Moscow State University in the early 1930s, an education that caused both men to bite the silver spoons stuck between their respective teeth. As Lardner put, they were "won over" to the Soviet system, and both men promptly joined the Communist Party upon returning home to America.

Working at Selznick International, the two young Communists harbored ambitions beyond being a reader or a publicist. According to Schulberg, they were given "an undercover chance to work on *A Star Is Born*." Selznick asked for suggestions on the Wellman and Carson script, and the two young men happily obliged. "I worked all night," Schulberg reported, "got some ideas that I thought might do, and kept a seven o'clock appointment—the next evening—in the producer's office. But in some way, word of what I was doing must have gotten out."

Wellman burst into the meeting "sore as the devil," Schulberg recalled. "He said he didn't want a punk like me fooling with the stuff he'd written."

Wellman immediately jumped above his pay grade to fire the two members of The Young Turks. Schulberg happened to be no fonder of the director-writer than was Irene Mayer Selznick, who called Wellman "a shoot-up-the-town fellow, trying to be a great big masculine I-don't-know-what. David had a real weakness for him. I didn't share it."

Schulberg chalked up Wellman's nickname "Wild Bill" to the writer-director being "slightly crazed as a result of a steel plate in his head."

Selznick rehired Schulberg, as well as Lardner, but with the caveat "to be secret about it" regarding their work on *A Star Is Born*. So many different typewriters contributed to the script that Schulberg likened his task to "laying linoleum, different people working on different squares."

Like Parker and Campbell before them, Schulberg and Lardner attempted to give Vicki and Norman's relationship a sharper, harder edge. In a memo to Selznick dated October 23, 1936, only weeks before the movie went before the cameras, the two Moscow State U alums asked to drop the courtroom scene where Norman's arrest leads to his humiliating rebuke by the judge. The two writers wanted to use instead a well-known moment from Colleen Moore and John McCormick's marriage: his attempt to negotiate a new contract for both of them with Warner Brothers, which, at the time, was a less prestigious studio than First National Pictures.

Schulberg and Lardner took that anecdote and wrote a scene where Norman, fired by his studio, holds a meeting at a Poverty Row company. Even there, his fading stardom doesn't in any way impress boss Max Hofburg, until Norman mentions that his movie star wife will join him in his move to Hofburg-Triumph Pictures.

As Schulberg and Lardner explained it in their memo to Selznick, "Our idea has the advantage of keeping the story in motion picture terms—that is, the [car] crash could happen to anyone, while our problem is peculiar [sic] to a falling motion picture star. It also presents the possibility of a comeback to Maine, his successful resistance to which strengthens his sacrifice and gives it something of a lift. In addition, it more or less crystalizes in one scene the conflict between their respective careers an ambitions."

At the time, the film's heroine had not yet been rechristened Vicki Lester. She was still being named Mona Lester, a not-so-subtle play on Mona Lisa.

The new scene takes place at Hofburg-Triumph Pictures, and "Maine winces at the shabbiness of the studio as [he and his agent] go in." When Max Hofburg questions whether Mona Lester will follow her husband to his studio, Norman shoots back, "My dear fellow, you seem to forget that I made Mona Lester." Hofburg barely waits for the actor to leave his office before giving the scoop to Louella Parsons, who promises him a Page One story. Schulberg and Lardner even gave the Hearst gossip columnist some dialogue. "Sure, it's a banner line," Parsons tells Hofburg, " 'independent producer announces Mona Lester co-starred with husband.' "

When the Parsons item appears in her newspaper as promised, a distraught Mona Lester asks her studio chief, Oliver Niles, "What can I do?"

"Something you should have done long ago," Niles tells her. "You must deny this story right away. You've got to say that Norman lied—that from now on, your careers are entirely separate."

Norman overhears the conversation, and even when Niles promises finally to greenlight her dream project—a movie version of *Joan of Arc*—Mona decides to turn her husband's lie into the truth. Otherwise, "It would finish him for good, Oliver." She explains, "I've borrowed too much from life, Oliver. I owe some of it back. I owe it to Norman. This is his chance."

There's only one problem with the new scene, as Selznick saw it. Throughout the rewriting process of *A Star Is Born*, it was crucial, in Selznick's mind, that Norman Maine remain "likable" to audiences. To have the character use his wife's career to further his own fortunes is the antithesis of "likable."

Schulberg and Lardner did use another well-known anecdote lifted from the turbulent Moore-McCormick marriage and turned it on its head to write the film's most famous and, ultimately, most controversial line.

At the end of the 1937 *Star*, when Vicki Lester is introduced on stage shortly after her husband's death, she announces to the public, "Hello, everybody! This is Mrs. Norman Maine," as if to assert her primary identity: being a wife, even if her husband is dead. The line also concludes the 1954 version. In the 1976 remake, it is spoken by an announcer and is softened to "Ladies and gentlemen, Esther Hoffman Howard." In the 2018 remake, Lady Gaga's character introduces herself as "Ally Maine" to the audience before she performs.

In their original screenplay, Wellman and Carson envisioned Vicki Lester returning to her home in North Dakota after Norman's suicide, ready to give up her career. It is Grandma Lettie who insists she return to Hollywood, and Vicki ultimately agrees. The end.

Selznick wasn't satisfied with that finale. He wanted something more "heart grabbing." To achieve the necessary emotional response, Schulberg and Lardner delivered a series of final scenes, each of which takes a small step toward what was finally performed and filmed. In an early draft of their finale, unlike the original treatment by Wellman and Carson, Lester returns to Hollywood for her latest movie premiere at Grauman's Chinese Theatre, with Grandma Lettie in tow. The old woman, decked out in her North Dakota finest, tries to prevent her famous granddaughter from seeing Norman Maine's footprints in the theater's legendary courtyard. The old woman fails in that bit of subterfuge, and Vicki accidentally glances at the block of cement with its "good luck" message from her dead husband. She almost collapses, but at the last moment regains her strength, puts on a smile, and walks triumphantly into the theater. The end.

In a subsequent version of the scene, Schulberg and Lardner added the character of a radio interviewer, who asks Vicki, after she has recovered her composure, to say something to her adoring public. She obliges, announcing with great emotion, "Hello, everybody! This is Vicki Lester." The end.

A few days later, Schulberg and Lardner came up with the alternate "Hello, everybody! This is Mrs. Norman Maine!"

Both versions of "Hello, everybody!" were filmed, and the rest is history, although the authors (or author) of that final line remains open to question. Several obits of Schulberg and Lardner credit them with "Hello, everybody! This is Mrs. Norman Maine." Ron Haver, who restored the 1954 remake of *A Star Is Born* in 1983, credits the famous line to John Lee Mahin. A perusal of all the versions of that 1937 screenplay at the Selznick archives makes it impossible to discern precisely who wrote the film's many different endings.

Success has many fathers, and Colleen Moore offered up her best friend as the author of "Hello, everybody! I'm Mrs. Norman Maine." The actress wrote, "Adela Rogers St. Johns was with me when I made the call. Later, when she wrote an original story from which the picture *A Star Is Born* was made, she used my gambit [Hello, this is Mrs. John McCormick]." She went on to call it "a very effective scene, and though its original was for a somewhat different purpose, it, too, was effective. John's job was saved." The only problem is, nothing Rogers St. Johns ever wrote featured a similar line of introduction.

According to Lardner, Selznick "decreed" that he and Schulberg "were now screenwriters," giving some credence to their authorship of the famous final line. Nothing else in the final screenplay can definitely be attributed to them. The various endings of the script are unsigned except Wellman and Carson's original fade-out in North Dakota.

One definitive bit of nonsense is Wellman's claim that he had to "put back" a lot of his own copy in the final screenplay before he found it fit to direct. A perusal of all those versions of the script in the Selznick archives makes it clear that the script underwent major changes as other writers were brought aboard. Many of Wellman and Carson's original ideas fell by the wayside as Parker and Campbell—and to a lesser extent, Mahin, Schulberg, and Lardner Jr.—reworked the story.

Chapter 4

The script changes to *A Star Is Born* had other forces at work—and by a writer who clearly could not write, if his many memos are any indication of his talent. In the Pre-Code era of *What Price Hollywood?*, George Cukor and his screenwriters got away with a clearly intoxicated and homosexual take on the director character Max Carey, an interpretation that would not have been allowed by the Hays Code office only a year later. By 1936, that censorship board had already been renamed the Production Code Administration, and Will H. Hays let his top "troubleshooter" and a "tough Irish Catholic" take full charge of the organization's grip on the motion picture industry. Left out of Hays's colorful description of his chief censor was that Joseph Breen also happened to be a Nazi sympathizer who claimed the wrong kind of people had a stranglehold on that same business. "Ninety-five percent of these folks are Jews of an Eastern European lineage," Breen wrote in one typical screed. "They are, probably, the scum of the earth."

When he wasn't accusing Jews of taking over America, much less the movies, Breen repeatedly warned Selznick not to feature any scenes of drunkenness in his new Hollywood opus about alcoholism. In the final film, Norman Maine does sleep with a champagne bottle, and in another scene, he orders not one but two glasses of scotch and almost no soda: When the bartender fills the glass almost to the brim with alcohol, studio chief Oliver Niles cautions, "The word, you know, is pronounced 'when.'" Norman responds, "Bad dialogue, Oliver."

It is vintage Dorothy Parker. However, Fredric March's Norman Maine never acts more than a little tipsy. He also takes no more than a couple of sips of those two scotches and almost no soda. Only in the famous Academy Award scene, where Norman interrupts Vicki's acceptance speech and accidentally slaps her, does he look very unsteady. Even there, he appears to be more pissed off than downright drunk.

Breen took credit for Selznick making a movie about alcoholism in which the disease is never really depicted. He emphasized "the imperative need of your cutting to absolute minimum all scenes of drinking and drunkenness, wherever these may occur in the development of your story." Apparently, Breen ran his own private poll service when he referred to the "great numbers of protests from motion picture patrons in all parts of the nation against the unnecessary and offensive drinking scenes."

Selznick, for his part, worried more about the depiction of Norman Maine's suicide. Surprisingly, the touchy censor waved the white flag there. Breen wrote to the studio chief about how impressed he had been by the "unglamorous" way in which suicide is handled in three previous films produced by Selznick: *Anna Karenina* (jumping in front of a train), *What Price Hollywood?* (firearm), and *Dinner at Eight* (asphyxiation). In that last film, Breen did insist on some "details of turning on the gas" be cut when John Barrymore's character kills himself in a hotel room.

Selznick wrote back to Breen to thank him, adding, "I didn't realize I had a suicide complex until I saw this list, all of the pictures in which [sic] I produced. In any event, it would appear that there is no reason to worry."

Breen's memo to Selznick also mentioned the need for modesty, especially with regard to the costumes. Although he expressed concern about Janet Gaynor's swimsuit at the beach, Breen fretted most about Fredric March's going shirtless. He demanded that the actor's "breasts" not be exposed on the beach or in a brief shower sequence in the trailer on the couple's unglamorous honeymoon. By contrast, in the Pre-Code *What Price Hollywood?*, actor Lowell Sherman's flabby pectorals are fully exposed in a bathroom scene early in the picture and again later when the principal characters gather around a pool on a Beverly Hills estate.

In 1936, nothing was too trivial to escape what Breen might consider prurient. He even cautioned that a movie poster of coming attractions at the preview of Vicki Lester's film be "tasteful." He worried because the script indicates the advertisement would be for a South Seas tale featuring "a native girl." The censor, who found much to admire in Adolf Hitler, warned, "This should not be too revealing or suggestive."

Breen saved his greatest bugaboo for last. He demanded no depiction or use of code words for homosexuality be used. At Breen's insistence, Selznick would go on to cut a scene in *A Star Is Born* that featured a "pansy" character. In the finished film, three makeup-and-hair artists perform an extreme remodel of Esther Blodgett that turns her into Vicki Lester. Cut was the character of an effeminate costume designer, played by Joseph Schildkraut, who helps in that metamorphosis. Breen could only have been happy that a homosexual was not on board again to direct. It's more than obvious that Lowell Sherman's Max Carey in George Cukor's *What Price Hollywood?* is a "pansy."

Sherman possessed what Cukor called an "odious" quality. It's what was needed to play Max Carey. Odious, however, never helped any actor become a star, a status that always escaped Sherman in front of the camera. Behind it, he had somewhat more success, directing Mae West in *She Done Him Wrong* and Katharine Hepburn in *Morning Glory*. Adding to his overall unseemly hauteur on screen was a real-life brush with notoriety off camera. Sherman had the unfortunate timing of accepting an invitation to one of Fatty Arbuckle's parties, the fete that ended up taking the life of Virginia Rappe in 1921. Sherman's testimony at the trial helped exonerate Arbuckle of murder, but nothing said on the stand could prevent the obese comic from being ostracized by the Hollywood establishment. The year before Rappe's death, Arbuckle signed a contract with Paramount Pictures for one million dollars a year. After her death, he found himself abruptly without work.

Sherman claimed to have based his portrayal of Max Carey on John Barrymore, a brother-in-law. There were also glimmers in his portrayal of another chronic alcoholic. Marshall "Mickey" Neilan had been one of the founding members, along with Cecil B. DeMille, of the Motion Pictures Directors Association in 1915, later renamed the Directors Guild of America. Neilan's career covered it all: directing, acting, and screenwriting. He had even directed the adaptation of Adela Rogers St. Johns's novel that kickstarted the *A Star Is Born* franchise: *The Skyrocket*. He weathered that box office disappointment but not Howard Hughes's *Hell's Angels*. Caught in the transition from silent to sound movies, Hughes fired Neilan as the film's director and gave the project to Edmund

Goulding, who turned the 1930 aviator epic into a sound picture. Coincidentally or not, Neilan would be given a small speaking role as a bystander in *A Star Is Born*. He appears briefly at the Santa Anita racetracks when Norman Maine falls off the wagon after his stint in the sanatorium. One witness in the crowd remarks, "These has-beens give me the creeps." Neilan's unnamed character agrees but adds sympathetically, "He was great while he had it."

The Max Carey character in *What Price Hollywood?* has antecedents in Barrymore and Neilan, but the screenwriters added another dimension abetted by Sherman's acting. His Max Carey is only slightly less mincing and limp-wristed than Franklin Pangborn, the longest-running "pansy" in the history of the cinema. After Max Carey meets Mary Evans at the Brown Derby, he drunkenly extends an invitation to her to be his date for the premiere of his latest picture. The next morning, Max asks his butler, played by Eddie "Rochester" Anderson, "Did I bring someone home with me last night?" Anderson's manservant replies, "No, sir, someone brought *you* home this morning." To further emphasize Mary's aggression, Max looks aghast at the white tuxedo shirt that he slept in. The front has been signed by the young waitress, who made sure to give him her name, telephone number, address, and other data. Still sleeping on the couch downstairs, Mary is awakened by Max, who asks, "Pardon me, but what really happened last night?" She's still wearing the dress she wore to the premiere. "Oh, nothing much," Mary replies, completely nonchalant. "You just happened to pass out at the end of the picture."

Max makes Mary a star, and his lack of interest in the opposite sex is next indicated when he attempts to show his protégée, on the set of their new movie, how to perform a love scene with her male costar. Max embraces the actor, but Mary pays no attention to his direction. She's too busy chatting with her new fiancé, Lonny, who has become a frequent visitor to the set, much to Max's ire. The director lets go of the male actor long enough to scold the woman he made a star, saying, "Do you think I'm doing this because I like it?"

Even after Mary and Lonny are married, Max remains a frequent guest in their home. One evening, the now-unemployed director barges into their bedroom in a full drunken stupor, and when he sits down on Mary's bed (even in Pre-Code Hollywood, a married couple always sleeps in separate beds), Lonny tells Max, "Maybe you'd be more comfortable in *this* bed," pointing to where he sleeps.

On the subject of pansies, Franklin Pangborn plays a cameo in the first *A Star Is Born*. He portrays a radio announcer, and in a profile of Vicki Lester, he gushes into the microphone: "Her very warmth, they tell me, is enough to drive men mad." The words "they tell me" subtly separates him from the majority of his sex. Again, it is vintage Dorothy Parker.

Max Carey predates two other gay characters who take an inordinate interest in women they want to control but for whom they show no romantic affection. In Otto Preminger's 1944 classic film noir, *Laura*, Clifton Webb's Waldo Lydecker grooms Gene Tierney's Laura Hunt to be a titan of the advertising world in a makeover that's practically lifted from *What Price Hollywood?*. Waldo explains, "I gave [Laura] her start . . . I selected a more attractive hair dress for her. I taught her what clothes were more becoming for her. Through me, she met everyone."

Waldo resents Laura's impending marriage to Vincent Price's Shelby Carpenter, whose masculinity Waldo mocks by referring to him as "a male beauty in distress." When Laura subsequently falls in love with Dana Andrews's detective Mark McPherson, Waldo experiences another emotional meltdown, threatening Laura by saying, "You're the best part of myself, that's what you are. Do you think I'm going to leave it to the vulgar pawing of a second-rate detective who thinks you're a dame?"

Laura was followed by Joseph L. Mankiewicz's Broadway classic *All About Eve*, in which George Sanders's Addison DeWitt, yet another journalist, helps to launch the theater career of Anne Baxter's Eve Harrington. Addison writes fawning newspaper profiles of Eve and, in the process, attacks her aging mentor, Bette Davis's Margo Channing. As with Waldo in *Laura* and Max in *What Price Hollywood?*, Addison becomes incensed when his female prodigy threatens to marry another man, the successful playwright Lloyd Richards. He tells Eve, "I'm nobody's fool, least of all yours. I've come here to tell you that you'll not marry Lloyd, or anyone else for that matter, because I will not permit it . . . because after tonight you will belong to me."

Laura Hunt, Eve Harrington, and Mary Evans are "beards" for homosexual men desperate not to lose their respective heterosexual covers.

John McCormick wasn't homosexual, but his threats to Colleen Moore were just as melodramatic, if not more so, than those ultimatums made by the fictional characters Max Carey, Waldo Lydecker, and Addison DeWitt. "You're nothing without me. I made you a star, and I can break you just as easily," McCormick threatened Moore.

In the first remake of *A Star Is Born*, one character got the homosexual treatment, albeit with very subtle shading. Esther's good friend Danny McGuire appears in both the 1937 and the 1954 versions. As played by the gravel-voiced comedian Andy Devine in the first *A Star Is Born*, it's difficult to imagine this sidekick as having sex with man, woman, or goat. In the remake starring Judy Garland, screenwriter Moss Hart kept the name Danny McGuire, but Cukor cast the very congenial Tommy Noonan in the role. (Hart wanted to cast the far rougher character actor Ray Walston.) Most significant, in his screenplay, Hart excised the Grandma Lettie character, which he found "very dated" but kept her motivation to push Vicki Lester to return to Hollywood after the suicide of Norman Maine. Hart gave that pep talk to Danny McGuire.

The intense friendship but nonsexual intimacy between Garland's Esther and Noonan's Danny predates a hundred gay-best-friend-next-door characters that screen heroines relied on for advice, as well as a kind shoulder, once the Production Code had finally been banished in 1968. The character would be completely excised from the 1976 version of *A Star Is Born* but would return as a full-blown gay character in the 2018 remake. There, Danny McGuire is renamed Ramon, played by Anthony Ramos, and he is the one who welcomes Bradley Cooper's Jackson Maine to the drag bar called Bleu Bleu (an homage to the sign that hangs outside the Downbeat Club in the 1954 version). It's where Lady Gaga's Ally sings the Édith Piaf classic "La Vie en Rose." Ramon remains Ally's most readily available shoulder to cry on throughout the film.

In his *A Star Is Born* tome, film historian Ronald Haver writes that Noonan's Danny McGuire is "evidently in love with Esther." That female character's behavior toward him, however, only makes sense if McGuire is gay. Otherwise, her running off with Norman Maine after she sings "The Man That Got Away" at the Downbeat Club would be seen as a hard punch in the groin to any straight man. Of all the female stars in the *A Star Is Born* films, none is more sensitive and devoid of flaws than Garland's Esther/Vicki.

In the 1937 *A Star Is Born*, Vicki Lester wins an Oscar for her performance in the film *Dream Without End*. In a weird anachronism, the ceremony does not include the announcement of any nominees for best actress of the year. Vicki's win is delivered as if it were a given, squelching any sense of suspense. In the scene, the Oscar Vicki holds is the same statue that Janet Gaynor received at the very first Academy Awards in 1928. She won for her performances in no fewer than three films: *7th Heaven, Sunrise*, and *Street Angel*. *A Star Is Born* brought Gaynor her second and final Oscar nomination. The film was also nominated for five other Oscars, including best picture, best actor (Fredric March), best director (William Wellman), and best screenplay (Dorothy Parker, Robert Carson, and Alan Campbell). The film won an Oscar for best story, by Wellman and Carson, and also an honorary Oscar for its Technicolor cinematography, by W. Howard Greene. The category of best story was last given in 1956 when Dalton Trumbo won for *The Brave One* but was credited to the pseudonym of Robert Rich since Trumbo continued to be blacklisted for his past affiliation with the Communist Party.

Whatever claims Selznick made about who contributed what to the story and the screenplay, Wellman had nothing but praise for the moviemaker. He not only offered to give Selznick his Oscar for *A Star Is Born* but also insisted, "I didn't make pictures for him. I made pictures with him."

After his success with *A Star Is Born*, Selznick considered revisiting the film, not as a remake but as a sequel. He even toyed with the title *Another Star Is Born*. As he wrote in a 1941 memo, the sequel "would pick up the career of Vicki Lester where it was left off in the old picture." Gaynor and Selznick's wife, Irene, were close friends, and he wanted to take the actress out of a premature self-imposed retirement to play an established movie star who shepherds the career of a young actress. After her big comeback in *A Star Is Born*, Gaynor made two other films, but *Three Loves Has Nancy* and *The Young in Heart* were only modest successes. Gaynor effectively ended her career at age thirty-three to marry MGM's top costume designer, Adrian, in 1939. In his proposed sequel, Selznick fantasized about bringing back to the screen "the chic new Gaynor, as created by Adrian," as he described her. He also wanted the new film to feature "some new girl who would be launched . . . Wellman would again direct and Menjou, Andy Devine, etc. would also appear."

Selznick had ignored exhibitors' opinion when they responded unenthusiastically to his making of the first *A Star Is Born*. Apparently, he felt much less secure about the sequel. As he went on to write in that 1941 memo, "Please check with some of the sales force and a few important buyers and advise."

The advice he received did not encourage him, and he soon dropped the project. For her part, Gaynor had no interest in returning to the screen after her marriage to Adrian and the birth of their son, Robin, in 1940. Her reasons for going into retirement could have been written by any second-rate screenwriter of the era, parroting the current gender ethic that a woman's role was best played at home. "I had been working steadily for seventeen long years; making movies was really all I knew of life," she said. "I just wanted to have time to know other things. Most of all, I wanted to fall in love. I wanted to get married. I wanted a child. And I knew that in order to have these things, one had to make time for them. So, I simply stopped making movies. Then, as if by a miracle, everything I really wanted happened."

It was the kind of conventional sop that Adela Rogers St. Johns sometimes put in her short stories, magazine profiles, and screenplays. Her own life and career told another story, as did the life and career of her best friend, Colleen Moore. While both women took multiple husbands, they were always far more liberated than the female characters they inspired, wrote, or sometimes played on the screen. Moore, besides being the movies' first flapper, went on to write the first financial guide for women, aptly titled *How Women Can Make Money in the Stock Market*.

Awarded the Presidential Medal of Freedom in 1970, Rogers St. Johns combined her fluffy movie star profiles with hard reporting on sports, politics, and sensational courtroom dramas, like the 1935 trial of Bruno Richard Hauptman, convicted of kidnapping and murdering Charles Lindbergh's son. She capped her career in journalism with stellar reporting on the 1976 bank robbery and conspiracy trial of Patty Hearst. She also never shied away from making controversial statements about her sex. "I love my children, but I wish I hadn't any. It's impossible to combine career with raising children," she said.

A legacy of all the *A Star Is Born* movies is that at no point in any of the films does the female lead ever talk about having children.

Part Two

"I'm Mrs. Norman Maine Too."

Chapter 5

It would be difficult to say which novice producer, Sid Luft or Jon Peters, received worse press when their respective remakes of *A Star Is Born* were announced.

Before his film version with wife Judy Garland started shooting in the autumn of 1953, Luft took time to note, "Our daily life became a hornet's nest of publicity. The media was unrelenting."

Peters remembered, with even slightly more color, his career switch from hairdresser to movie producer with the 1976 remake starring his new girlfriend, Barbra Streisand. He noted, "When I left that business and went into this one, all I read was that I was a pimp and a conniver and a nobody latching onto a star's wings."

Luft held the minor advantage on his résumé of having produced a couple of B-movies from the late 1940s, *French Leave* and the equally forgettable *Kilroy Was Here*. While he liked to brag that he came up from nowhere, Luft worked as a test pilot for Douglas Aircraft Company and was an amateur boxer who fought less in the ring than in the bars, where he earned the nickname "One-Punch Luft."

Peters held the minor advance on his résumé of having done something successful in his life, like cutting women's hair in Beverly Hills and owning a few high-end beauty salons. While he liked to brag that he came up from nowhere, Peters, indeed, had been "a kid with dirty underwear going to beauty school."

In a contest of who would be the least likely to end up a movie producer, Peters easily won. He didn't even call himself a hairdresser in his early days. He called himself a "muff dyer." It was about the truth, because he primarily serviced working girls. "The prostitutes had red hair, red pubic hair, and red poodles. I made it so everything matched," he reported.

Peters, however, assumed the distinct disadvantage of plotting a power grab even greater and more outrageous than Luft's. Streisand's new boyfriend announced that he would not only produce *A Star Is Born* but would also direct the film and be its male lead. Frank Pierson, who ended up directing the second *A Star Is Born* remake, described Peters as a guy "whose motion picture experience was a previous marriage to an actress."

Luft carried his disadvantages too. Many falsely accused him of breaking up Garland's marriage to director Vincente Minnelli, but much more concerning, not to mention real, was his being taken to court by ex-wife Lynn Bari for nonpayment of child support. It wasn't a good look for a producer of B-movies who wanted to break onto the A-list, since Luft also made a habit of showing up at Hollywood's best boîtes with Judy on his arm while being sued by Lynn for not feeding their kid.

"A charming fellow, Sid," opined Jack Warner, whose studio went on to release all the remakes of *A Star Is Born*. "He's one of the original guys who promised his parents he'd never work a day in his life—and made good."

What made Luft the perfect producer in Garland's eyes

is what made Peters the perfect producer in Streisand's eyes. When Hollywood's most bankable female star first met Peters, she kept him waiting forty-five minutes at her home. He was there to do her hair or, more specifically, to make her a wig for an upcoming film. Ticked off at her chronic lateness, Peters threatened Streisand when she deigned to appear, telling her, "Don't ever do that to me again!"

No one had ever talked to Barbra like that before.

Nor had anyone within minutes of meeting Barbra tell her, "You've got a great ass."

In other words, she was smitten.

"He wasn't treating me like some unapproachable star. It was very disarming," Streisand reported. Which is why Streisand, in her memoir, titled the chapter on meeting Peters "What Was I Thinking?" It's clear she was not thinking from her head.

Garland was no doubt even hornier after being married to Minnelli for fewer than six years. It's not fair to blame that marriage's failure on Luft. Halfway into that Garland/Minnelli union, she rejected him as the director on her 1948 movie *Easter Parade*, picking the somewhat less illustrious but equally gay Chuck Walters instead.

Minnelli had an unusual résumé for a movie director. He cut his teeth by being a window dresser, a profession that's just to the right of hairdresser and florist in the gay world. It was at Marshall Field's department store in Chicago where Minnelli met a young man named Lester Gaba. Or as Dorothy Parker referred to the couple, "Here come Lester and Lester." Being inseparable and wearing makeup, the couple attracted gossip of a shade somewhere between blue and fabulous. MGM star Ann Miller spoke of Minnelli's sexual orientation but with a caveat. "He could poontang," she said of the director. "Liza is proof of that."

Luft also took his potshot at Minnelli's masculinity, saying the marriage to Garland broke up because the director "secluded himself and wouldn't explain why he let her alone so much." Luft didn't leave it there, going on to note, "Judy and Vincent's marriage was rocky. She was looking for romance." He never mentioned that Judy was looking for a meal ticket, for financial security, or to escape an abusive husband. For Garland, her soon-to-be third husband's trump card was his unabashed heterosexuality.

His daughter believed her mother's previous husband was straight, but Lorna Luft put Minnelli in the same category as the other men fawning over Judy. "They all treated her like a lady," the Lufts' daughter reported in her memoir. "They were all gentlemen. Sid Luft, on the other hand, was no gentleman. He was a weight lifter. He was a former test pilot. He was a gambler. He was a guy." In other words, her daddy was a proud ladies' man, and she went on to use a word that is sometimes code for gay, writing that Luft was "so unlike the *refined* men [Garland] usually favored."

There were a few other reasons for Garland to be filled with lust. As she put it to one reporter, "Sid kept telling me I was good, and he brought me back. He gave me an inner belief in myself and my talent."

Garland's best friend in Hollywood agreed. "Sid was a wheeler-dealer but not a bad guy," Lauren Bacall reported. "He and Judy were crazy about each other. He was very good for her; he gave her a reason to get it all together. He gave her a semblance of family life."

That's what Garland saw in Luft. Their daughter summed up best what Luft saw in Garland. "[M]y father saw her as both a lover and an opportunity—a conduit for reflected fame," Lorna Luft wrote.

Both those roles—lover and opportunist—played into Jack Warner's decision to let Luft produce the first remake of *A Star Is Born*. Luft himself noted, "[Jack Warner] wanted to show the money people that someone was there to ensure Judy's reliability, and who better than the husband of the star?"

Warner put it more bluntly, noting, "He could make Judy go home just by snapping his fingers."

Except when it mattered most. Luft would later admit, "[I]t was virtually impossible for her to sustain a work mode in front of the cameras without taking some kind of medication."

Both Luft and Peters claimed that they were the ones who thought up the idea of doing a remake of A Star Is Born.

"I discovered this project. I was the one who found it for Barbra and convinced her to do it," Peters said. No matter that his girlfriend had already rejected the script called *Rainbow Road*, written by Joan Didion and John Gregory Dunne. Anything that was pre-Peters in Streisand's life did not matter to the hairdresser-turned-movie-producer.

When Luft first suggested a *Star* remake to Garland, it sparked a similar déjà vu moment, only different. She informed him, "I wanted to do that picture at Metro after *Summer Stock*." She had performed in a radio version of *A Star Is Born* for Lux Radio Theatre in 1942, with her very giddy Esther Blodgett playing to Walter Pidgeon's nearly somnolent Norman Maine. Back then, Louis B. Mayer liked the idea of doing a remake, but Nicholas Schenck in MGM's New York office felt otherwise. As Garland explained, "[T]hey said the theme was too depressing, and my fans wouldn't want to see me as the wife of an alcoholic."

Luft and Garland found a far more congenial environment at Warner Brothers, where its eponymous head of production had fallen in love with the former MGM star after seeing her perform at the Los Angeles Philharmonic

Auditorium in the spring of 1952. Jack Warner believed he was the one to revitalize Garland's moribund movie career, and he credited Luft for her recent successes on the stage.

Perhaps he gave Luft too much credit there. It was the legendary agent Abe Lastfogel who first suggested that Garland reinvent herself by following in Danny Kaye's footsteps. The American comic, well known at the time for having played the title characters in such movie hits as *The Secret Life of Walter Mitty* and *Hans Christian Andersen*, had recently played the London Palladium to enormous acclaim. "Go to England, leave the country," the top agent at William Morris advised Garland.

That string of concerts at the Palladium, beginning on April 9, 1951, were so enormously successful that Garland went on to perform throughout "the boonies," as she dubbed Scotland and Ireland, followed by her opening on October 16 that year at the newly renovated Palace Theatre in New York City. Originally scheduled for eight weeks, the Palace stint ran an astounding nineteen. Garland closed there on February 24, 1952, and the following month, she received a special Tony Award for her "important contribution to the revival of vaudeville."

"The atmosphere was explosive, more glorious than the Palladium. Judy was now a symbol of victorious America," Luft reported.

Even more glorious was the $25,000 a week for four weeks that Garland earned playing the Los Angeles Philharmonic Auditorium, up from her $15,000 a week at the Palace. The shiny cherry on her L.A. sundae was the appearance of a Hollywood kingmaker in the audience. Jack Warner took uncommon pleasure in sticking it to Louis B. Mayer, who fired Garland in 1950 after fifteen marvelous but bumpy years at MGM. Warner enjoyed taking his rival's rejects and giving them a spectacular comeback. He did it with Joan Crawford in *Mildred Pierce* the previous decade, giving the former MGM actress her one and only Oscar, and Warner thought he could do it again with Garland if he put her in *A Star Is Born*.

Without Warner, Garland's career might have gone in another direction. She might have stayed right where she was, on stage. After her Broadway success at the Palace Theatre, Garland had been in talks to star in a new stage musical based on George Bernard Shaw's play *Pygmalion*.

But being a star in America is not starring on Broadway, even if the musical ends up being called *My Fair Lady*. "Being a star is being a movie star" is how Barbra Streisand once described it before making the movie version of *Funny Girl*. To reclaim Garland's movie star status, Luft joined with a producer of not much distinction. What made Edward L. Alperson vital to Garland's comeback was his recent purchase of the rights to *A Star Is Born*. David O. Selznick, strapped for cash, held an auction in early 1952 to sell off a few assets. What neither Luft nor Alperson bothered to check out in the fine print of this sale was that Selznick cleverly retained the rights to *A Star Is Born* in no fewer than thirteen countries, including such not insignificant markets as Germany and Japan. Fortunately, the producer of the first *A Star Is Born*, not to mention *Gone with the Wind*, looked to do a remake of *A Farewell to Arms*—and Warner Brothers conveniently held those rights, having bought them from Paramount, which made the first film adaptation of Ernest Hemingway's war novel in 1932. A swap was made, plus Selznick had to pay a fee of $25,000, all of which put the first remake of *A Star Is Born* on the fast track at Warner Brothers.

"How Sid went about it is one of the reasons I fell in love with him," Garland said of Luft's work on the only movie they would ever make together. Her gratitude there went a long way toward forgiving him for the abortion she endured before opening at the Palace. The couple had not yet married—that big date still months away, on June 8, 1952—and a pregnant Garland would have created a scandal, not to mention put a crimp into her Broadway debut. Garland chastised Luft, "Obviously, you don't want my baby."

His reply: There's no business like show business. "Of course I want your baby, but we've got a show to do!" he said. Luft suffered nightmares about the potential newspaper headlines, such lurid gems as NOT DIVORCED and CANCEL THE PALACE and LUFT'S ILLEGITIMATE CHILD. Garland did as her nervous lover advised, but Luft was otherwise engaged when she visited the abortionist. Regarding that inconvenient pregnancy, he later admitted, "I handled it like a clod."

On the subject of Garland and Luft doing a remake of *A Star Is Born*, many industry insiders were skeptical. Producer Arthur Freed, who had worked with the star on everything from *The Wizard of Oz* to *Easter Parade* at MGM, did not mince words. "I can't believe those two alley cats are making a movie," he said in a quote that quickly made the rounds in Hollywood circles, high and low.

Freed's doubts aside, the couple turned into two tigers when it came to putting together an impressive team to make their movie. "I wanted George," Garland said of George Cukor. "The picture had to be the greatest; it couldn't be merely good. I had too much at stake." In the end, merely good might have been better. The movie she, Luft, and Cukor made suffers from an elephantiasis of length and budget, if not spirit, that ultimately doomed it at the box office and sank Garland's movie career along with it.

Cukor and Garland had worked together in her earliest days in Hollywood, and for a while it looked as though he might direct the seventeen-year-old in *The Wizard of Oz*. He even guided her through the early days of preproduction on the classic musical, and it was Cukor who gave the teenage singer-actress a far more natural look as the iconic Dorothy who sings "Over the Rainbow." He started by getting rid of the blond wig the makeup department at MGM stuck on her head. The scene in *A Star Is Born* where three cosmetologists perform a radical and ghastly makeover of Esther Blodgett, complete with auburn wig and padded nose, is the same unfortunate fate that Cukor spared Garland on *The Wizard of Oz*. Back in 1938, he was her Norman Maine, minus the romance, the alcoholism, and the suicide.

Cukor avoided doing remakes throughout his career but broke form with the first *Star* remake. According to the director, it was not their *Wizard of Oz* encounter that made him want to direct Garland. His wish came a full decade later when he asked her to sing "Happy Birthday" to Ethel Barrymore on the great actress's seventieth birthday, the party hosted by Cukor at his Cordell Drive home. "She did it with such feeling and emotion that I thought Ethel would dissolve in tears," the director recalled. "Anyone who could sing like that, I thought, had the emotional ability to be a great dramatic actress. That was the first time I got the idea I wanted to direct Judy."

And then there were the songs. "There has to be some compelling reason for making a picture all over again, such as the addition of songs in the case of *A Star Is Born*," Cukor noted. There were the songs and, of course, there was Garland, whom he likened repeatedly to Laurette Taylor, most famous for creating the role of Amanda Wingfield in Tennessee Williams's *The Glass Menagerie*. Cukor had directed Taylor on Broadway in Zoe Akins's play *The Furies*. That was 1928. The following year, Cukor moved west when Paramount gave him a contract to coach silent film stars on how to speak now that microphones hung like guillotines over their heads.

The songs in *A Star Is Born* were crucial to Cukor. Equally important was Garland herself. As he pointed out, the remake would be the first film in which "she was sad, and the first time she ever cried and she ever screamed." Cukor wanted to be there for those fireworks, even though she had already shown signs of sadness in *The Wizard of Oz* and *Meet Me in St. Louis*, and she cried in *The Clock*, among other films.

Sid Luft invited the director to a lunch at Romanoff's in Beverly Hills, and the about-to-be-an-A-list producer didn't even have to broach the reason for their meeting. Before they could order Bloody Marys, Cukor told Luft, "If you want me to do a picture with Judy, I will."

For the movie's songs, Garland wanted composer Harold Arlen and lyricist E. Y. "Yip" Harburg who together wrote "Over the Rainbow." Harburg, unfortunately, didn't make the cut, being blacklisted in the film industry for his suspected Communist ties. In the end, Garland had to settle for no less a dream team than Arlen and Ira Gershwin.

As soon as Moss Hart heard about the *Star* remake with Garland, Cukor, Arlen, and Gershwin aboard, the esteemed playwright and stage director set up a meeting with his agent. "I'd very much like to write it for Judy. I've known her a long time, and I'd enjoy it," Hart told Irving "Swifty" Lazar. Hart knew Garland and counted her a friend. He and his future wife, Kitty Carlisle, had entertained Mr. and Mrs. Vincente Minnelli in New York City when they were newlyweds in 1945. Hart, rumored to have much better jewelry than Carlisle, bonded with Minnelli. The two men knew each other from Minnelli's early days on Broadway, where, after his stint at Marshall Field's in Chicago, he designed sets and costumes for major Broadway impresarios like Florenz Ziegfeld and Earl Carroll.

Garland didn't hold Hart's very close friendship with Minnelli against him. A major name on Broadway, Hart also enjoyed success on the other coast. Two plays he wrote with George S. Kaufman, *You Can't Take It with You* and *The Man Who Came to Dinner*, were turned into hit movies. Even better, Hart had won an Academy Award in 1948 for his adapted screenplay *Gentlemen's Agreement*, based on Laura Z. Hobson's best-seller about anti-Semitism. Together with Cukor, Hart fit the description of the "refined men" whom Garland "usually favored," according to Lorna Luft.

Regarding his take on remaking *A Star Is Born*, Hart came up with the novel idea to stick closely to the 1937 screenplay, except for his decision to dump the Grandma Lettie character. He explained, "It was a difficult story to do because the original was famous, and when you tamper or change the original, you're inviting all sorts of unfavorable criticism. It had to be changed because I had to say new things about Hollywood—which is quite a feat in itself as the subject has been worn pretty thin. The attitude of the original was more naive because it was made in the days when there was a more wide-eyed feeling about the movies. Finally, the emphasis had to be shifted to the woman, rather than the original emphasis on Fredric March."

Because the remake would star Judy Garland, and because he was hired to write the screenplay even before Warner Brothers signed a male lead, Hart changed the source of Esther Blodgett's ambition. In the first version, Janet Gaynor's character is hell-bent on becoming a movie star even before she leaves her home in the sticks. In Hart's version, Esther appears happy to be a band singer who entertains vague fantasies about cutting a record one day—until Norman tells her, "Your dream isn't big enough." He's the one who gives her the idea to think bigger, to leave the band, to become a major movie star. With his help, of course.

The change in emphasis put the character more in line

with Garland's MGM persona: an immensely sympathetic heroine who eschews the pronounced aggression shown in performances from other leading ladies of the day—actresses like Bette Davis, Joan Crawford, Rosalind Russell, and Barbara Stanwyck. A kinder, gentler Esther Blodgett also played into post–World War II attitudes toward women and the strict gender conformity of the 1950s. As soon as the Japanese bombed Pearl Harbor, women entered the workforce in unprecedented numbers to keep the American economy alive; however, after the war, those same women were expected to step aside for men, leave the workforce, return to their homes, have babies, and take care of everybody else in the process. That submissive ethos created problems for a movie titled *A Star Is Born*, since famous people are by nature required to have the drive and ambition to grab the spotlight at any cost and not let it go without a fight. Hart eliminated most of those hard edges by making Norman Maine the one who creates that dream for Esther. He has enough ambition and braggadocio for both of them.

Before Hart's script went before the cameras, there were other forces at play to soften not Esther but the story itself. Joseph Breen continued to run the Production Code Administration. He had both mellowed and hardened from his days of touting Hitler and dealing with David O. Selznick on the first *A Star Is Born*. While this censor no longer harbored deep concerns about the exposure of male "breasts" or blatant displays of inebriation replete in the Hart screenplay, Breen launched into a whole new set of moral diatribes. He wrote to Jack Warner, "We'd like to suggest that you not play the marriage sequence in the jail, in order to avoid an undignified atmosphere concerning the wedding ceremony." Intriguingly, this scene is lifted almost verbatim and visually from the first *A Star Is Born*.

Back then, Breen expressed no objection to the jailhouse nuptials.

Elsewhere in his memo, Breen ordered that the line "sucking up to the columnists," delivered by studio publicist Matt Libby, be taken out. There weren't any "pansies" in Hart's screenplay for Breen to complain about, the newly neutered Danny McGuire character too subtle a homosexual for the censor to notice. "Sucking" is definitely a more obvious lavender reference.

Breen saved his biggest criticism for a subject that also didn't bother him back in 1936. "Danny's eulogizing of Norman's suicide is unacceptable," he wrote, and went on to point out that the Production Code specifically forbade "the glorification and justification of suicide."

He wanted to cut the speech that Danny McGuire delivers to Vicki Lester: "Took guts to do what he did when he found he couldn't lick it—but he did it! And the one thing he was proudest of—the only thing he ever did in his life that paid off—you . . . you're tossing right back into the ocean after him. Who gives you that right? Because it hurts?"

Apparently, Breen no longer possessed the power he once had—at least not over Jack Warner. In the finished film, Esther/Vicki and Norman are married in a jailhouse with two seedy prisoners looking on behind bars. Danny McGuire is also present, acting more as bridesmaid to Esther than best man to Norman. Late to the wedding, Matt Libby feels he has been double-crossed by the couple. He had planned to turn the nuptials into a big media event and deeply resents being lied to by the two movie stars. McGuire lectures the flack, "They have the right to get married quietly if they want." Libby disagrees. "No, they don't," he insists, and adds that Norman "knows better than that. Mr. Public Nuisance could stand some decent publicity for a change, believe me. I've spent ten years covering for him, killing bad stories, sucking up to the columnists to smooth away his insults. Who do you think they're going to blame for not letting them cover this today? Him? Nah! Me! I'll look just like a fool . . . just wait your turn!"

In the end, only a few words from Danny McGuire's suicide speech were eliminated. Like Grandma Lettie in the first *A Star Is Born*, McGuire convinces Vicki not to give up her career in the movies. Jack Warner, however, held firm regarding the words "sucking up." He let the publicist character continue to perform oral sex, albeit figuratively, on members of the press. Warner knew how to handle Breen. He excised a few words to placate the censor's moral outrage and then got on with making his movie without further interference from a Nazi-loving Catholic.

For this studio chief, there emerged far more immediate problems with the upcoming production of Judy Garland's comeback film. According to Warner's very unreliable memoir *My First Hundred Years in Hollywood*, the first sign of trouble came when Sid Luft rejected Humphrey Bogart to play Norman Maine. Luft, for his part, remembered it differently. "I brought up the name Bogart," he reported, "but Jack just brushed him off quickly. His thinking was that the contrast facially between this young, pretty girl and this older, withered-up man was just too much."

The thought of Bogart playing Norman Maine is tantalizing. The actor, who, in 1952 won an Oscar for his performance in *The African Queen*, had been under contract to Warner Brothers since the 1930s. Even more convenient for his starring opposite Garland in the musical remake, Bogart loved the original *A Star Is Born* so much that he screened it every Christmas at his home on a 16mm movie projector. Nothing quite perks up the holidays like a movie that ends with a suicide. The tough-guy actor offered no excuse for his addiction to *A Star Is Born*, except to say, "I don't know. It just makes me cry." It could have been that Bogie identified with Norman Maine's alcoholism or the character's attraction to a much younger actress whose career he helped nurture in the industry. In many ways, the film replicated his own relationship with Lauren Bacall— except for the fact that Bogart never fell out of favor in Hollywood or with the public.

Bogie even went so far as to ask Luft, "How about me doing the Norman Maine part?" The Lufts and the Bogarts were good friends, and no woman in Hollywood was closer to Judy Garland than Lauren Bacall. That Bogart wasn't cast in *A Star Is Born* remains a mystery.

Warner's remark about Garland being "this young pretty girl" flew in the face of what she looked like at age thirty-one, and as for Bogart being "this older, withered-up man" at age fifty-four, he had enjoyed great success on-screen romancing Bacall, two years younger than Garland, in no fewer than five movies, including the certified classics *To Have and Have Not* and *The Big Sleep*. After Warner or Luft didn't accept Bogart's invitation to costar in *A Star Is Born*, the tough-guy star didn't take that rejection well. He never liked Jack Warner. "Hate" might be a better word. "I'd rather work for a crude son of a bitch like Harry Cohn any day of the week," Bogart said. "At least you know where you stand. Jack Warner you can't believe."

Pissed off, Bogart finally left Warner Brothers to become a free-agent actor. One of his moves after Warner Brothers was crossing the Hollywood Hills to pass under the fabled gates of Paramount Pictures and star in Billy Wilder's 1954 romantic comedy *Sabrina* opposite Audrey Hepburn, seven years younger than Garland. Perhaps if the fifty-four-year-old Bogart had played opposite Garland, his grizzled face would have made her look less middle-aged at thirty-one.

His casting would also have played into one of the enduring strengths of the *A Star Is Born* legend and why it keeps being reborn. As Lorna Luft described the film's universal appeal, "[A]t its basic level, it examines the father/daughter dynamic." Implicit in that statement is how the child often ends up taking care of the parent, which is also very much what Esther/Vicki does with Norman Maine.

Bogart was expert at playing daddy to ingenues, his nick-naming Bacall "Baby" just one prime example. More important, he remained a bona fide box office star in 1953. Garland, on the other hand, was attempting to make a difficult comeback. Even in her last few films at MGM, Louis B. Mayer wisely paired her with such box office champs as Gene Kelly (*The Pirate*, 1948), Van Johnson (*In the Good Old Summertime*, 1949), and Fred Astaire (who came out of his brief, self-imposed retirement to replace an injured Kelly in *Easter Parade*, 1948). *Easter Parade* is yet another story of an older man who helps a much younger woman launch her career, this time in vaudeville. Astaire even had a few months on Bogart, both men having been born just before the turn of the century.

Bogart would have provided the box office insurance that both James Stewart and Cary Grant provided for Katharine Hepburn in her big comeback in 1940, *The Philadelphia Story*, after she got hit with the "box office poison" label in the previous decade.

While Bogart wanted to costar with Garland in *A Star Is Born*, he was never quite sure about her husband's involvement with the film. Bogart even went so far as to ask him, "Sid, what makes you think you can be a producer?"

Garland's husband didn't hold back. "I got more fucking class than any cocksucker or motherfucker in this room," Luft told Bogie.

Everyone from Laurence Olivier to Marlon Brando rejected the Norman Maine role. Luft claimed that Cary Grant was Garland's "preferred costar." And Judy wasn't the only one who felt that way. "Everybody wanted Cary to play Norman Maine in *A Star Is Born* with Judy," George Cukor remarked.

Regarding a remake of *A Star Is Born*, Grant was mildly curious at best. Or perhaps he felt indebted to Cukor for putting him in the 1935 movie *Sylvia Scarlett*, a big misfire starring Katharine Hepburn in male drag that beguiled neither the critics nor the public. However, one good thing did emerge from this movie disaster: It proved that Grant could act and possessed real screen charisma after his playing handsome but bland leading men opposite Marlene Dietrich (*Blonde Venus*, 1932) and Mae West (*I'm No Angel*, 1933, and *She Done Him Wrong*, 1933). Or perhaps Grant wanted to show his acting chops after making the 1952 box office dud *Room for One More* opposite his current wife, Betsy Drake, and that same year a mindless piece of fluff called *Monkey Business* opposite a chimpanzee.

Curious or indebted or simply polite, Grant read aloud Moss Hart's *A Star Is Born* script for Cukor at his house, with the director playing all the roles not named Norman Maine.

Cukor told him afterward, "Can there be any doubt? This is the part you were born to play."

"Of course, that is why I won't," Grant replied. The star's biggest commercial disappointment to date with his name above the title came when he essayed the equally downbeat role of a Cockney drifter, one of the actor's greatest and most uncharacteristic performances. He made *None but the Lonely Heart* in 1944, and never again would he abandon his heroic debonair image. Playing a drunk, out-of-work movie star in a musical where Judy Garland got to sing all the songs did not exactly fit his honed and hard-won image.

Before the ultimate no arrived, Grant demanded $300,000 plus 10 percent of the gross to costar in *A Star Is Born*. Jack Warner countered with $450,000 and no percent of the gross. Grant was no longer a top box office attraction in the early 1950s; later in the decade, he successfully reestablished himself with *An Affair to Remember* and Alfred Hitchcock's *To Catch a Thief* and *North by Northwest*. But those box office successes were years away, and it's likely that the star made such lofty salary demands because he never harbored any real intention to remake *A Star Is Born*, especially with Garland. Betsy Drake gave the most probable reason for Grant rejecting the role of Norman Maine. "Judy was a drug addict," Drake said, and Grant, the ultimate professional, knew that her conduct on the set would be anything but. In the end, after the Lufts had wined and dined the Grants several times at their home, Cary turned out to be less than a gentleman. He sent his wife to the scene of those many dinners to give Sid and Judy the bad news. Betsy told the couple that Cary Grant would not be starring in *A Star Is Born*.

Garland later remarked, "God, I wish I could get back some of those dinners!"

The offer to play Norman Maine then went out to an actor much less well-known to American movie audiences. James Mason would soon be seen on screen as Brutus in *Julius Caesar*, opposite Marlon Brandon's Marc Antony, having appeared previously in only a few films made in Hollywood.

Mason considered Garland a friend. He wrote in his

memoir, "I got to know her very well when I first arrived in Hollywood, because one of the first films I appeared in at MGM was *Madame Bovary*, which was directed by her husband at that time, Vincente Minnelli, and I developed a fond relationship with her."

Getting his second choice to play the male lead—or perhaps third or fourth—Cukor never saw Norman Maine quite the way Mason did, and the actor felt the disconnection.

"I fancied that the Norman Mayne [*sic*] whom Cukor had in mind had all the colours of John Barrymore, whereas I was putting together an actor who resembled much more closely some of my own drunken friends," the actor wrote in his memoir, repeatedly misspelling his character's last name. "In fact, this was the best that I could offer him. Stylistically, a Barrymore figure might have been preferable, but I had never liked what I saw of Barrymore."

The screen's first Norman Maine knew the work of John Barrymore very well. Fredric March played the legendary actor's fictional doppelgänger Tony Cavendish in *The Royal Family of Broadway*. That film version of George S. Kaufman and Edna Ferber's hit play, a roman à clef about the Barrymore tribe, had been codirected by Cukor, who never could get his old actor-friend with the great profile out of his head. John Barrymore remained stuck there when Cukor told David O. Selznick about meeting the actor in a Culver City sanatorium, and Barrymore continued to live there in another anecdote the movie director told regarding the first remake of *A Star Is Born*.

Before filming began, Cukor wrote to Moss Hart, telling the screenwriter he wanted a very specific scene written into the film, one where Norman Maine comes out of his portable dressing room "[l]ooking like hell, a drink in his hand . . . He should present a very discouraging picture and looking unfit for work, not drunk, however."

As the director explained it, such a scene happened in real life when Cukor was shooting *Romeo and Juliet* in 1936. Barrymore, cast as Mercutio, had a real fan in the film's costume designer. Oliver Messel looked forward to meeting the legendary actor, who, at first look, proved something of a disappointment to the designer. Cukor recalled, "Oliver had designed a most dashing costume for Mercutio, and when he saw a rather seedy gentleman well past middle age with the suggestion of a pot belly, rather woozy on beer, his heart sank; he felt all was lost. Then Jack put on the costume. By some alchemy, he was now tall, slender, supple, and young."

Cukor instructed Hart, "I would like to get some of that effect here, as Norman comes out of his dressing room—an insignificant, uninteresting little man."

A few minutes of that deleted scene are included in the special features section of the DVD restored version of *A Star Is Born*. It is also mentioned briefly in the memoir *Under the Rainbow*, written by John Carlyle, who was cast as the assistant director in the scene.

"A Chinese junk, surrounded by seventy-five extras squatting and smoking that very early morning, loomed up on the back lot at Warners," Carlyle wrote. "James Mason, as the inebriated Norman, cavorted in a pirate costume on the decks above us. Our goal was to talk him down, subdue him gently, and take him off to his dressing room. The extras did not always look alert or put out their cigarettes."

When the scene got cut from the movie, Carlyle called it "the worst thing that ever happened to me!" He wasn't the last gay man to feel that way regarding *A Star Is Born*. A similar feeling also beset another actor decades later when the third remake of the film went before the cameras.

Beyond one actor's extreme heartbreak, such scenes help to explain why the budget for the first remake of *A Star Is Born* started at $2.5 million and ended up being $5,019,770, topped at the time only by David O. Selznick's 1946 epic *Duel in the Sun,* which cost just a quarter of a million more. Even as a musical, *A Star Is Born* is a simple story, and it's obvious that everyone involved, from Luft and Garland to Cukor and Hart, not to mention Jack Warner, appeared to have forgotten that great doesn't necessarily have to be gargantuan.

Garland could not be blamed for expensive scenes in which she did not appear. However, lost today is just how controversial, as well as unreliable, the star named Judy Garland was before *A Star Is Born* began production—controversial not only in Hollywood but also across America. Selling out a bunch of performances in a theater in New York or Los Angeles was one thing. Movie theaters were another, and the middle of America between the two coasts wasn't accustomed to reading about washed-up movie stars addicted to drugs, undergoing electroshock treatments, and attempting suicide in a country that was still very pre–*Hollywood Babylon* but more than ready for Kenneth Anger's tell-all scandal sheet.

The negativity surrounding the remake of *A Star Is Born* in its preproduction phase shocked its new leading man. "There were no great expressions of joy about the Lufts' project movie," James Mason reported. "One would hear people say, 'They're supposed to start shooting next week, but Judy'll never make it.'"

Only *Cleopatra* in the following decade got off to a worse start, felled by bad weather in England and followed by Elizabeth Taylor's near-fatal tracheotomy.

Chapter 6

After a few false starts, George Cukor began filming *A Star Is Born* in mid-October 1953, with Garland already having committed her "The Man That Got Away" vocals to tape on September 4. Of all the songs in the film, this one was her favorite, which may be why the recording of it proved to be both brilliant and harrowing. The American Film Institute puts "The Man That Got Away" at number eleven on its list of The Greatest American Movie Music, with Garland's rendering of "Over the Rainbow" placed at number one. One can't argue with the Harold Arlen and E. Y. Harburg hit from *The Wizard of Oz* that came to be Garland's theme song. But should "The Man That Got Away," by Harold Arlen and Ira Gershwin, really rank under Henry Mancini and Johnny Mercer's wistful ballad "Moon River" from *Breakfast at Tiffany's* or the Bee Gees disco anthem "Stayin' Alive" from *Saturday Night Fever*? It's just anyone's opinion.

Regarding "The Man That Got Away," Arlen's music, Gershwin's lyrics, and Garland's riveting delivery of the song is the brilliant side of it. Harrowing was the record-

ing that quickly ended Garland's long working relationship with the songwriter who wrote the luminous "Have
Yourself a Merry Little Christmas," as well as the rollick-
ing "Trolley Song," from her 1945 classic *Meet Me in St.
Louis*. In the following decade, Hugh Martin worked as
Garland's pianist at the Palace Theatre. Again, they got
along so well that she and Sid Luft spoke to Martin about
writing the score for their movie dream project. When that
job on *A Star Is Born* went instead to Arlen and Gershwin,
Garland approached Martin with some trepidation regarding a much less prestigious assignment on the film.
"Would you consider doing the vocal arrangements and
being my vocal coach?" she asked. Before Martin could
swallow his pride, he grabbed the opportunity to work
again with an artist he idolized.

He knew all about her perfectionism. On Martin's
"Have Yourself a Merry Little Christmas," Garland found
some of his original lyrics too downbeat. Martin obliged.
He substituted "It may be your last / Next year we may all
be living in the past" with the far more optimistic "Let
your heart be light / Next year all our troubles will be out
of sight."

Garland voiced no such problems with "The Man That
Got Away" as written by Gershwin and Arlen, who reported that when he first played it for her and Luft, "They
went wild with joy!" What the composer did not tell Garland and Luft—or, for that matter, Gershwin, with whom
he was collaborating for the first time—is that the song's
tune was not original. Arlen had written it a few years before, and Johnny Mercer wrote the lyrics for what was
then a song titled "I Can't Believe My Eyes." Garland also
never questioned the ungrammatical use of the word "that"
in the title and lyrics. Unlike many others who have attempted to correct it over the years, she got it instinctively.
As Gershwin explained his slightly clunky word choice,

"The title is as a paraphrase of the angler's 'You should have seen the one that got away.'" Arlen and Gershwin would not be so lucky with a few other songs they wrote for *A Star Is Born*, songs that ended up never being recorded, much less filmed. How different the unfortunate saga of what came to be dubbed "a star is shorn" might have been if one of those three songs would have been used to conclude the first half of the film.

The delivery and placement of the song "The Man That Got Away" is crucial to the story. It follows Esther and Norman's first meeting at a gala benefit at the Shrine Auditorium, where he has shown up late and inebriated. After getting into an altercation with publicist Matt Libby, Norman stumbles onto the stage where Esther is performing with a big band and two male singer-dancers. Thinking fast, she saves Norman's reputation by making it appear that his being there on stage with them is part of the act. Enchanted by this singer, Norman spends the night searching for her, only to find Esther performing with another, smaller band at the Bleu Bleu club. (Curiously, this venue is referred to verbally in the film as the Downbeat Club.) He hears her sing "The Man That Got Away," which proves apt. After he convinces her to leave the band and become a movie star with his help, he disappears for weeks. For Esther Blodgett, Norman Maine is the man that got away.

Hugh Martin heard this torch song being sung "with moody, understated emotion." He recommended that Garland sing it in B flat.

"Put it in C," she insisted.

"If you sing it in C," he cautioned, "you're going to have to yell by the time you get to the end of the bridge."

Incensed, Garland said in no uncertain terms that she never yelled when she sang. "The Man That Got Away" would be sung in C.

Martin wasn't the only one who wanted a much more subdued interpretation. "If she does a tour de force in the first thirty minutes, I have no picture!" George Cukor fretted. "There's no place to go from there. She's demonstrated that she's a star too soon. Too soon!"

It would not be the only time Cukor disagreed with his star—or the powers that be at Warner Brothers. However, like Vincente Minnelli before him, Cukor survived in Hollywood by being the essence of a "company man." It's what Luft called Garland's ex-husband, and like Minnelli, Cukor knew that longevity counts for almost everything when dealing with despotic moguls like Louis B. Mayer and Jack Warner. After being fired from no less an assignment than *Gone with the Wind* because Clark Gable wanted a more macho director (i.e., a heterosexual man named Victor Fleming), Cukor immediately picked himself up to begin work and typecast himself as a woman's director on the ultimate women's picture, *The Women*.

Garland recorded "The Man That Got Away" in the key Martin wanted but didn't give it her best. When everyone, including the assembled orchestra, heard the playback, Garland let it be known, "Hugh, you're so fucking wrong!"

She insisted the higher key worked better and asked her arranger-vocal coach to second that opinion. Instead, he told her, "I don't know why you ask me, Judy. I'm always so fucking wrong."

"You're so fucking right," she shot back.

Martin realized he wasn't in the Palace Theatre or St. Louis or Kansas anymore when this one-sided catfight transpired on September 4, only three days after what was supposed to have been the film's start date. Postponements were the only constant. September 7 turned into September 16 and turned into October 12. The news about the Garland/Martin dustup traveled faster than the ever-changing start date. *Variety* reported in its September 5 issue that there was "a heated verbal hassle" on the set of *A Star Is Born*.

When Martin hightailed it back to New York City, the battle between him and Garland appeared not only in *Variety* but also in major newspapers' gossip columns, all of which helped reestablish Garland's reputation for being difficult and dismissive of highly talented colleagues.

Cukor finally got around to committing "The Man That Got Away" to film on October 20. He shot the song in WarnerScope, using a set that divided the Downbeat Club into three distinct fields of color—salmon, lavender, and electric blue. The color blue made sense since a neon sign outside the venue calls it the Bleu Bleu club. Wearing a pink blouse and gray skirt, Garland lip-synched the song and moved across the set surrounded by musicians in one moving shot. Cukor always envisioned the song being performed in a single take. He admitted it wasn't easy. "You have to be strong. I wanted to do it with Judy because I knew she could sustain it," he said.

Garland, in film after film, honed her own special technique for sustaining the emotion. "In making a movie, there's no audience to play to, only a large crowd of technicians," she said. "I would try to make the electricians and the cameramen and the others react to the song. . . . Only when they had shown the emotion the particular song was supposed to evoke did I feel that I had reached them."

Garland got what she wanted. For Cukor, there were compromises. Few of his ideas for the number, other than it being done in one shot, were realized. Before the shoot began, he told his cinematographer, "I want to see her, but I don't want to see the musicians. I don't want to see their instruments. I don't want to see their faces. I don't want to see anything about them. I just want to see her alone."

Those musicians are very visible, even in the October 20 production of "The Man That Got Away," which required not one but two reshoots. Most problematic, Warner-Scope proved unsatisfactory. It tended to spread images, and that wasn't good for photographing Garland's occasionally expanding hips. The switch required a change in cinematographers too. With $700,000 down the drain, Sam Leavitt replaced cinematographer Winton Hoch to reshoot "The Man That Got Away" over a period of three days, from October 27 to 29. The replacement cinematographer used CinemaScope, a new wide-screen process 20th Century Fox developed, owned, and put to use in its most recent epic. Audiences accustomed to watching a tiny black-and-white screen on their new TV set did not care that *The Robe*, starring Richard Burton and Jean Simmons, told one of the most turgid stories ever committed to film. Americans addicted to weekly doses of *I Love Lucy* and *The Milton Berle Show* now found themselves lured back to movie theaters featuring stadium-size screens in glorious, saturated color.

Camera lenses weren't the only thing that changed on *A Star Is Born*. On the second attempt to film "The Man That Got Away," both Esther Blodgett and the Downbeat Club looked slightly different. Garland eschewed pink to wear a very wrinkled brown dress designed by Mary Ann Nyberg, and Gene Allen's production design now featured a nightclub with only two distinct fields of color. Garland began the song seated against a salmon background and then moved among several band members to sing in front of a gray background, framed by two bright blue pillars.

Over three days, Cukor required Garland to perform twenty-seven takes of "The Man That Got Away."

Cukor had never directed a musical, much less a film in color, much less one using a new, cumbersome technology. Filming *The Robe*, Jean Simmons complained that she had never experienced such heat on a movie set, since the wide-screen process required extreme lighting. On *A Star Is Born*, considering that the temperamental Garland was making her much-anticipated return to the screen, wiser minds might have considered using not only a time-proven technology but also a director with experience making a musical in color, someone like her ex-husband Vincente Minnelli. No one can argue with the brilliance that is the final achievement, but "The Man That Got Away" took no fewer than three attempts by Cukor, plus over a million dollars, to get it just right.

The saga of "The Man That Got Away" didn't end on October 29, 1953. In March of the following year, after more than three months of production on *A Star Is Born*, Cukor decided to shoot the song a third and final time with Garland wearing a far more flattering blue dress with white Peter Pan collar and tie designed by Jean Louis, and her Esther moves through a nightclub that features only one field of color: salmon, with a thin strip of gray on the right side of the screen. Garland lip-synched literally dozens of takes—most of them featuring her signature right-hand-through-the-hair sweep performed twice—to get the one that appears in the movie.

In the first remake of *A Star Is Born*, Garland never looked or performed better than in "The Man That Got Away." The problems with WarnerScope, her dress, and the set cannot in any way be blamed on her. It is arguably the greatest performance of a song ever put in any movie, regardless of AFI's list of great American movie music. Perhaps she gave too much too soon with "The Man That Got Away." As the production progressed, the daily reports from Eric Stacey, head of production at Warner Brothers, began to show an increase in the number of days she missed and a decrease in the number of hours she worked on the days when she managed to show up.

In the beginning, James Mason, always highly professional, missed a few days when an ear disorder induced extreme dizziness. In true Method actor form, he used the condition to great effect in some of his character's early scenes of inebriation. More often, he endured an "inordinate number of 'driving' shots" in cars to give "the impression that we were hard at work," as he described the obfuscation of working around an often-absent leading lady.

Then again, what did Jack Warner expect? As Mason explained, "The higher-ups tended to forget that they had undertaken this operation knowing full well that Judy did not have a reputation for reliability."

Often left out of the criticism of a ballooning budget was Moss Hart's script, which turns Norman Maine's hunt for Esther Blodgett into a marathon of false starts after she delivers "The Man That Got Away." Dumbstruck, Norman asks Esther, "Do you always sing like that?" It then takes forty-five minutes of screen time for her to become a star when she performs the "Born in a Trunk" medley at the preview of her first movie.

There were other reasons for the budget on the first remake of A Star Is Born film to explode. Cukor demanded endless takes, the filming of "The Man That Got Away" being just one example. As Sid Luft described it, "George Cukor's directorial style often involved milking a scene." Moss Hart put it another way, grousing that Cukor "directed just the way he tells stories, passing the point or not making the point of some scene."

The director's penchant for take after take was only half of it. Early in production, Jack Warner hit the persnickety Cukor with a "no excess printing" edict. If Garland was going to do twenty-seven takes of a song, Warner made sure that Cukor had to pick two or three takes to go to print, not all twenty-seven.

Once upon a time, Cukor made his reputation for being an economical director, like Alfred Hitchcock and Otto Preminger, who kept budgets low to prevent a box office failure from becoming a box office disaster. Something about *A Star Is Born* turned Cukor into an expensive perfectionist on the level of Erich von Stroheim, who demanded that extras wear special silk underwear on his 1922 silent classic, *Foolish Wives*, advertised as "the first million-dollar movie." Earl Bellamy, an assistant director on *A Star Is Born*, described one such extravagance: Esther and Norman's jailhouse wedding in the film. Hart lifted it almost word for word from the 1937 screenplay, and the scene closely resembled Garland and Luft's own wedding on June 8, 1952. Like the characters in the film, the real-life couple registered under their real names— Frances Ethel Gumm and Michael Sidney Luft—in Hollister, California, a small town south of San Francisco best known for calling itself "the earthquake center of the world" and inspiring the motorcyclist riot that Marlon Brando immortalized in *The Wild One*.

Cukor was a stickler for detail. If the script asked for a private wedding in a small town, he believed the wedding had to be filmed in a real small town. "Cukor wanted to go away, far away from Los Angeles, because it was kind of a secret affair, their marriage," Bellamy recalled, "and we needed a town that was so small that nobody in the place would recognize them; nobody would even know they were there." Cukor may have known the difference between Podunk, California, and a back lot in Burbank, California, but the audiences did not.

Songs are an added expense for any movie, but Warner Brothers in the 1930s made its reputation on smart, sassy little musicals that eschewed the colorful (and far more expensive) extravaganzas that the Arthur Freed unit would bring to MGM, beginning in 1939. Jack Warner caught gargantuanitis with *A Star Is Born*, an ailment that would infect his career up to the very last film he made at his studio, the epic mistake that was *Camelot* in 1968.

James Mason pointed out one budget-exploding problem early in the film's shooting schedule. George Hoyningen-Huene, the film's color coordinator, relied on such classic paintings as *The Dancers* and *The Dancing Class* for inspiration to create the film's spectacular opening sequence at the Shrine Auditorium in Los Angeles. Much of the backstage action recalls those Edgar Degas works of art, and Cukor's direction and Sam Leavitt's cinematography is unquestionably brilliant.

Elsewhere, however, Mason failed to admire the color coordinator's influence on the movie. "Cukor had a habit, aided and abetted by his friend George Hoyningen-Huene, of relating his films or parts of them visually with the work of some painter," the actor noted. Apparently, beyond the great Degas, the color coordinator on *A Star Is Born* much admired a minor eighteenth-century Swiss painter named Henry Fuseli, who often depicted the supernatural in his art. Hoyningen-Huene sought to bring some of that otherworldly mystery to one of Norman Maine's hangovers early in the film. The designer thought this could best be achieved not by Mason's performance but a bevy of female extras dressed in Halloween costumes.

"I had not learned of this until I ran into a strange-looking girl in one of the corridors of the studio," Mason reported. He wondered which film on the Warner Brothers lot employed this bizarrely costumed extra. What horror film was *that*? Mason thought he would be the only actor pretending to endure a hangover in the scene—until meeting this colorfully attired extra. "She told me she was playing the part of a curtain. She seemed to think that this explained everything," he noted. "It was revealed that Cukor was going to mix these peculiarly painted girls with the curtains so that they could move as if in a breeze. I would think in my drunken haziness that I saw a girl, and then . . . Ah, it's just a curtain."

It's just one of many expensive scenes that were filmed and then cut.

Regarding the film's escalating budget, costumes to be worn (or not) by Garland and Mason contributed to the expenditures. Mary Ann Nyberg created a white dress for the pivotal Academy Awards scene, where Norman accidentally slaps Vicki. Garland liked the gown so much she wanted it for her own personal use and threw a fit to carry it off the studio lot and home with her that night. "Look at this thing!" she yelled, using reverse psychology. "How can you expect me to wear this? It makes me look like a white whale." Garland refused to wear the dress on the set. At private parties, however, she had no problem looking like Moby Dick's cousin in the outfit. Garland wore another costume off the set and subsequently ruined it for use in front of the camera.

For the Academy Awards scene, she instead wore a dark-purple gown designed by Nyberg. What surrounded Garland, however, bore no resemblance to any Oscar ceremony of recent vintage. Having starred in a movie titled *A World for Two*, Garland's Vicki Lester competes for best actress against only three other actresses (there are not the usual five nominees) at a dinner banquet complete with tables and waiters at the Coconut Grove nightclub in the Ambassador Hotel. It's a venue that had not been used by the Academy since 1940 when Garland, at age sixteen, received the honorary Academy Juvenile Award, previously presented to Jackie Cooper and Shirley Temple, among other actors under age eighteen.

Sid Luft also used the film to fill his own closet. Jack Warner complained, "As soon as Mason reported for work, Sid read the script and noted two or three wardrobe changes for the male star. He went to the tailor and ordered twelve suits—nine wardrobe changes that Mason didn't wear." While much of what the film mogul wrote in his memoir is nonsense, Lorna Luft, the producer's daughter, verified this anecdote in her memoir.

More controversial is Warner's accusation that Luft emptied the set of the Malibu living room—where Vicki sings "Someone at Last" to cheer up an unemployed Norman—and used those furnishings to fill the Lufts' nineteen-room mansion in Holmby Hills. Lorna Luft recognized that decor from her childhood but defended her parents. She claimed that the sofa, tables, rug, and various tchotchkes had been paid for ten cents on the dollar as part of her father's written contract with the studio.

The greatest difficulty in controlling the budget on the first remake of *A Star Is Born* remained its star. Garland's erratic behavior is immortalized in many memos from Eric Stacey to Jack Warner, who liked to have the title "colonel" put before his name, even though he never achieved that rank in the armed forces. One such memo from the production head details how money routinely got flushed down the backlot gutters. "Late last night, Mr. Luft informed that that [*sic*] Miss Garland would be unable to come to work today, Saturday, to continue in the Malibu home. This information was received too late to cancel any of the crew that had been called." And since it was a weekend call, the entire crew received overtime for no time spent doing their respective jobs.

The actress Amanda Blake performed in the opening sequence at the Shrine Auditorium, playing a radio host who interviews celebrities making their entrance. In some respects, what went on behind the scene (Garland being difficult, Mason being respectful) stood in stark contrast to what was being captured in front of the cameras (Esther Blodgett being respectful, Norman Maine being difficult).

"Judy was very out of control," Blake recalled, "and certainly her husband who was producing could never control her, but James [Mason] was always wonderful, very patient when she was late on the set."

Even Lorna Luft, born a year before *A Star Is Born* went into production, noted how Garland made a habit of misbehaving. "My mother was used to having everyone cater to her, including her sisters. She knew how to throw a tantrum," she noted.

Jack Warner, dismissive of Garland's husband from the get-go, eventually lost patience with the star who so enchanted him in 1952 at the Los Angeles Philharmonic. The phone call that broke the studio chief's streak of patience came on a weekend when Warner performed his Sunday ritual of playing eighteen holes of golf. More than anything else, Warner didn't like having his putting on the green interrupted. Suddenly, he had no problem scolding his temperamental star, telling her over the phone, "Judy, you've given us a lot of trouble. We gave you everything you wanted, and now you're calling up to complain to me. I don't like to be disturbed at my home. Don't bother me again. You were utterly spoiled by the people at MGM. You've cost us a hell of a lot of money by going over schedule on this picture. That's all!"

If anyone had reason to complain, it was her costar, who always stood firmly in Garland's corner. "To get something as unique as Judy's talent, some patience and certain sacrifices were needed," Mason believed.

Moss Hart also never wavered in praising Garland's great talent. It was one of the few facets of the production he didn't harshly criticize. During the shoot, he wrote several hissy-fit memos to Cukor and Warner to complain about cuts to his script. At one point, he even bragged, "I've apparently stirred up quite a hornet's nest out there, and I am rather pleased that I have."

A manic-depressive, the writer experienced one of his signature mood swings when he visited the set to do some rewriting. In a letter to his wife, Kitty Carlisle, who remained behind in New York City, Hart wrote that never before had he hit "the low point I had reached in California."

He arrived at this nadir early one morning in a bar across the street from the Warner Brothers studios. The writing session there had already gone on for hours. "Then at five in the morning, I had quite a skirmish with Judy, who wanted me to rewrite a love scene," Hart revealed.

In letters and private conversations, he was quite the critic, because Hart made a habit of lashing out at such gifted talents as the "terribly affected" Leonard Bernstein and the "lost lady" Barbara Stanwyck, as well as the new movie *On the Waterfront*. He "hated" the yet-to-be-released picture directed by Elia Kazan and was angered by the glowing reports from the press and celebrities alike. His outrage didn't end there. He wrote, "I also felt that Marlon Brando had become a caricature of himself and seemed like a parlor imitation that Sid Luft does of him."

After seeing a rough cut of *A Star Is Born*, Hart found himself suddenly stuck in yet another deep depression. "I was terribly shaken by what I saw," he wrote. "I thought James Mason was terribly uneven—good in some things, extremely bad in others." He felt the same way about Cukor's spotty direction.

In a memo to Jack Warner, Hart expressed anger at the film's editing, especially the scene that follows "The Man That Got Away," where Norman tells Esther to dream big, to be a movie star. "I want to protest as strongly and vigorously as I can at the way this scene has been cut. It is their big scene together, the scene that kicks off their relationship and the scene that established Norman Maine as the kind of person he really is. . . . Whoever cut it has calmly proceeded to take all the character and juice out, leaving it as dull and cliché as possible. . . . I hardly think I deserve this kind of dismissal."

The only thing Hart liked about the early cut of *A Star Is Born* was its female star. If Garland had been difficult to work with or caused the film to go over budget, the film's screenwriter did not care. "The only saving grace, it seemed to me, was that Judy was spectacular. She is an extraordinary actress of depth and emotion and very rarely goes over the edge into sentimentality," he wrote.

In Hart's eyes, Garland could do no wrong. "She can be quite difficult and perhaps the achievement of the entire picture is that fact that she has gotten along so well with George that they are going to be able to finish it. . . . I can forgive her anything," he wrote. Like Cukor, he compared Garland to the stage actress Laurette Taylor. The director and the screenwriter agreed on one thing, and that was Judy Garland.

"She works intensely and can only sustain the pace for short periods, but it's well worth it, for she is a revelation in her emotional scenes," Cukor said.

Garland stood first in line to second that opinion. She liked to boast, "Someone told me I work as if I have only ten minutes left to do everything in."

Except for that one early morning phone call in a bar off the Warner Brothers lot, Hart never had to work with Garland on a daily basis. Cukor did, and finally, even his extreme admiration of this gifted artist left him exhausted, if not broken. Garland pointed to her artistic integrity as the reason for the film going over budget, and she threw her director under the same careening, out-of-control leviathan. She paid him the dubious compliment of also being uncompromising.

"I'd be the last to deny the picture took an awful lot of time and went way over the budget," she said. "But there was a reason for all that. I'm a perfectionist; George Cukor, who directed, is a perfectionist; and so is Sid. We have to have it right, and to make it right took time."

Cukor saw it somewhat differently, having experienced firsthand both Garland's brilliance and her unprofessionalism. He expressed his frustration in a letter to good friend Katharine Hepburn, written during the last month of production on *A Star Is Born*. (Or what Cukor thought was the last month of production.) Garland often claimed being too sick to show up on the set, but the next day, Cukor would pick up the *Los Angeles Times* to read reports that his ailing star had been seen at the horse races with Sid Luft or singing and dancing at the Mocambo.

"About three weeks ago, strange, sinister, and sad things began happening to Judy," Cukor wrote to Hepburn. "This is the behavior of someone unhinged, but there is an arrogance and ruthless selfishness that eventually alienates one's sympathy. She's always saying that the trouble with her is that she's honest and direct, and that everyone lies to her. The fact is that when she's in this state, the truth isn't in her; she's devious and untrustworthy. I found that not only had she no regard for anyone, but if you're forced by your work to be at the mercy of such erratic goings-on, you find yourself responding in an all-too-human way."

From the Palladium in London, to a tour of Scotland and Ireland, then opening at the Palace Theatre, and winding up in California at the Los Angeles Philharmonic Auditorium and later San Francisco's Curran Theatre, Garland had performed spectacularly with few incidents. The movies, however, are another kind of medium. Perhaps her perfectionism did not allow her to perform at less than 101 percent when her singing would be preserved for posterity on celluloid. A debilitating paranoia set in, making it impossible for her to deliver or even show up.

And then there were all the pills she took, the vodka she

drank. To get through the workday, Garland needed to down a cocktail of Seconal and Dexamyl. Those drugs were prescribed by Dr. Fred Pobirs, the same doctor who recommended that Garland undergo a series of shock treatments to ready her for production on *Annie Get Your Gun* back at MGM before the studio fired her. On the set of *A Star Is Born*, a nurse accompanied the star. Garland introduced Margaret Gundy as her secretary. Everybody on the set just called her Gundy. It was yet another example of life copying the screenplay copying life. It began with John Barrymore being cared for by a nurse named Kelly, who became Cuddles in both the 1937 and 1954 versions of *A Star Is Born*. And once again, it was Garland's life replicating not the Esther Blodgett/Vicki Lester character but Norman Maine.

Reviewing her own performance, Garland found nothing not to admire in *A Star Is Born*. "I never really liked myself on the screen before. But now I go to the rushes, and I actually enjoy them," she said. "I even cry a little at the sad scenes. The four years have done me a lot of good. I got out and met the people and sang before live audiences. It improved my timing, and my voice is better too. I think I look better. I don't have that 'little girl' look anymore."

Chapter 7

The remake of *A Star Is Born* wrapped on March 17, 1954. Or, at least, most people working on the film, including George Cukor and Moss Hart, thought it had wrapped. "The picture was, in fact, too long," the director admitted. And he wasn't the only one thinking it.

Hart fired off yet another angry letter to Jack Warner: "I have had a goodly number of reports from people to whom you have shown the picture—all completely laudatory but all complaining about length, particularly in the beginning. I am not at all certain that they give you the complete truth—it is what I might term 'projection room truth'—i.e., you get their praise but not their reservation, and their chief reservation in spite of their genuine feeling about the picture is length—harmful and unnecessary length. So much so that I am apprehensive that what appears to be a fine picture might be jeopardized by a too-loving eye or an unwillingness to relinquish some parts for the good of the whole."

Rather than listening to his director and screenwriter, Warner took the advice of Sid Luft, whom he had otherwise found completely incompetent. Late in the production, the film's inexperienced producer experienced an epiphany, as if he had never before read Hart's screenplay. "I discovered a big hole in Moss's script. . . . There was no musical number to transform Vicki within the storyline. The audience needed to see why she became a star," Luft insisted.

Or, as Garland explained, "Our picture will show why the girl reaches the top." It's a plot element that she found lacking in the first *A Star Is Born.*

Lorna Luft gave another reason her parents added a big musical number. "Mama's ambition for her picture had been supercharged by the grand success of her ex-husband Vincente Minnelli's *An American in Paris,*" she reported. "For her movie, Mama wanted something comparable, preferably even to outshine it."

In fact, despite Sid Luft's claims to the contrary, Hart had written the spot for just such a song in his screenplay's original outline. He saw the need for six songs. They are listed as follows, with number three being the song that "will show why the girl reaches the top":

1. *Benefit show—Esther and orchestra*
2. *"Dive" song—Esther and small group*
3. *Movie rehearsal song (happy type), partial, reprised complete at preview*
4. *Song in recording stage (marriage proposal with interruptions)*
5. *Honeymoon song in motel, to be reprised later*
6. *Malibu beach home song (funny song, she tries to cheer Norman up)*
7. *Reprise of 5, probably sung over suicide or at end*

Hart's final screenplay stuck to most of those suggestions. "Gotta Have Me Go with You" shows how Esther rescues Norman at the Shrine benefit. The dive song is "The Man That Got Away." The marriage proposal comes after Esther, now renamed Vicki Lester, sings "Here's What I'm Here For" in a recording studio, the song being conducted by Warner Brothers's own music director, Ray Heindorf, in a bit of real-life casting. Vicki first sings "It's a New World" on their honeymoon in a motel. The funny song that cheers up Norman is "Someone at Last," which also acts to recap Vicki's latest movie musical, now in production. Not listed but written and filmed is "Lose That Long Face," a musical number from that movie; she sings it before and after having an emotional breakdown regarding Norman's chronic alcoholism. The studio chief Oliver Niles, played by Charles Bickford, is so moved by her dressing room outburst, confession, and plea that he decides to offer Norman a second chance.

Not included in the final film is song number three, the movie rehearsal song that is to be reprised at the movie preview where a star is born. The sentence "A star is born" is spoken only in the 1937 film and in none of the remakes.

Despite Garland and Luft's claims to the contrary, the audience learns of Esther's phenomenal talents precisely when Norman does: as soon as she sings "The Man That Got Away." Clearly, a reprise of that song would have achieved the required effect at Vicki's movie preview if Cukor had not already used the moment earlier when Norman summons Oliver Niles to his dressing room to complain about the decor. It's a ruse. During the actor's contrived attack, Niles "accidentally" eavesdrops on Vicki singing the song a second time as the strains of "The Man That Got Away" stream through the dressing room windows. Niles is outraged that Norman wastes his precious time on interior-design aesthetics when he has bigger issues. Foremost among his troubles, a star singer has reneged on her commitment to appear in a new musical film, and he needs to replace her, pronto. During their argument about sofas and window treatments, Niles hears Vicki's singing and says to Norman, "Not bad. Who is she?" Norman tells him, "You have her under contract." The studio chief finally understands. "A light begins to break," he says.

In place of song number three is a brief sequence where Vicki rehearses a dance number from the song "Black Bottom" in the "Born in a Trunk" medley. Despite Luft's critique about "a big hole in Moss's script," Harold Arlen and Ira Gershwin wrote no fewer than three songs for Vicki Lester to sing in the film-with-in-a-film moment when she watches herself on screen at the big preview. The problem was, Garland didn't like "Green Light Ahead" or "Dancing Partner." Initially, she approved of "I'm Off the Downbeat," but Luft convinced her otherwise.

Gershwin fretted, "Don't know what to do about it." His initial reaction was to write another song. As he put it, "Give them what they think they want." There were two problems with that seemingly easy solution: Arlen was busy writing the music for a new Broadway musical, *House of Flowers*, and while performing those chores, the composer ended up in the hospital with a bleeding ulcer.

Without consulting Arlen and Gershwin—or Hart or Cukor, for that matter—Luft enlisted Roger Edens to fill this imaginary hole in *A Star Is Born*, and together with Lenny Gershe, the new songwriting team came up with "Born in a Trunk."

"It was, in fact, the story of Judy's life," Luft believed.

And it would last nearly as long. The medley tells the story of a young singer who achieves fame by becoming a star in vaudeville. Gershwin did not kick up a fuss regarding what he considered a "messy situation." He went so far as to wonder that "lost is the hope of the producer that the film would be released by now." With Arlen out of commission, he could only opine, "[T]here's too little sleep left as is."

Before "Born in a Trunk" went into production, Jack Warner treated a few of his top directors to a private screening of the unfinished remake of *A Star Is Born*. Among them were Elia Kazan, busy directing *East of Eden* with James Dean at the studio. After that screening on May 17, Kazan dashed off a note to Moss Hart. While he thought "Judy has superb moments" and there were "some especially good scenes," Kazan delivered a negative critique. "I thought Cukor had directed it without a sense of proportion," he wrote. "Everything had been blown up or glamorized. Numbers which were supposed to be the essence of informality were informal on such a huge scale! I also thought he had put too much self-pity into the feelings of the two leads."

Despite his thumbs-down opinion of Luft, Jack Warner approved the added expense of $250,000 to film "Born in a Trunk" and gave the go-ahead in late April.

And, of course, it didn't go as Luft promised. Even in the middle of May, with filming still a month away, Warner had already returned to form to complain to Luft, "Have you any ideas when rehearsals will start? My impression is that the number should be in front of the cameras by the first week in June or before, if possible."

If nothing else, Luft knew how to work Warner to get what Garland wanted. He even asked that the filming take place at night, despite the enormous overtime charges, because his wife functioned more reliably after six o'clock in the evening. Warner, his masochism getting the better of him, agreed.

Forget about Cukor and Hart, who were never consulted about the added sequence. "Born in a Trunk" emerged as a major act of subterfuge. Edens had been Garland's "original trainer and overseer and a lifelong friend," according to Lorna Luft, but one who remained under contract to MGM. He could take no credit for his work on "Born in a Trunk." Edens wrote the music, and Gersche provided the lyrics to the original song "I Was Born in a Trunk" that is part of the medley. Gersche also wrote the dialogue and recitative that Garland delivers to string together such standards from the 1910s and 1920s as "I'll Get By," "You Took Advantage of Me," "Black Bottom," "El Manicero (Peanut Vendor)," "My Melancholy Baby," and "Swanee."

The medley clocks in at fifteen minutes. It could have been even longer. Also filmed but cut was "When My Sugar Walks Down the Street (All the Birdies Go Tweet-Tweet-Tweet)." That jazz standard from 1924 shows how Garland's character in "Born in a Trunk" came to replace Mom in her parents' vaudeville routine.

To no one's surprise, the original budget of a quarter of a million dollars ballooned to $350,000, and instead of taking a couple of weeks to film, as originally planned, "Born in a Trunk" started filming on June 30 and ended a full month later, on July 29 at 2:45 in the morning.

Sometime before the final-final wrap of both "Born in a Trunk" and *A Star Is Born*, Hedda Hopper let her readers at the *Los Angeles Times* know precisely what she thought of such profligate waste in the movie business. The gossip columnist with the crazy hats never liked Garland, and the feeling was mutual. Whenever the star had a major or even minor scoop to deliver, she sent it directly to Hopper's primary rival, Louella Parsons at the *Los Angeles Examiner*. During the film's production, Hopper often took the opportunity to trash the *Star* remake, and after "Born in a Trunk" had been in production for a couple of weeks with no end in sight, she lambasted the decision to shoot the medley, which she misreported as a dance number in her column.

"When I asked why Warners would spend money on a ballet sequence in *Star* when the picture already cost $4,500,000 and runs three hours and twenty minutes," Hopper wrote, "I was told that after that much, why quibble over another $200,000 to make it better?"

When Gershwin saw *A Star Is Born*, he liked the finished film, calling it a "big hit." He offered a somewhat more reserved opinion about the treatment of his and Arlen's songs, writing "Generally the songs come off okay or better." He saved his biggest criticism, unsurprisingly, for "Born in a Trunk," calling it a "big mistake (but all none of my business)."

In an interview conducted ten years after the film's release, George Cukor finally offered his true opinion of the medley. "That huge fifteen-minute "Born in a Trunk" number threw everything out of kilter," he opined. But being a company man, he kept those thoughts to himself in the summer of 1954. He even went so far as to say, "I didn't direct it. I don't know who did."

He did know, of course. It was directed by Richard Barstow, the film's choreographer, who grabbed the directorial reigns with all due speed. His previous major credit had been as choreographer of the circus numbers in Cecil B. DeMille's 1952 film, *The Greatest Show on Earth*. That assignment made sense, since Barstow's career began at the Ringling Brothers and Barnum & Bailey Circus, where he choreographed clowns, acrobats, elephants, and other critters. His career as a film director essentially began and ended with *A Star Is Born*, and it shows. Why Garland trusted him remains a mystery. Only a few months earlier, when the erstwhile circus choreographer directed the unimaginatively staged "Lose That Long Face" number, Garland wanted to know, "Where's George?" When told that Barstow would both choreograph and direct the musical number, she launched into one of her vintage tantrums, walked off the set, and got into her limousine, where she proceeded to down a bottle of vodka. Now, in June and ready to film "Born in a Trunk," she voiced no problem snubbing Cukor and working with Barstow. Again.

James Mason came up with a novel idea for a much shorter number to replace "Born in a Trunk," which he also called a "liability . . . all the film needed at this spot was a few feet of Judy belting a show-stopping number," he wrote. "The obvious thing for Jack Warner to do was to ring up Louis B. Mayer—assuming they were on speaking terms—and, having broken the ice with a couple of locker room jokes, say something like, 'Hey L. B., I'd be very grateful if you could find me a few feet of some Judy Garland musical number that they couldn't find a place for in one of your musicals. Nothing important. A finale of some sort would work best.' "

The easiest solution would have been to cut "Born in a Trunk" to bring the film down to a manageable length. Of course, Garland's core fans could not tolerate such a thing. In the final version of the film, she sings no fewer than seven songs by no fewer than seven different songwriting teams in that medley, and as wonderful as some of those standards are, they are not unlike Maria Callas deciding to interject in the middle of *La Traviata* a slew of arias by a number of Italian opera composers not named Giuseppe Verdi.

Brilliant, maybe. Wrong, absolutely.

Cukor took one look at a rough cut of the film with the addition of "Born in a Trunk" and fired off a letter to Hart. "Neither the human mind nor the human ass can stand three and a half hours of concentration," he wrote. In Ron Haver's book *A Star Is Born: The Making of the 1954 Movie and its 1983 Restoration*, the author uses Cukor's quote to reference the director's impression that the film needed an intermission. In fact, Cukor referred instead to the sheer length of the original film, not the need for a popcorn or restroom break.

One of the director's close friends put his criticism of the film in slightly more graphic terms. "Every song was attenuated to such a length that I thought I was going mad," Noël Coward wrote. "One in particular, 'Born in a Trunk,' started brilliantly, but by the time it was over and we had endured montage after montage and repetition after repetition, I found myself wishing that dear, enchanting Judy was at the bottom of the sea."

Cukor, after sitting through the film's first preview in August 1954, strenuously objected to the editing. Especially upsetting were the number of scenes now lost between Esther singing "The Man That Got Away" and her landing a contract at the studio. These are the very sections of the movie that Warner would chop out post-premiere. Before those final cuts were made, Cukor did manage to convince Warner to reinstate much of the "lost" footage. "After a lot of wrangling, I won my point," Cukor wrote to Hart. "How right I was to kick up that fuss. . . . I won't go into detail about how heavy a hand he used in his depredations—how inept and insensitive—because you might rupture another disc."

The director did think some cuts were needed. As Cukor also explained to Hart, "What made my job of per suasion a wee bit more difficult was everybody saying to Warner, 'Don't cut a single inch of it.' This was absolute nonsense. . . . I wish the picture were a little shorter."

Perhaps fifteen minutes shorter, which would have left "Born in a Trunk" on the cutting room floor.

Surprisingly, Cukor suggested that "Here's What I'm Here For" and Norman's subsequent marriage proposal to Vicki in the recording studio be cut. "Charming and original as it is, it seems to me now—after the passionate love scene on the terrace of the nightclub—to be anticlimactic, back treading, as it were. I suggest that this scene might be cut, but Jack Warner was adamant," Cukor wrote. The director also reported that he had been able to cut twelve minutes from the film. Despite all the hassles of directing the film's temperamental star, Cukor found the effort completely worthwhile. "Judy generates a kind of hysteria from an audience. This was especially noticeable at the first preview in Huntington Park," Cukor added, his written diatribe to Katharine Hepburn about Garland's bad behavior now academic, if not forgotten.

At a second preview, fifteen minutes were trimmed, the film running 181 minutes, the length that audiences would see at its premiere in Los Angeles on September 29 and in New York City on October 11, 1954.

On the eve of the film's September premiere, Jack Warner came down with a bad case of buyer's remorse and fired off a memo about the difficulties bringing Judy Garland back to the movies. He wrote to Mort Blumenstock, the studio's head of national publicity, to take special care with her: "It is quite apparent that being off the screen for five years . . . Judy Garland is not a favorite . . . nor is she even known to many teenagers," who, at the time, were the largest movie-going block in the country.

Chapter 8

Shortly before the movie opened, *Life* magazine put Judy Garland on its September 13 cover with an article titled "New Day for Judy." The picture magazine reported that "Garland's energy and talent create, then overcome obstacles in *A Star Is Born*." The profile went on to rave that "the year's most worrisome movie has turned out to be one of its best." But a hornet caught in the ointment of its pages is a photo of an angry Garland on the set, pointing her finger in defiance at someone, or something, just out of the camera's range. Under the incriminating photo, a caption reveals, "Judy bawls out a studio technician."

At the film's premiere on September 29 at the Pantages Theatre, twenty thousand fans, along with almost every star in the Hollywood firmament, showed up to welcome Garland back to the screen. Everyone from Bogie and Bacall to Liz and Marlene attended the premiere, but two famous faces who failed to make the pilgrimage were George Cukor, busy in Pakistan scouting locations for his next picture, *Bhowani Junction*, and James Mason, apparently watching TV somewhere in Beverly Hills.

Jack Warner shot off a wire to the male star playing hooky: "There's an old adage. One must put something back if they want to continue taking something out." *A Star Is Born* is the only movie James Mason ever made at Warner Brothers while its eponymous king ruled there.

The coverage of that premiere by *The Mirror* could have been written by the studio's publicity department. "Filmdom Hails Judy's Comeback," reporter Roby Heard wrote. "The largest turnout of stars of many years paid tribute to the turbulent singing actress who was considered washed-up in pictures four years ago." However, as with the *Life* magazine profile, *The Mirror* couldn't help but follow a compliment with a slap at Garland's controversial past, adding, "She was a far cry from the temperamental star whose tantrums led to an end of her long MGM career."

The reviews were uniformly positive, except for the most influential hometown newspaper. Edwin Schallet in the *Los Angeles Times* wrote that *A Star Is Born* was "overstressed" and "potentially a target for strong critical resistance."

That mixed-to-downbeat review didn't presage well for Garland's trip east for the New York City premiere on October 11. As *The New York World-Telegram* reported it in the newspaper's headline, MILLIONS MISS JUDY'S ARRIVAL. The anonymous reporter revealed that "Judy Garland arrived at Grand Central fifteen minutes late from the coast this morning and kept NO fans waiting. The Warner Bros. publicity office had hinted delicately that 'several thousand teenagers from fan clubs in three states' were expected to be on hand to welcome Judy. But when Miss Garland arrived at 9:15 on the Century for the premiere, most of the welcomers were reporters."

One fan who did show up was a teenager named Arthur Bell. "I saw *A Star Is Born* opening night at the Paramount

in 1954 and got Judy Garland's autograph later that evening at the Waldorf Towers," Bell wrote in his *Village Voice*
column three decades later. "She was sweet and asked her
fans what they thought, and I remember keeping my mouth
shut. What I thought then and I think now is that the
movie's a mess. Garland overacts—in certain scenes I want
to shake her shoulders and feed her downs."

For the moment, snappish comments in the *Los Angeles
Times* and the *World-Telegram* could be dismissed along
with one teenager's negative opinion about *A Star Is Born*.
When it finally opened to the general public, a top box office analyst saw nothing but good news. *Variety*, the bible
of the entertainment industry, reported a bonanza of
$700,000 in seventeen theaters in the film's first week of re-
lease, calling those numbers "[a] showing a little short of
phenomenal . . . Boffola box office, period . . . Fort Knox,
move over."

The keepers of America's gold reserves didn't have to
worry. *Variety*'s ebullient analysis of the film's box office
potential turned into a notoriously bad prediction only a
month later. Those original seventeen theaters were all located in the biggest cities in the country, three of which—
New York City, San Francisco, and Los Angeles—were
places that Garland had scored great publicity with her
live appearances on stage. As soon as the film expanded to
theaters beyond the nation's major urban areas, the box
office immediately hit a wall. Exhibitors blamed the suddenly tepid grosses on the film's length. Instead of half a
dozen screenings a day, theaters were limited to only two
or three. That might work for a blockbuster like *Gone
with the Wind* but not a comeback film starring Judy Garland.

When *A Star Is Born* opened in New York City, *The
Toast of the Town* (a.k.a. *The Ed Sullivan Show*) clocked
in over twelve million TV viewers every Sunday night. The

exceedingly laconic host of television's most popular variety show opined on the movie in his syndicated newspaper column. "It would have been much more palatable to the general public had it been lacking twenty minutes in running time," Ed Sullivan wrote. He took special aim at the "Born in a Trunk" number, which "was designed as a tour de force for the Garland character. In consequence, the picture has not done as well at the box office as expected."

Instead of dropping "Born in a Trunk," Jack Warner found another twenty-seven minutes to delete. His older brother Harry, the moneyman at the studio, demanded it. Removed were "Here's What I'm Here For" and "Lose That Long Face," as well as Norman's protracted hunt for Esther after their meeting at the Downbeat Club. The film's production designer recalled the slashing of *A Star Is Born*. "Jack Warner and others were snipping away at it," Gene Allen said. "We were a long way away [in Pakistan on the movie *Bhowani Junction*], and we couldn't stop anything."

Bosley Crowther in *The New York Times* offered a critique of the new, shorter film, calling it *A Star Is Shorn*. Sid Luft remembered, "The film's grosses fell off as word circulated about the nearly half hour of deleted material." The fact is, the film never performed well outside the major urban centers.

Just before the release of *A Star Is Born*, the moody Moss Hart experienced a rare, sharp mood upswing. Forgetting his many fights with Jack Warner, he wrote to the studio chief to gush, "There's a reason you are the greatest showman in Hollywood." When Warner cut *A Star Is Born* and the film began to tank at the box office, Hart not only fell completely out of love with the movie mogul but also sank into another of his dark funks. In early December 1954, he returned to the City of Angels to have dinner at the legendary Beverly Hills restaurant Romanoff's, where he saw everyone—Judy Garland and Sid Luft, Janet Gaynor and Adrian, Clifton Webb and Barbara Stanwyck. Very unimpressed, he wrote, "the entire place was like a great cross section of Hollywood. It was as though one had never left it, or these people were painted on the walls." *A Star Is Born* would be Moss Hart's last screenplay.

After seeing the new cut version, Cukor refused ever again to watch what some critics called his masterpiece. "The story of what happened to *A Star Is Born* is rather sad," he recalled years later. "After the initial release, the studio found that its length restricted the number of daily showings, so they cut it further, and I think disastrously."

Cukor, however, kept deeply negative words like "disastrously" to himself for a good ten years. In 1963, Jack Warner paid him back for his loyalty by letting him direct *My Fair Lady*, which won the legendary director his one and only Academy Award despite the film being a lackluster copy of the Broadway production minus Julie Andrews. After the glow of that Oscar triumph sufficiently faded, only then did Cukor unleash his true feelings about the man who reduced *A Star Is Born* to a mere understudy, in his opinion. "Jack Warners's last crime!" he announced. "I've been used to cuts in pictures that I've done, but this one strikes me as irreparable and tragic. Maybe *tragic* is too pompous a word—but it was awfully sad and unnecessary."

In the end, even Sid Luft had to admit why the cuts, miserable as they were, could not be avoided. "We did too much of everything," he said. "Too much movie and too much music. It was good too much."

The Academy Awards in March 1955 remained the last chance for *A Star Is Born* to regain some box office momentum. The six nominations received included ones for Garland's and Mason's respective performances in the lead actor categories, but Cukor's direction and Hart's screen-play failed to make the cut. Most important, the Academy snubbed the film where it meant the most: a nomination for best picture. *On the Waterfront* and *The Caine Mutiny* dominated the nominations that year and also receiving a best picture nomination were *The Country Girl*, *Three Coins in the Fountain*, and *Seven Brides for Seven Brothers*. In the public imagination today, only *On the Waterfront* holds anywhere near the esteem and popularity of *A Star Is Born* even in its truncated version. So much for the stay-ing power of a best picture Oscar nomination.

In 1955, *A Star Is Born* suffered from a major image problem. In the weeks leading up to the Academy Awards on March 30, the movie looked to be a big money loser, unlike that year's five best picture nominees. Even in the original 1937 film, a nastiness lurks around the edges of *A Star Is Born*, and Academy voters didn't like smelling any criticism of their profession, especially the fact that a star today is often an actor out of work tomorrow. Jack Car-son took the brunt of it. His brutal portrayal of studio flack Matt Libby angered Hollywood's many publicists who were Academy members. They didn't vote on the nominees, but they voted on who won in all categories. Carson offered apologies. He even revealed that he had talked to Cukor and Luft during production, trying to convince them about "letting me make a pitch for [Nor-man] Maine at the end [of the film], but they wouldn't go for it." His comment "a pitch" refers to the scene where Tommy Noonan, playing Vicki's good friend Danny McGuire, talks to her after Norman's suicide. She wants to retire. He thinks she should make a public appearance where it all began, at the Shrine Auditorium. "As a monu-ment and tribute to her late husband," Carson explained. "That's the sequence I wanted to do. It would have taken some of the sting off me."

Cukor and Luft nixed that idea, and, still deeply stung, Carson begged to be made master of ceremonies at the eighth annual Panhandle Dinner staged by the Screen Publicists Guild. As newspaper reporter Harold Heffernan wrote, "The publicists were not only highly indignant at Jack's vitriolic impersonation of one of their craft, they were outspokenly antagonistic."

Garland was in no condition to do any such press maneuvers to assuage rumors that "she had aged Jack Warner ten years," as one reporter put it. Busy being pregnant with her third child, she committed to one assignment to help promote the film. The Academy asked her to present the award for best song, and she quickly accepted, wanting to hand Oscars to Harold Arlen and Ira Gershwin for "The Man That Got Away."

Her own Oscar was less assured. Good friend Lauren Bacall recalled the pressure for Garland to win. It would help the film's sinking box office figures, and a best actress Oscar would return some of the comeback luster that the film possessed at its Hollywood premiere. "She knew it was then or never," Bacall noted. "Instinctively, all her friends knew the same. Judy wasn't like any other performer. There was so much emotion involved in her career—in her life—it was always all or nothing."

Pre-Oscars, those friends felt some encouragement when *Look* magazine gave its award for best actress to Garland. But there were omens that Garland did not have a lock on the Academy Award. At the much less prestigious Golden Globe Awards, while Garland won for best actress in a musical or comedy, Grace Kelly won for best actress in a drama, *The Country Girl*.

Joey Luft arrived ahead of schedule, the day before the Oscar bash, on March 29. Bacall sat in the audience at the Pantages Theatre that night to accept if Garland were to win. Still recuperating in the hospital, Garland agreed to have the big moment televised, which would have been a first for any winner. The ceremony itself had been telecast for the first time only since 1953.

Because Cedars of Lebanon in Los Angeles refused to allow TV cameras inside the facilities, NBC built a tower outside Garland's hospital window to capture the big moment. Microphones were another story. Technicians quickly turned the hospital room into an obstacle course of wires, one of them running right up the Oscar nominee's nightgown.

And then from the stage of the Pantages Theatre, William Holden announced the nominees for best actress. The winner was one of his most recent female costars. "Grace Kelly, *The Country Girl*," he said.

Bacall didn't have to budge from her seat as the future princess of Monaco ascended to the stage to accept the award. Garland's best friend later remarked, "And though she put on a hell of a front, this was one more slap in the face. She was bitter about it, and, for that matter, all closest to her were."

There's some circuitous irony in the fact that Bacall had been picked to accept the Oscar if Garland were to win. The scene replayed itself fifty-five years later when Bogart's widow was nominated for best supporting actress for her performance in *The Mirror Has Two Faces*. In one of the Academy's biggest shockers, Bacall watched in tears as Juliette Binoche accepted the Oscar for her performance in *The English Patient*. Not lost on many in the motion picture industry was how much Bacall resembled Garland in their respective moments of Oscar defeat. Both actresses' on-the-set behavior had alienated those Academy voters who were not the big above-the-line talent. For years, the publicists, cinematographers, designers, and other names unfamiliar to the general public had been on the receiving end of extremely arrogant and bad behavior from these two actresses.

Bacall's appearance at the 1955 Oscars is open to some debate. Newspaper reports on the day of the ceremony announced her as the designee to accept the award for Garland if she won. Those same reports had Bing Crosby subbing for Garland to present the award for best song. Bacall remembered it differently. In her memoir, she claimed to be at home, watching the event on her TV set. In the end, *A Star Is Born* won not one Oscar, even for best song. The Academy voters instead chose the treacly theme song for *Three Coins in the Fountain*, written by Jule Styne and Sammy Cahn.

Garland didn't get the kind of publicity she wanted on Oscar night 1955. But she knew how to use her defeat to tell a good story, one the press would enjoy. "There I was, weak and exhausted," she recalled of the pending snub from her peers. "As I lay there in bed, the door burst open and in came a flock of TV technicians . . . Then they strung wires all around the room, put a microphone under the sheets, and frightened the poor nurses almost to death by saying, 'If you pull the venetian blinds before they say "Judy Garland," we'll kill you.' . . . I didn't have time to be disappointed. I was fascinated by the reactions of the men. They got mad at me for losing and started lugging all their stuff out of the room. They didn't even say good night."

Left out of her story was that either Garland or Luft—or, most likely, both of them—needed to approve all those rude TV technicians being there in the first place. As Luft explained, "I held Judy's hand as the TV technicians wired her up for the win." It was publicity, pure and simple, and sometimes publicity can turn bad. Very bad.

The abuse she suffered at the hands of NBC technicians

now joined her other ultimate victim story. According to Garland, her much-despised mother had tried to abort her during the pregnancy. "She did everything to get rid of me," Garland said of Ethel Gumm. "She must have rolled down nineteen thousand flights of stairs, jumped off of tables, and for some reason I was a very stubborn child and was not about to be shaken loose." Garland's ability to tell a good story never escaped her.

The cult of Judy Garland began with her getting fired from MGM and burnished itself with the lows of suicide attempts and electroshock treatments and then the highs of her Palladium and Palace successes, followed by *A Star Is Born*, which possessed both the highs of its spectacular Hollywood opening night and initial critical praise, followed by its box office failure and the Oscar rejection.

Writing for the Museum of Modern Art, Gary Carey analyzed the cult surrounding this unique talent: "Garland brought to the role personal qualities that she could not strip from herself as an actress, and I think that this is what a great number of her fans are responding to." Carey went to explain that while it is "a striking performance, and one cannot remain unaffected by it," the nakedness of the acting is "wrong for the character." Norman Maine, not Vicki Lester, is the damaged one. She's the sane, uncomplicated force that drives the narrative. Instead, Garland's Vicki Lester communicates "a powerful neurosis at work."

Which was the way Cukor had directed her, most specifically in the scene where Vicki breaks down in her dressing room before and after performing "Lose That Long Face." It's the moment in *A Star Is Born* where the actress, her gamin face covered in fake freckles, tells Oliver Niles, "You don't know what it's like to watch somebody you love just crumble away." Before the cameras rolled, Cukor had told Garland, "You know what this is about. You really know this."

Lorna Luft agreed with her mother's director and screen-writer. "Moss Hart understood when he wrote the sequence that Mama was both Norman Maine and Vicki Lester, that she would be speaking of her own failures and drug dependency."

What Garland's performance communicates in the second half of *A Star Is Born* is the Norman Maine side of it, not the Vicki Lester side of it. Garland knew only the one half, the crumbling part. She did not know the watching part of it.

This actress's extreme emotionalism on screen would continue to divide fellow collaborators and audiences alike. In the following decade, when Garland and Montgomery Clift performed in Stanley Kramer's *Judgment at Nuremberg*, both assigned cameo roles, the star of *A Place in the Sun* and *From Here to Eternity* watched from behind the camera as his colleague played a German housewife who had been called to testify against the Nazis. Garland broke into lots of tears and deep, wrenching sobs on the witness stand, and watching her perform, Clift started to tear up too. In the film, he played a man castrated by the Nazis due to his mental challenges. Kramer, seeing Clift's emotional reaction, walked over to comfort the actor, famous for his understated performances on screen.

"Wasn't Judy magnificent?" Kramer asked.

Clift shook his head. "Aww, Stanley," he replied, "she did it all wrong!"

Both Garland and Clift would receive their respective final Oscar nominations for *Judgment at Nuremberg*, and neither of them would go on to win.

Garland's life story, even more than her emotive acting

style, was a big reason gay men became a huge segment of her cult. It began with her Palace Theatre performances and reached its apotheosis with the rocky reception of *A Star Is Born*. These were men who migrated to and lived in the urban centers where Garland performed live on stage and *A Star Is Born* drew record crowds for a few weeks at least. These were outcast men who could identify with a woman who suffered and then survived to triumph only never to be fully accepted by her peers and the general public.

A requirement for any female icon to enter the pantheon of gay idols is to be copied by drag queens. Strong actresses like Barbara Stanwyck and Jean Arthur never achieved that status because their physical features and mannerisms were too unremarkable to be imitated by men wearing makeup, wigs, and dresses. Even Rosalind Russell didn't possess the required size—until she starred in the 1958 movie comedy *Auntie Mame*, and it's that character, more than the actress herself, who is imitated by transvestites after the release of the movie. The young Bette Davis of *Jezebel* or the young Joan Crawford of *The Grand Hotel* are also not imitated. Rather, both stars had to leave defiantly or be fired by their studios (Davis at Warner Brothers, Crawford at MGM) to suffer and then survive in comeback vehicles like *All About Eve* and *Mildred Pierce*, respectively. And it's these middle-aged women with their features more hardened and outlined by extreme makeup and hairstyles that drag queens not only want to but also can emulate. Garland was only thirty-two when *A Star Is Born* opened in movie theaters, but she looked middle-aged, and it was her more exaggerated appearance and gestures that female impersonators can easily duplicate.

In her Palace Theatre performances, Garland made a habit of sitting on the lip of the stage, a pose she put into the "Born in a Trunk" number. It achieved full camp status in Mel Brooks's 2001 stage musical *The Producers*, when the gay and Hitler-loving director of the show-within-the-show emulates Judy by sitting on the stage of the St. James Theatre in New York City.

Also at work is a vivid androgyny that Garland exploited and gay men respond to. It's there in the top hat and tails she wears at the beginning and end of "Born in a Trunk," and it's there in the film's most iconic moment. It comes when she splays her hands to frame her face to replicate "a big, flat close-up" in the "Someone at Last" number. Vicki Lester performs the song to entertain a depressed Norman Maine, but the female character could just as easily be auditioning for Mary Martin's trouser role in *Peter Pan*, which opened on Broadway the same month that *A Star Is Born* had its premiere in New York City.

By its very definition, a cult can never worship a star who's beloved by everyone or even a sizable minority of the public.

Part Three

"I'm Esther Hoffman Howard."

Chapter 9

Just how bloated was the final cost of *A Star Is Born* starring Judy Garland? Two decades later, despite inflation, Barbra Streisand and Jon Peters made their version for only half a million dollars more. When shooting on their 1976 version finished, First Artists and Warner Brothers even went so far as to take out a double-truck ad in *Variety*: "Jon Peters—Congratulations on producing one helluva concert in Phoenix. It will be a dynamic part of your production of *A Star Is Born*, the movie millions will see at Christmastime. Our thanks for your many contributions to the film that has finished on schedule, on budget, on target—a sure winner!" Who cared that the two companies' respective presidents, Philip Feldman and Frank Wells, who signed the advertisement, mixed up Phoenix and Tempe, where the rock concert actually took place?

Streisand and her boyfriend made the film for the production company First Artists, which she founded with Paul Newman and Sidney Poitier in 1969. Two years later, Steve McQueen joined to make it four movie stars who wanted to take control of their product and, perhaps, revolutionize the film industry in the process. Something similar had been attempted in 1919 when four of the biggest names in the movies—Charlie Chaplin, Douglas Fairbanks, D. W. Griffith, and Mary Pickford—formed United Artists.

At First Artists, the four movie stars signed an agreement to make three films each for no more than six million dollars each. "We had to stick to a budget," Streisand explained. "Otherwise, it was out of your pocket." Regarding her remake of *A Star Is Born*, she added, "I did end up going a million over—for the music and editing."

Streisand had very definite ideas of what she wanted her *Star* to be. "The women in the previous films were more passive," she noted. "I wanted my character to not be afraid to say exactly what she thinks and challenge the men."

Streisand's character in the film is also not afraid of being a proud Jew and goes by the name Esther Hoffman. From the beginning, the actress made her Jewish heritage central to her public persona in an era where Jewish comedians like Jack Benny (né Benjamin Kubelsky) celebrated Christmas on his weekly TV show and only seasoned middle-aged male comics like Alan King (né Irwin Alan Kniberg) could get away with telling jokes about their Jewish heritage on late-night TV talk shows. Ashley Feinstein worked as Arthur Laurents's assistant on *I Can Get It for You Wholesale*, the musical that marked Streisand's Broadway debut in 1962. Even then, "Barbra had no compunction about letting people know she was Jewish," Feinstein said.

In many ways, Esther Hoffman is Streisand: a Jew, a singer, a star, a feminist. In only one aspect was the character her alter-ego, and that had everything to do with Esther's relationship with the fading rocker John Norman Howard. Behind the scenes, Streisand's relationship with Jon Peters looked anything but liberated, one that was as dramatic as the marriage between Judy Garland and Sid Luft that delivered the first remake of *A Star Is Born*, as stormy as the doomed marriage between Barbara Stanwyck and Frank Fay that inspired the first *Star*, and as power-fraught as the marriage between Colleen Moore and John McCormick that did the same for *What Price Hollywood?*.

The one big advantage Streisand had over Garland, Stanwyck, and Moore was that she never made the tragic mistake of marrying her new lover, which did not prevent her from giving up enormous control to Peters on the second remake of *A Star Is Born*. Peters, who could be even more violent than either McCormick or Fay, didn't limit his physical threats to Streisand. He also menaced her chosen director and screenwriter, Frank Pierson. Peters did manage to deliver a couple of big pluses: He was not a chronic alcoholic, like McCormick and Fay, and, as that advertisement in *Variety* emphasized, he produced *A Star Is Born* on schedule and only slightly over budget, unlike Luft, who went way over budget on his *Star* remake.

Garland had once warned Streisand, around the time they performed together on CBS's short-lived *The Judy Garland Show* (1963–64), "Don't let them do to you what they did to me." Clearly, Garland didn't mean Luft, and Streisand didn't make the connection to Peters.

No sooner had Peters set up house with Streisand, during the summer of 1973, than he took charge of her latest album. They met because she wanted him to design her wig for the movie *For Pete's Sake*. It didn't seem to matter that he had never designed wigs before. Being a hairdresser, Peters felt the need to convince his newest client of his heterosexuality. In addition to his "great ass" comment within minutes of meeting her, he let it be known that his services also included sleeping with his female clients after he cut, dyed, and blew out their hair. Chief among those women was Sonja Henie, the Norwegian Olympic skater-turned-movie-star, who happened to be thirty-three years his senior. Peters called Henie "the woman who had the most influence in getting me to Beverly Hills." She had previously been Adolf Hitler's favorite pinup, although Peters knew her simply as "a rich old broad" who could often be seen riding behind him on his Harley-Davidson on Rodeo Drive in Beverly Hills.

Peters also bragged that he was the inspiration for the hairdresser-lothario whom Warren Beatty played in *Shampoo*, even though the two men who wrote that screenplay—Beatty and Robert Towne—insisted they had based the character on two other famous Beverly Hills hairdressers, Gene Shacove and Jay Sebring.

To further bolster his hetero bona-fides, as well as his Hollywood connections, Peters married actress Lesley Ann Warren, best known at the time for starring in Disney musicals like *The Happiest Millionaire* and *The One and Only, Genuine, Original Family Band*. When Streisand described the kind of wig her kooky housewife character in *For Pete's Sake* needed, she mentioned the haircut "on this very attractive woman" she saw recently at a party given by her friend Carol Burnett. Peters remembered the woman with obvious fondness, and as Streisand told the story, he "managed to suggest that he knew her *very well* . . . more than just as a client . . . as if he were worried I might think he was gay."

Peters played his games with Streisand, and she played right back.

"Would you ever go out with me?" he wanted to know after complimenting her rear end and letting her know he was straight and promiscuous.

"No, you're not my type," she replied without much thought. "I like men who are older, more sophisticated. I see myself with a doctor or a lawyer."

In nearly every film of hers to date, it had become de rigueur for the leading man to tell whatever character Streisand happened to be playing, from Fanny Brice in *Funny Girl* to Katie Morosky in *The Way We Were*, that she was "beautiful." Those male actors were paid to say it. Peters was not paid to say it, although she would pay big time when he picked the title *Butterfly* for her 1974 album. "He said I reminded him of a butterfly . . . beautiful but always just out of reach," Streisand recalled.

Peters's reach, in fact, quickly became all-encompassing. She even let him choose the image for her album cover: a common housefly sticking its black proboscis into a long stick of very yellow butter. Her choice had been a psychedelic portrait, which Peters relegated to the album's back cover. *Butterfly* turned into one of Streisand's worst-selling albums of all time.

It didn't matter. Some things are better than record sales. And better than being called "beautiful" for Streisand was being called "sexy."

"Jon has a way of seeing me," she said at the time. "He knows me as a woman, as a sexual being, and I'm tired of being just a funny girl, a self-deprecating waif."

Peter kept telling her, "I want to bring out your sexy side."

Despite calling herself a feminist, Streisand wrote of her new lover, "[H]aving a man in my life made a big difference. Now I had someone to shield me, and we could do things together."

Her Broadway mentor noticed something else about Streisand after she met the man who would go on to produce her remake of *A Star Is Born*. "Peters taught her to have fun," Arthur Laurents observed.

When she fell in love with Peters, Streisand had already signed to make *Funny Lady*. It marked the fourth and last film on her contract with Ray Stark, a signed agreement that began with *Funny Girl*, a classic Broadway musical and film based on the life of the producer's mother-in-law, Fanny Brice. She didn't want to make *Funny Lady*, but doing it would rid her of Stark, whom she despised. Regardless, Peters didn't have to think long to level a nasty crack that his girlfriend was once again playing "Ray Stark's mother-in-law." On the Fanny Brice scale of sexual desire, Peters would go on to hate *For Pete's Sake* even more than *Funny Girl* or *Funny Lady*, saying that in her latest film Streisand now "looked like Ray Stark's grandmother" despite wearing a cone-like mound of mousy hair that he designed for her.

Peters took full credit for their relationship being "a discovery period for her," he said. "And she started to realize that she could do it, she could take control of her life. I was the tool, in a way. The halfback. I was the one who ran interference for her—because there were a lot of changes she wanted to make, but she couldn't always articulate it."

In some ways, Peters's control over Streisand could be excused as narcissism. She identified with him, explaining, "Jon is so strong! I [also] never had a father; I was always in charge of myself. I came and went as I pleased. I can't stand for someone to tell me what to do."

Ditto Peters. "I'm a fella who, when I was nine years old, watched my father die in front of me," he said.

Through her agent Sue Mengers, Streisand had already read and rejected Joan Didion and John Gregory Dunne's screenplay *Rainbow Road*, a rock and roll update of *A Star Is Born*. "The lead characters didn't even exchange a word until fifty-two pages in," Streisand complained of the screenplay. Plus, "I don't particularly like doing remakes."

When Peters pursued *Rainbow Road* with her, she let him know, "You idiot! That's been made three times already!" Peters had never heard of *A Star Is Born* much less seen it, or them.

Mr. and Mrs. Dunne, who were better known in Hollywood as the Didions, also had not seen any of the *A Star Is Born* movies, nor did they feel any need to. "Warners wanted us to see the movie. But we assiduously refused to do it," Dunne said. "We knew what it was about."

The screenwriter couple spent weeks traveling with Jethro Tull and Uriah Heep to soak up all the color of the groupies, the journalists, the roadies, the sex, the drugs, the rock and roll. Even before they hit the road, Dunne, who came up with the concept, saw it as "James Taylor and Carly Simon in a rock and roll version of *A Star Is Born*."

But as with one of their previous movies, Dunne and Didion were not committed reporters or even very good researchers. On *The Panic in Needle Park*, their first screenplay—Didion called it "Romeo and Juliet on heroin"—the couple spent their mornings wandering around the seedy Upper West Side of Manhattan to scout locations and interview drug dealers and addicts. "They went to Abercrombie & Fitch and bought all these jungle outfits," their director-friend Billy Hale recalled. "They were going into the heart of darkness."

The couple didn't spend an inordinate amount of time walking around tiny Needle Park (a.k.a. Verdi Square Park) on Broadway and West Seventy-Second Street. At about noon each day, they took time to break for lunch and escape to the safer side of town to dine at La Côte Basque; a few years later, Truman Capote would do for it with his short story "La Côte Basque 1965" what he did in the previous decade for a high-end jewelry store on Fifth Avenue with his novel *Breakfast at Tiffany's*. *The New York Times* called the restaurant a "high-society temple of French cuisine," which was good enough for Dunne and Didion to make it their Ma Maison, a somewhat less exclusive eatery in Hollywood that they continued to frequent even after its sous chef John Thomas Sweeney was convicted of voluntary manslaughter for strangling their actress-niece, Dominique Dunne of *Poltergeist* fame.

By 1973, *Rainbow Road* had become one of the most-read unproduced screenplays in Hollywood, having been rejected by Liza Minnelli, Diana Ross, and even Cybill Shepherd. Actor-director Mark Rydell worked with Dunne and Didion to get the screenplay into shape. He called it "a savage look at the rock world."

Rydell's opinion was a minority report.

"I thought it was awful," said Peter Bogdanovich, who, at the time, counted Cybill Shepherd as his girlfriend. "I showed it to Cybill. She likes to sing. I thought she might like it. She didn't like it much either."

Since *Rainbow Road* would require songs, the screenplay also made the rounds to music producers. One of them, Richard Perry, wanted nothing to do with the project. "It really didn't catch the contemporary rock-pop milieu. Everything in it was clichéd," he said.

Unlike Streisand and almost everyone else in the movie business, Peters loved *Rainbow Road*. He even told his new girlfriend, "What a great story!" Deeply in love with the hairdresser, she soon began to see the project the way he did. "It's the innocence or the lack of knowing certain facts," Streisand said to explain her about-face on the project. "He came to it with a kind of purity and in a way that I started to think, 'This seems to work every twenty years.'"

All her talk of feminism and women's liberation did not prevent Streisand from turning her career over to Peters. Her super-loyal and longtime manager, Marty Erlichman, had been with Streisand since her pre-Broadway days at the Bon Soir cabaret in Greenwich Village. When he found himself at odds with Peters, he chose to step aside sometime into the production of *A Star Is Born*. He and Streisand would later reconcile. Ehrlichman didn't think the rock milieu was right for his longtime client. Sue Mengers agreed and felt betrayed when Peters talked Streisand into doing *Rainbow Road*.

Also not happy was Cher, who auditioned no fewer than three times for the film in her pre-*Silkwood* days. "Barbra Streisand and Jon Peters just walked in and took over the project," said the better half of Sonny and Cher. "Barbra doesn't know shit about rock and roll."

The people at Warner Brothers, on the other hand, were ecstatic. Here was yet another chance to recycle a valuable property in their vaults, and, more important, as one executive there explained, "It doesn't matter if the picture is good. Shoot her singing six numbers, and we'll make $60 million."

Streisand had her own ideas about the project, of course, after Peters convinced her it was a brilliant idea to remake *A Star Is Born*. Renamed Esther Hoffman, her character would eschew any glamorous makeover and that included a WASP-y name change to Vicki Lester. This Esther would be a strong woman, say exactly what's on her mind, often dress up in men's suits to perform on stage, and take off those same clothes to make love with all the freedom of a man. Most important, Streisand's Esther would tell John Norman Howard to stop being a helpless alcoholic and cocaine addict and get his life together.

Streisand then turned the film over to her boyfriend.

Decades later, Streisand described the fragile psyche of Jon Peters. "And it was so important for his ego that I didn't fight him or make him feel bad by pointing out that he needed help on everything," she reported.

The frangible ego of the male of the species has always

been one of the most potent elements in all the *A Star Is Born* incarnations. Whether he's named Norman Maine or John Norman Howard or Jackson Maine, he sacrifices himself through suicide to save the career of the woman he loves. Less acknowledged but equally present is the need to end his life because he can't face the humiliation. The person he loves is a woman, and she has gained the upper hand. She possesses more power, influence, and respect, and he can't live with that debasement of his male pride. With Streisand's *A Star Is Born*, it would be the first time that this dynamic also played out behind the scenes and forced its female star to regain her own self-respect by playing an alter-ego on-screen that reflected how Streisand should have handled her boyfriend away from the camera but could not. She knew Peters "was a novice with no experience" in the film industry. No matter that "he didn't want to share the producer credit with me. That should have set off alarm bells, but I could see how desperately he wanted that stature," she wrote years later in her memoir.

Streisand wanted Esther Hoffman to "challenge the men," but beyond the cameras, she could not really challenge Peters.

When Streisand gave him an inch, her boyfriend went for the full mile. He insisted on that producer credit sans her name anywhere near this credit. He also wanted to direct and costar in *A Star Is Born* with Streisand, who kept looking to other people to dissuade Peters from ruining their movie.

Chapter 10

One of the first directors of the film—after Warren Beatty, Peter Bogdanovich, and Mike Nichols turned down the second remake of *A Star Is Born*—was Jerry Schatzberg. He came to the project via John Gregory Dunne and Joan Didion, having brought their first screenplay, *The Panic in Needle Park*, to the screen in 1971. "His influence over her was very strong," Schatzberg said of Streisand and Peters. In a dynamic that would play out with other directors, screenwriters, editors, and songwriters working on the project, Schatzberg talked to Streisand and Peters "about one thing, and then I'd come in the next day and everything would be changed, and I wasn't privy to their conversations. He was like Rasputin or Svengali with her. She ogled him, aahed over him. She was a woman in love. He would come up with something, and she would say, 'I think that's a great idea,' and she'd come back to me."

When the film finally began shooting on February 2, 1976, director Frank Pierson would experience a similar whiplash of Streisand's opinions. And a few months later, when editor Peter Zinner began his work on the film, Friday night agreements between him and Streisand turned into Monday morning changes.

Schatzberg's stoicism in the face of such a variable power dynamic was nothing short of Job-like. He didn't quit the project even when Streisand asked him, "What do you think of Jon playing opposite me?"

Peters loved *Rainbow Road* because the lead male character was "a man I identify with, really. It touches on the facts of my life—the street fighter and overachiever. The macho thing is very much me. I fought for what I believed in and was not above using violence."

Streisand found herself identifying with the female character, and as with Peters, the story of *A Star Is Born* forced her to relive aspects of her fraught childhood. "I did have this dream to be seen, to be heard, and it wouldn't have felt good if I hadn't achieved that, because as kid I was very ignored," she said. "I walked into rooms, and nobody looked up. And it leaves something in a child. I've got to be acknowledged. I've got to be seen." In other words, like Peters, Streisand needed to be born a star.

She also could have been talking about Peters when commenting on Esther's attraction to John Norman Howard. "I don't think she was attracted to John's reckless behavior," Streisand said of the female character. "She fell in love with him despite that. She is attracted to the man that she thinks he can become." It was the kind of thing women used to say in the days before Simone de Beauvoir and Betty Friedan, about their needing to remake the imperfect men they loved instead of selecting the right dude from the get-go.

When Peters told Streisand, "Hey, I can do this part. I got the looks and the energy!" she did not look at him in horror. She did not laugh in his face. Instead, she melted to reply, "You can do anything, Jon." Streisand somehow thought her boyfriend's astrological sign and the various red vehicles he drove made him perfect to play the lead male role. As she described John Norman Howard, a character that other people had conceived and written, she noted, "He drove a red Ferrari and had a red Jeep, which my Jon does, and he was a Gemini, which Jon is. It was kind of a mystical thing—it was destined to be."

Peters could not have agreed more. Besides, "The whole world is waiting to see Barbra's and my story," he added.

Schatzberg came up with a quick response to Streisand and Peters starring together in *A Star Is Born*. "I don't want to shoot a documentary about you two," he replied.

And there were other very major problems with Peters playing the role of John Norman. He had never acted before, except at age ten as an extra in the exodus scene from Cecil B. DeMille's *The Ten Commandments*, shot on the backlot of Paramount Pictures. Also, Schatzberg wondered aloud if Peters could sing. It had been decided that in this *A Star Is Born* Streisand would sing live and not lip synch, which she hated doing for one simple reason. "I'm a very bad lip syncher," she revealed. "I believe, as an artist, of being in the moment. I work in a very spontaneous way; I work in the moment. I can't lip synch to something I recorded three months before." Incredibly, Judy Garland lip-synched dozens of takes to her September 1953 recording of "The Man That Got Away," and in most of those takes, despite changes in costumes, sets, and lighting, her lip-synching is flawless. Streisand agreed, saying of Garland, "She's great!" and had elevated lip-synching to "an art."

But she wasn't Garland. She was Streisand. "Every time I sing, it's a bit different," she said.

It had always been so. On the 1962 Broadway musical *I Can Get It for You Wholesale*, Arthur Laurents criticized the nineteen-year-old Streisand for being "undisciplined" and refusing to give the same performance twice after the show had been set. "You will never be a star!" the stage director threatened in rehearsals.

While Streisand eschewed lip-synching, Peters thought it would be his ticket to costarring with her in *A Star Is Born*. He told Schatzberg he could be "dubbed," and the director could "shoot around me."

"Look, you can do that with a singer to make it look like his acting has more energy," Schatzberg replied. "You can't do it with an actor to make it look like he's a singer."

Peters eventually took himself out of the running to costar. He offered a novel excuse, saying, "I like to make it on my brain, not on my looks. I'm more interested in the concept and the making of the film, not as an actor."

Talking him out of directing the movie took more time. Streisand's longtime manager looked to the head of Warner Brothers to put his foot down, to bail them out, to get rid of the boyfriend who fantasized himself to be a director. "Can you believe Jon Peters wants to direct the movie?" Marty Erlichman asked John Calley.

"As long as Barbra Streisand is in it," Calley answered, "I don't care who directs it."

Calley would probably have let Streisand and Peters write the screenplay, direct, produce, and play all the roles in *A Star Is Born*. He wanted a Barbra Streisand movie musical. Period. The executive recalled his very first meeting with the hairdresser side of the project. "[Peters] came in and said that in his and Barbra's view, the screenplay was moving away from being suitable for Barbra. I agreed with them," Calley said. "Forget about whether the screenplay was good or not, the issue was 'Is it right for Barbra?' [Peters] said, in effect, 'It's very simple: Either we get to take over the screenplay and make it work for Barbra, or we take a walk. It is entirely up to you. Do whatever you like.'"

Calley more than loved having a Barbra Streisand

movie musical on his tally of upcoming movies. He needed such a film, because, as he put it, Warner Brothers had "no real alternatives. We were most anxious to do the film with Barbra. . . . I felt that the worst thing that could happen was that if they took a shot at the screenplay and failed, we'd lose them anyway, but if they succeeded . . ."

Calley made clear his position on Streisand and Peters as a package. "I told Jerry [Schatzberg] to stay loose and see what the two of them were able to do with the screenplay," he said. Schatzberg thought about it overnight, then phoned Calley the next day to say, "Listen, I don't want anyone else developing my screenplays."

That decision put Schatzberg's job as director in limbo. If Peters wasn't going to play John Norman Howard, then Peters felt he must direct the actor who played John Norman, because only he understood the character. "It's a story I felt only I could tell. I wanted to deal with it and not interpret it through another person. Barbra felt this was a wise choice too," Peters insisted. That he had no previous experience behind the camera deterred him even less than acting in front of the camera. "Directing is a thing I've done my whole life!" he boasted. "It's getting people to do what I want them to do!"

Until Barbra felt otherwise. Negotiations went on for three months, but eventually Freddie Fields delivered the bad news to Peters. The president of Creative Management Associates wanted the project to stay at First Artists. Fields didn't mind being the fall guy to take the pressure off Streisand on the subject of who would not direct the film. Peters had to settle for being the producer, although years later, Streisand admitted that, essentially, she was both producer and executive producer despite receiving only the latter credit.

"In 1976, people in Hollywood weren't used to a woman being in control," Streisand said.

At the time, Peters put on a brave face when his public announcements about also directing and starring in the film conveniently evaporated. He realized the limits of his influence over Streisand. "How could I direct her and keep our relationship?" he said. "I had to decide which was more important, our love or the movie."

Schatzberg stayed on board as director even when Dunne and Didion left the project in the summer of 1974. The couple was less upset than they were relieved. "You have to understand the way she saw it," Dunne said of Streisand. "It was her life on the line. If the picture went down, she went down with it. She just had to do what she thought was right." It also helped that Dunne and Didion received a $125,000 fee for their original screenplay and two rewrites. "The third draft was little more than a re-hash of the second draft," Dunne admitted. "It's tough to tailor a part for a star. We were all played out at that point." And besides, as the writer put it, "Barbra and Jon saw the picture as being about their own somewhat turbulent love affair. It began to look like a long summer."

Played out, yes, but the Didions played their hand very well. The two screenwriters received an incredible 10 percent of the gross. No one in Hollywood wanted the second remake of *A Star Is Born* to be a bigger hit than the couple who wrote *Rainbow Road*. "We came out smelling like a rose," Dunne said. "I really hope the movie gets made; we have such a nice chunk of it. And I'm sure relieved to be out of it."

Schatzberg finally followed his two screenwriter friends and called it quits when Jonathan Axelrod came aboard as screenwriter. The novice twenty-four-year-old writer fit Streisand and Peters's new edict for their movie. Besides being yet another client of Sue Mengers, as well as a stepson of veteran screenwriter George Axelrod (*The Manchurian Candidate*, *Breakfast at Tiffany's*), he was young.

Indeed, "young" turned into their new mantra. "We should have someone young on this picture," Streisand kept repeating.

The young Axelrod had at least one real idea. "My original idea was to reverse the roles, make her like Janis Joplin," he revealed. In other words, Streisand would be playing the John Norman Howard character, in essence, the big star whose last successful deed is to discover the talented newcomer. And then she commits suicide to save the career of the new male star.

Axelrod wrote and wrote and wrote, often putting down on paper what Peters told him, but eventually someone taking dictation was not enough. Streisand not playing the ingenue but rather the destitute rock star led to real problems, such as, how many songs can a burned-out performer sing in one movie? Axelrod soon found himself bumped off the A-list of screenwriters before his career there had begun, and he went on to produce TV movies for the Hallmark Channel. As Peters explained it, "Axelrod was the right person at the beginning, because he was my interpreter. What you read in that script, I wrote. Now I need a real writer." Suddenly, the new prevailing idea was not to make radical changes, beyond taking the story from Hollywood to the world of rock and roll. "Now we're going to make it much closer to the 1936 [sic] version, the one with Janet Gaynor," Peters said. "That's what we want to achieve."

In other words, "young" was no longer the operative word, but with so many changes in the story, Streisand grew frustrated if not downright desperate. She even turned to her fifty-seven-year-old Broadway mentor. Surprisingly, Arthur Laurents agreed with Jonathan Axelrod. "I told her she should play the other part, which was much more interesting," Laurents said of the John Norman Howard role. After reading four versions of the new

A Star Is Born, he liked only the screenplay titled *Rainbow Road*. "But you're not going to do that," he added. Streisand wanted to know why. "Because it's tough," Laurents explained. What he didn't tell her was what he also really believed. "Barbra wanted what I guess all insecure women want—to be romantic princesses," he said.

Streisand and Peters eventually settled on a writer who was somewhere between the respective ages of Arthur Laurents and Jonathan Axelrod. Forty-year-old Frank Pierson also had the advantage of writing screenplays that actually turned into movies. He got his start in the entertainment business as a script editor on the 1950s TV Western *Have Gun—Will Travel* and went on to write the screenplays for *Cat Ballou*, *Cool Hand Luke*, and *Dog Day Afternoon*. As part of the audition process for writing the latest remake of *A Star Is Born*, Streisand complained to him that the scripts "keep getting worse and worse. I don't know what to do. Do you?"

More basic, she asked, "What's the story about?"

Before their meeting, Pierson prepared a few ideas on the subject, and for a story that's about rock music, he quoted a famous and persecuted Irish homosexual who had passed away at the turn of the century. He quoted Oscar Wilde: "An actress is a little more than a woman; an actor a little less than a man."

No matter that the latest *A Star Is Born* was about two singers, not two actors. As Pierson described his new scenario to Streisand and Peters, "The woman in our story is ambitious to become a star, but it is not necessary. . . . For the man, his career is his defense against a self-destructive part of himself that has led him into outrageous bursts of drunkenness, drugs, love affairs, fights, and adventures that have made him a legend. His career is also what gives him his sense of who he is. Without it, he is lost and confused; his demons eat him alive." Somehow, Pierson translated these two career observations into Esther Hoffman being more than a woman and John Norman Howard being less than a man.

When it came to reading scripts, Peters didn't. "I had actors act it out," he said.

What Peters had acted out for him went like this: He saw the two singers in *A Star Is Born* as people "trapped by their money and success, trying to relate to each other and really get into their feelings." He also believed that Esther "becomes a super superstar by realizing what's the most important thing to both of them: communicating. Wanting to have children. Not the thousands of agents and press agents and all that stuff that control their life. He's a boy who spent the first thirty years of his life fighting—very aggressive—and then met this woman and fell very much in love and realized that this was his chance to live. But he accidentally dies. For us, the understanding of it—through film—is a very heavy thing. Do you know what I mean? That's why the script has to be perfect. Because it has to be right for us."

Streisand developed a much more direct way of letting Pierson know what she wanted the script to be. "I could tell you what to write," she told him.

None of the aforementioned ideas expressed by Pierson or Peters would have much to do with what ended up in the final screenplay. Peters especially hated the idea of John Norman taking his own life. He asked, "Does he have to commit suicide? That's such a turnoff. Why can't it be an accident?"

Having written several successful screenplays, Pierson knew his way around a negotiating table and how to handle crazy notes from narcissistic movie people. He knew how to massage the problem as well as the egos. On the subject of suicide, which is essential to the story, Pierson told Peters, "Well, he doesn't make some dumb theatrical

gesture to make way for tomorrow and he can't walk into
the water, not after *Jaws*. He dies of drink and dope and
pushing his luck. Like Janis. She didn't fire off a gun, but
does anyone doubt she killed herself?"

Peters adored Janis Joplin, who had died of a heroin overdose in 1970 at age twenty-seven. He understood what "a
very heavy thing" Pierson was telling him, which didn't
conflict too awfully much with his deep, deep identifica-
tion with John Norman Howard. He wouldn't commit
suicide, so John Norman can't commit suicide. "I hate him
if he kills himself and leaves her all alone, this little girl,"
Peters said of the movie that was supposed to take
Streisand from being a malleable funny girl to a feisty, liberated woman.

Streisand also confused her own story with that of Esther Hoffman's. As Pierson saw the situation, "They talk
about themselves, and I realize they see their own story
gloriously told in song and dance and color, a $6-million
home movie," he noted.

Surprisingly, Streisand didn't disagree with that assess-
ment. Pierson, in fact, had read her mind. "People are
curious; they want to know about us," she told the screenwriter. "That's what they come to see! I don't want you to
use too much. I don't know if I should tell you this or not,
because someday they'll want to do my life story, and I
don't want to use it up."

What she did not mind using up was her many negative
thoughts about her own fan base and how it adversely affected her life. "There's a lot of jealousy of famous people
among the general public," she said. "Everybody wants to
be recognized. Everybody has dreams, and some people
achieve their dreams and the others are angry. These kinds
of fights with [famous] people are very real. It's reverse
discrimination. Because people have watched their movies
or bought their records. They think they know you, but

they don't really. Sometimes people expect you to be their little puppets, get up and sing a song, but we don't do that unless we feel like it. The performer isn't owned by the public. It just doesn't feel good."

Pierson didn't include himself in that rude, intrusive, and possessive fan base. Amazingly, he had never seen a Barbra Streisand movie until a few days before he met the star face-to-face. Better late than fired, he finally caught up to *Funny Girl*; *Hello, Dolly!*; and *The Owl and the Pussycat*. To his amazement, he became a bigger Streisand fan than Pauline Kael before *Funny Lady* turned the influential *New Yorker* critic into an ardent Streisand hater. Pierson may not have liked most of the movies he saw that weekend, but he did find that Streisand the actor possessed "her own clear force and direction regardless of what may have gone wrong or silly around her." He went on to beatify, "She is a primitive force and an elegant delight; I'm humble and amazed. What a fantastic picture we can make!"

Streisand and Peters were excited about the screenplay Pierson wrote, so excited they even accepted his demand that, if they wanted what he wrote, they had to take him as the film's director. Pierson boasted Academy Award nominations for his *Cat Ballou*, *Cool Hand Luke*, and *Dog Day Afternoon* screenplays. As for directing movies, his one effort, *The Looking Glass War*, based on the John le Carré novel, was a success with neither the critics nor the public.

Streisand made a deal with Pierson. "You can direct," she told him, "but you have to understand something. I'm personally responsible for this project . . . every penny of it. My company, Barwood Films, is making it for First Artists, and then I have to answer to the larger company, Warner Brothers. Any dollar we spend over the $6 million budget comes out of my own pocket. So, I'm going to be involved in every decision. You can have the credit, but we basically have to codirect."

Peters, in a momentary lapse of egotism, seconded that idea. "You and Barbra make the picture," he told Pierson. "I'm here to expedite. You need somethin', I'll kick ass to get it."

Streisand soon found that her boyfriend was "way out of his depth and later he admitted it." Peters said later, "My instincts were good, but my abilities weren't. Barbra literally had to bail me out."

She agreed with him there. "I saved him then, and I've saved him several times since. But I was taken aback when Jon still wanted all the credit as producer," she noted.

Caught in the middle of their fraught relationship, Pierson decided to be optimistic against all signs to the contrary. Whatever resentment Streisand harbored about her boyfriend's mania regarding credits, Pierson took the brunt of her dissatisfaction, if not her rage, which had been building for at least a decade. As she told Pierson, "Ray Stark always used to bully me, the son of a bitch. You'll pay for every lousy thing Ray Stark ever did to me!"

One of those paybacks came when they picked the film's cinematographer. He and Streisand told conflicting stories regarding Robert Surtees. According to Pierson, when he suggested the three-time Oscar winner, Streisand said, "He's old. We should have someone young on this picture. What does he know about backlight? Did he sign his contract?"

"Backlighting" turned into not only a deal-breaker but also a mantra on the scale of "young." Over lunch one day at her home, Streisand sat with her back to the window with the sunlight streaming into the dining room. "This backlight? Through my hair? You love it?" she asked Pierson. It was a rhetorical question. "I want a lot of backlight. I see myself this way. I know my face; I can feel the light when it's right. This side is good," she said, turning to give him a profile view of her left side. "The other side my mouth has this curve here; it's no good. I'm better for comedy on this side, but for anything else, always on the left."

Pierson dared to tell Streisand that her obsession with the left side of her face had become "monotonous" in her movies. She disrespectfully disagreed.

Streisand wanted lots of backlighting, because she thought such light would look great when shot through her new Afro hairdo. "It's like there's a theatrical aura around certain people, certain performers," she said of the halo effect. She saw Esther Hoffman and John Norman Howard as those kinds of special, chosen people.

For her part, Streisand insisted that Surtees was part of the filmmaking team early in the process. "I hired Bob Surtees even before we had Frank [Pierson] on board, and I showed him pictures of backlighting," she recalled. "I tore out pictures from magazines of this kind of lighting."

On the little subject of who should be Streisand's costar, Kris Kristofferson had been in talks to star with Cher back in the Pleistocene when the movie was still being called *Rainbow Road*. In the beginning, the new team wanted someone other than Kristofferson. Streisand had had an affair with Kristofferson back in the late 1960s. She put him in the expanding category of "one of my flings," and no one knew better how jealous Jon Peters could be when it came to her old boyfriends than his current girlfriend.

Streisand and Peters's first choice to star opposite her was the king of rock and roll himself. "It was real life," Streisand said of casting Elvis Presley. "He was fat, he was going down, and it would be exciting." She went so far as to call their pairing "monumental."

Peters was equally psyched. "The man's been an idol of mine since I was nine! Imagine Barbra Streisand opposite the king of rock and roll!" he exclaimed. It didn't bother him that his idol was a drug addict. He looked on the bright side of the king's extreme substance abuse: "Perfect. He'll really understand the part!"

Presley and Streisand had met only once before. "He had come to see me in Las Vegas when I opened there in 1969," she recalled, "and I was polishing my nails the whole time. It was an odd meeting."

Now it was her time to set up the meeting with rock royalty, and again it was Vegas, where Presley was currently performing, at the Las Vegas Hilton. Meeting the king, Streisand and Peters could not believe the man in front of them managed to get through several performances a week on a Vegas stage, much less another few weeks of living on this planet. He drank too much, took too many pills, and ate a steady diet of peanut-butter-and-banana sandwiches.

Streisand, like her boyfriend, remained optimistic in the face of Presley's seriously unhealthy condition. "He was going through hard times then," she said. "He'd gained weight and was losing esteem. We thought, 'Why not go for him? He's really going through this time in reality, and to tap into that might be magnificent.'"

Peters agreed. He found Presley so overweight that "he looked almost pregnant. . . . He was dying, really," Peters said. In other words, "He was John Norman Howard."

Despite the king looking like an expecting, morbidly obese drug addict, Streisand and Peters left it to Colonel Tom Parker, the rocker's longtime manager, to put a kibosh on the deal. "I think Elvis Presley really wanted to do it, but the Colonel talked him out of it," Streisand said.

The Colonel might have had more common sense than Streisand and Peters and knew what Presley could handle at this late stage in his life. Parker looked askance at the movies or any medium that would expand his client's already severely bloated face to larger-than-life proportions. In Hollywood, Presley hadn't exactly lit up any of those wide screens in recent years. One of his last efforts there came in 1969 with something titled *The Trouble with Girls*, released as a double feature alongside the equally forgettable *Flareup*, starring Raquel Welch. Even more ignoble, the Presley picture got relegated to the bottom half of that tepid pairing

Although it did not figure into their thinking, Streisand and Peters owed a major debt to the King. Starting with *Love Me Tender* and *Jailhouse Rock* in the late 1950s and followed by more than a couple dozen movies in the following decade, Presley single-handedly made rock and roll commercially viable at the movies. In the process, his vast film oeuvre basically retired movies about Broadway or Hollywood, subject matter that peaked spectacularly in the early 1950s with *All About Eve*, *Sunset Boulevard*, *Singin' in the Rain*, and *The Bad and the Beautiful*, with Judy Garland's *A Star Is Born* being the first nail in the coffin of such films. The public had moved on, and to remake *A Star Is Born*, the film's milieu needed to eschew Tinseltown for the grittier glamour of rock and roll that Presley turned into a movie staple.

With Elvis out of the picture, Streisand wondered aloud, "What about Brando? I always wanted to play with Brando. Why does it have to be a musical?"

Duh, it had to be a musical because Warner Brothers wanted it to be a musical since only Streisand's singing six songs guaranteed that the film would be a box office blowout. Her starring in a movie and not singing remained a far more open commercial question. *For Pete's Sake* had been a minor success, *Up the Sandbox* a total dud.

No matter, the meeting with Brando did not go well. According to Peters, the legendary star of *On the Waterfront* and *The Godfather* put the make on Streisand, and

Peters ended the meeting by playing Judas. He planted a kiss on Brando's face.

Exit Marlon.

Finally, it came down to Kris Kristofferson and Mick Jagger, who squelched his movie star potential with a box office dud four years earlier. Nicolas Roeg's crime drama *Performance*, about a London gangster (Peter Fox) and a reclusive rock star (Jagger), would eventually reach cult-class status but not soon enough to impress either Peters or Streisand, who felt the lead singer for the Rolling Stones didn't have the right looks. They had to wonder, would Jagger and Streisand make a photogenic couple? Streisand tended to score with leading men of the distinctly Wonder Bread line of beauty, guys like Robert Redford and Ryan O'Neal. More important, would Jagger blow her off the screen in their musical sequences together?

Re-enter Kristofferson. "He's an actor. He's beautiful to look at," Streisand declared. "He can sing and play the guitar. And he's a Gentile, which seems to work with me—the Jew and the Gentile." She also noted that Kristofferson had "great teeth."

Back in the 1960s, Streisand redefined what it meant to be beautiful for a woman. When it came to leading men, however, she eschewed being a trailblazer to embrace the status quo regarding hunks. Years later, she expanded on her aesthetic regarding the male body. "All my men are really attractive. All of them," she insisted. "I love beauty, whether it's in a vase, a piece of furniture, or a design. There are some people who are very fortunate to be beautiful."

Regarding the casting of Kristofferson, there were the usual negotiations. Streisand wanted her name to be alone above the title. Kristofferson wanted to share that top spot. Having basically exhausted leading men who could sing, act, and measure up to Streisand's high ideals regarding male beauty, Kristofferson won by default to share billing above the title.

No sooner had he signed than another candidate miraculously surfaced. When Bruce Springsteen appeared on the cover of both *Time* and *Newsweek* in the last week of October 1975, Streisand and Peters obsessed over The Boss. They worried that Kristofferson's folk-country roots weren't in vogue anymore.

Streisand and Peters brought on Rupert Holmes to write the entire score for *A Star Is Born*. Her intense work ethic on the movie, however, unsettled the songwriter, who had arranged and produced the singer's 1975 album, *Lazy Afternoons*. After writing five songs for *A Star Is Born*, Holmes flew back to New York. "I think he was a bit overwhelmed," Streisand admitted, "which left me in kind of a lurch. How was I going to get the rest of the score?"

Upset at Holmes's abrupt departure, Streisand found herself crying in the bathroom one day when Peters asked her, "Why don't you write your own songs? Why don't you just try?"

For a while, he may have regretted such a suggestion. "I drove everybody crazy," Streisand said. At all times of the day and night, she kept asking Peters and their children, "What do you think of this bridge?" She took guitar lessons, even cutting the beloved long nails on her left hand (but not her right) to pluck the chords. She didn't read music. "I just play by ear," she said. Eventually, she came up with the music for what lyricist Leon Russell would title "Lost Inside of You" and another melody that lyricist Paul Williams would title "Evergreen."

At one songwriting session, when Russell went to relieve himself in the nearest powder room, Streisand started playing "a kind of classical theme" she had written years ago. When Russell returned, he told her, "Play that again." With her repeating the tune on the piano, he started to hum a countermelody. She quickly turned on a tape recorder, which not only immortalized the music they made together but also their congratulations to each other.

"What did that come from?" he asked incredulously.

"That's amazing!" she exclaimed excitedly.

Their mutual admiration fest at the piano turned into the movie's big love scene between Esther and John Norman.

Streisand's encounter with Paul Williams was equally fortuitous but far more frustrating.

Williams expected the worst when Streisand told him she had written "something," but he soon found himself enchanted with her tune. "This is your love theme for the movie!" he gushed, much to Streisand's childlike delight. He even gave her the title "Evergreen" on the spot.

Then several weeks passed. When Streisand expressed her angst at having no lyrics for her beloved song, Williams complained, "How can I write when I have to talk with her all the time, and nothing ever gets finished because before I finish the damn song, she's already asking for changes?" Curiously, the "Evergreen" lyrics would be the last thing he wrote for the score, much of it written with his frequent collaborator, Kenny Ascher.

What Williams wrote for the new *A Star Is Born* is arguably more hip than what John Kander and Fred Ebb wrote for Streisand in *Funny Lady* or what she sang in her other movie musicals. Regarding his and Ascher's contributions for *A Star Is Born*, Williams explained, "We didn't write rock and roll for her. Kristofferson was the rocker in the movie. I mean, 'Watch Closely Now' is pure, hardcore rock and roll. I think for Kenny Ascher and I, two middle-aged guys who write songs like 'You and Me Against the World,' we did pretty good."

Kristofferson did not agree, at least with regard to the music written for him. Having been told he needed to channel The Boss, Kristofferson wanted to know, "Who shall I say says my music isn't rock—Barbra Streisand's hairdresser?"

Peters took offense. "It's crap," Peters said of Kristofferson's music. "I don't care who says it!"

Chapter 11

The debate between Kris Kristofferson and Jon Peters regarding what's rock and what's not exploded into a near fistfight at the film's big outdoor concert.

John Norman Howard has helicoptered Esther Hoffman to the event to wow her after their first meeting in a club where she performs with the Oreos, played by Venetta Fields and Clydie King, their long hair straightened in contrast to Barbra Streisand's big perm. Or, as the star delicately described the trio, "Two chocolate girls and me, white in the middle. . . . Both [women] had sung on my recordings many times." Kristofferson made changes to his character's signature song, "Watch Closely Now," much to the disapproval of Paul Williams. Kristofferson also wanted to perform with his own band, which Streisand wanted to put through the usual audition process. Kristofferson complained, "They're stuffed in this little room playing stuff they've never heard before. Barbra was listening and instantly said, 'We gotta get studio musicians,' the kind who read charts, like in Vegas shows."

Streisand eventually relented, letting Kristofferson perform with his own band. When she retaliated by giving
them almost no rehearsal time, he retreated to his trailer to
fume, "Goddamn it, I've been trying to make this stuff
sound like music. I've got to go and play it in front of sixty
thousand people, but she doesn't give a damn."

Peters disagreed with him there. The hyperbolic Peters
claimed that seventy thousand people showed up.

Frank Pierson never wanted to film the concert live.
"Let's get stock footage of Woodstock, and stuff like that,
and use it as the big scene with all the people," he told his
producer. "We can't afford to pay them."

"Well, make them pay!" Peters shot back. "We'll put on
a concert."

"Jon was very right," Streisand recalled. "We made
money doing the scene." Indeed, those sixty or seventy
thousand people paid $3.50 each to watch them film the
pivotal concert scene in *A Star Is Born*. After all costs were
covered, the concert turned a profit of $25,000, all pro-
ceeds going to the March of Dimes.

Most concertgoers that day showed up to see headliners
Peter Frampton and Santana and camped out all night to
enter the arena at Arizona State University's Sun Devil Stadium at seven in the morning. Hours passed without any
music being played in heat that quickly climbed to ninety-
plus degrees. The Sun Devil Stadium in Tempe, Arizona,
lived up to its name. It was hot as hell. "No more filming!
No more filming!" the crowd started to chant, even though
the cameras had not yet captured anything on film.

Rock promoter Bill Graham staged the concert. "I'm
paying him a fortune, but he's worth it," Peters said. "He's
tough. He's like me; he's a street fighter."

But even street fighters know when they're badly out-
numbered. Graham nearly had a seizure when he heard the

"No more filming" chant. He made his desperation clear to Peters. "Do you know what you're doing? They're going to kill us!" Graham yelled.

Finally, Streisand came to the rescue, and, scared to death, she told the unruly crowd that she would sing something. Her repertory of songs didn't match what the lovers of Peter Frampton and Santana wanted to hear. "I'm always insecure. Maybe they won't like it," she fretted. "They've come to see rock and roll artists. I'm too traditional." Even worse, she hated performing live. Back in her *Funny Girl* days on Broadway, she never experienced stage fright. "There was a lot to prove; I kind of enjoyed it. So, the fear is something else," Streisand recalled. "As I got older, I got more scared." Something happened when she became a big star. She felt people in the audience didn't like her, were out to get her. They paid not to be entertained but to see her fail, which, in its cruel way, is another form of entertainment.

There, at Sun Devil Stadium, facing that huge crowd, Streisand had no choice but to sing "People" and "The Way We Were." Of course, it worked. The hardcore rockers melted into a bunch of Broadway babies and ended up giving her a rousing standing ovation, even though most of them had already been on their feet for hours. She followed those standards with a couple of new songs from *A Star Is Born*, "The Woman in the Moon" and "Evergreen." Regarding the latter song, which she wrote, Streisand told the crowd, "I hope you like it. If you don't, I'll be crushed."

Instead, they loved it. "Do you really like it?" she asked, sounding about ten years old. "I'm really glad you like it, because that's the first time I ever sang that song in front of people!"

Among the live rock acts hired by Graham, Frank Pierson gave himself a couple of two-hour sessions and four cameras to get on film the moment on stage when John Norman Howard, smashed out of his mind on drugs and alcohol and ego, attempts to impress Esther with his singing, and when that doesn't achieve the required effect, he hops on a fan's motorcycle and crashes it into the sound equipment. Peters had wanted to hire Evel Knievel (potential cost: $25,000) to perform the motorcycle stunt, but wiser minds prevailed.

Amid all the downtime and the crowd shouting "No more filming!" and Streisand singing her greatest hits and soon-to-be hits, Kristofferson somehow went from angry in his trailer to nonchalant on stage. When record producer Phil Ramone groused that he had to record the concert performance live—"What you hear in that stadium is what you'll hear in the film. What we don't get we'll never get. It's like driving on slick pavement," he informed everyone—Kristofferson suddenly acted as if he could not have cared less. "I just want to tap-dance and fart my way through," he said, resorting to his good old country boy persona despite being a Rhodes scholar and having been pissed as hell in his trailer only an hour earlier. Violent mood swings that day became the norm.

Eventually the motorcycle crash went off without a hitch—except for one. The crowd didn't want to watch some stuntman on a motorcycle. They wanted to watch Barbra Streisand. She had to scold them. "You can't look at me. You wanna look at me?" she screamed, then let out a big laugh before letting them know, "Well, fuck you!" She was getting into this rock and roll thing. Years later, she called the filming that day "chaotically smooth."

Part of the chaos had to do with something Streisand could not control. Warner Brothers had flown 150 reporters to the concert to observe the filming. Such press junkets were usually reserved for the release of the movie and take place a couple of weeks before the premiere to plant interviews in local newspapers and TV and radio programs.

That day at Sun Devil, those reporters ended up with more copy than a dozen press junket chitchats. Forgetting about the live microphones on the concert stage, Streisand shouted at her costar, "You're not doing what I tell you to!"

Kristofferson shouted right back, "Shit! I got the director telling me one thing and you telling me another. Who's the director? Get your shit together!"

"Listen to me!" she continued to shout. "I'm talking to you, goddammit!"

"Go fuck yourself!" Kristofferson shouted back.

That's when Jon Peters entered the fight, shouting, "You owe my lady an apology. If we didn't have a movie to make, I'd beat the shit out of you!"

Peters should have known better than to argue with someone who graduated summa cum laude and owned a Phi Beta Kappa key. "Listen," Kristofferson continued, unafraid of the producer's tightened fists that hung like ripe pomegranates ready to burst at his hips, "if I want any shit out of you, I'll squeeze your head."

The 150 reporters that day, their tape recorders spinning overtime, got their story. And there was more to come. When Streisand, Peters, and Kristofferson weren't screaming at each other on the concert stage, they went after each other when interviewed off camera by the assembled press.

One of those reporters at the press junket was Arthur Bell from *The Village Voice*, the same Arthur Bell who got Judy Garland's autograph at the New York City premiere of *A Star Is Born* and kept his mouth shut when she asked her gaggle of fans what they all thought of her latest movie. Two decades later, Bell, the first openly gay journalist to have his own eponymous column ("Bell Tells") in a major publication, found himself equally impressed for all the wrong reasons with what he witnessed that day in Tempe, Arizona.

Sitting with a dozen other reporters, he looked glaze-eyed when Streisand answered softball questions about being a feminist. "I'm all for women's liberation: Do it because you feel it," she said. "All women should call their own shots, not in a militant manner but with the conviction that they've got a helluva lot to offer other than looking pretty and passive."

A tough, no-nonsense journalist, Bell swatted aside these kinds of celebrity bromides. He dared to ask Kristofferson what he was doing there since the rocker-actor looked bored out of his mind. "Going crazy," Kristofferson replied. "I hope I don't wipe out two careers in one day."

Before Streisand could answer Bell's question why she took the credit of executive producer, her costar answered for her, "Because she doesn't want to take every other credit."

Streisand, as her smile hardened, recovered enough to say, "I'm being very modest. I just want to be executive producer and nothing else."

Kristofferson lowered a few inches in his seat. "Shit," he whispered loud enough for Bell to record his expletive. The Warner Brothers publicists could only hope that most family newspapers and magazines would not publish all the four-letter words spoken the day.

Otherwise, Kristofferson remained philosophical. He later remarked, "I knew Barbra was writing the script and the picture's big songs and had total control of everything, but Frank [Pierson] was called the director, and I figured I'd just do my usual tap dance between two haystacks, trying to keep both star and director happy. I'd never been in no movie where they were the same person."

After the big concert at Sun Devil, the film production moved to the houses of Beverly Hills and Whitley Heights, as well as the sound stages of Warner Brothers in Burbank. The switch in locales didn't help the working relationship between the two stars. Kristofferson continued to rub Streisand the wrong way. She often needed menthol blown into her face to cry. She used it in all her previous films before working with Sydney Pollack on *The Way We Were*. A former acting teacher, Pollack knew how to bring out all the tears. Frank Pierson was not Pollack, who had been a protégé of the famed acting guru Sanford Meisner at New York City's Neighborhood Playhouse, a theater that Streisand much admired. In *A Star Is Born*, when Esther finds John Norman in bed with a female journalist, Streisand could not cry, even though Kristofferson had no trouble coming up with the requisite wetness in his eyes. He apologized, "Jesus, Barbra. I'm sorry. I wish I could do something to help you. It's my fault. I'm not giving you what you need."

Incensed, Streisand took Pierson aside. "Did you hear what he said, the ego!" she huffed. "He thinks what he does controls what I do!"

Kristofferson would eventually own up to his own severe shortcomings. "I was out of control, no doubt about it," he confessed. During filming, he made it a habit to consume no less than a quart of tequila and two six-packs of beer a day on the set. That he could remember his lines, much less stand up straight, was a minor miracle.

The Warner Brothers publicity department made one smart decision. They did not invite 150 reporters to watch Streisand and Kristofferson film either their big love scene or the big nude bath that followed it.

In this *A Star Is Born*, before Esther becomes a star, she beds John Norman. It was just one aspect that distinguishes the film from its two predecessors. In the 1937 and

1954 versions, it is not obvious that the respective couples have sex even *after* they get married. In the second remake of *A Star Is Born*, after Kristofferson's John Norman tells Streisand's Esther, "You're a helluva singer" and follows it with "you have incredible eyes" and "you've got a beautiful mouth" and "you have a great ass"—for some reason, the character never mentions her breasts or painted toenails—they have sex thirty-three minutes later.

Stardom takes another fifteen minutes. Against her new rocker boyfriend's prodding, Esther doesn't want to sing at a "Native American benefit concert" that John Norman headlines. He insists, she surrenders, and at first, the audience resists her attempt to sing with their impolite in-unison clapping. Not knowing that she is expected to perform that night, Esther just happens to be wearing an elegant Ralph Lauren men's suit, and gaining her strength much the way Fanny Brice does to begin "I'm the Greatest Star" tentatively and ended it in socko fashion, she quickly wins over the unruly audience by her amazing performance.

Streisand recalled, "I sing 'The Woman in the Moon,' not 'Man in the Moon.'"

In the film, John Norman has even engaged the two other Oreos to back her up, much to Esther's surprise, and she becomes an overnight star, besieged by fans and reporters and managers alike as the two of them make their getaway, leaving the two other Oreos to find their own way home.

Much as Sid Luft found a big hole in Moss Hart's script for the 1954 remake, Streisand pointed to a flaw in Frank Pierson's screenplay. "He somehow couldn't write a love scene," she declared. It fell to her to remember the tape recording she made months before with Leon Russell when they composed the song "Lost Inside of You" and he asked, "Where did that come from?" and she exclaimed, "That's amazing!" Playing screenwriter for a moment, Streisand replicated that scene at the piano with Kristofferson. Their two characters fall in lust, and even though Esther has already checked out his tacky waterbed—she touches it cautiously with her foot as if checking for fungus—John Norman shows respect by carrying her instead to a far more romantic setting of antique pillows strewn across the polished parquet floor. It is there that they consummate not only the writing of their song but also their love.

As Streisand explained it, "This is how the two characters should come together, the melody and the counter-melody, around their music. They're in harmony with each other. I took [the dialogue] from reality—'Where did that come from?' and 'That's amazing!'—and made it happen in terms of his carrying her [to the pillows] and the music continues, and they make love for the first time, and that's how that scene was born." She called their making music together "a safe place where there's mutual respect and wonder and admiration about what's coming out of the other one's brain."

Esther and John Norman having sex showcases one of the film's many deliberate role reversals. Streisand explained, "There's a moment in the love scene when Esther looks down at John Norman and undoes her belt. I was thinking of Clint Eastwood . . . you know how the guy always unbuckles his belt before having sex. That's why I wanted Esther to be on top. Why should a man always be the one doing the unbuckling?"

It's just one of many scenes in the second remake of *A Star Is Born* that had much to do with Streisand and Peters's life together off camera. "A lot of Esther and John's relationship was based on me and Jon, too, what happened to us," she said. "There was a certain rawness, grittiness, to our relationship that should be part of this [movie] relationship, a ferociousness, an animalistic . . . whatever you want to call it."

After their first bout of lovemaking, Esther and John Norman clean up in a suds-filled bathtub. "We took that from real life," Peters noted. "Barbra and I have an enormous stone tub at home with a big, broad rim on which we put lighted candles when we bathe together." The scene in the movies, indeed, used enough candles to light the Sistine Chapel before the invention of the light bulb.

Streisand visited the set the day before the bathtub shoot only to see that her instructions had been ignored. She wanted the bathroom walls to be black tiles with pink trim. Instead, Streisand got a bathtub with pink tiles and black trim. She envisioned a dissolve to black from the previous lovemaking scene, which would not be possible with bright-pink tiles. The crew spent the night repainting the bathroom tiles.

In one of his smarter moves, Frank Pierson made sure that Peters did not visit the set the day Streisand and Kristofferson pretended to make love or pretended to bathe together nude. Peters whined, "You think it's easy? Some dude making love to your woman?"

To play drunk, Kristofferson got drunk. To play naked, Kristofferson got naked before sliding into the bathwater. Streisand, wearing a slip and no top, ordered her director, "For God's sake, find out if he's going to wear something. If Jon finds out he's in there with nothing on, naked . . ." Her boyfriend had already laid down the law. "Jon insisted he put on some trunks," Streisand reported.

As it turned out, the film's producer feared more than Kristofferson's naked body. "Fucking bastard is going to pee all over Barbra!" Peters said.

Someone in the costume department came prepared. Streisand may have been wearing clothes from her own closet, but Kristofferson did not own a pair of skin-colored trunks. Pierson handed the naked actor just such a costume to put on.

"What the hell are they afraid of?" Kristofferson wondered, his attempt at realism thwarted.

In yet another role reversal dictated by Streisand, her Esther applies makeup to Kristofferson's John Norman in that big stone bathtub. "When someone is truly masculine, they're not afraid of their feminine side," she explained. "I was always interested in the gender question, that men like peacocks might want to have their feathers painted. It's interesting to explore the differences in the sexes, to put on him rhinestones and makeup."

Later in the film, it is Esther who proposes marriage to John Norman, but to make the occasion special, she wears an antique white lace dress, not a Ralph Lauren suit. "Esther is really the driving force in this relationship. She sets the terms," Streisand said. "I was interested in being more sexually aggressive in this film . . . a different kind of character than I'd ever played."

There is a problem with so much role reversal, however. It begs the question: Why does this woman want or need a man? Esther Hoffman is a singular, independent talent for whom only stardom remains a missing ingredient in her life. Key among Streisand's changes to her role was something that had been in the original 1937 screenplay of *A Star Is Born*, a scene that dramatizes Vicki Lester's anger at Norman Maine's for his dissolute behavior. Dorothy Parker and Alan Campbell wrote such a scene, when Vicki screams at Norman, "Don't you blame me for that!" And she goes off on a tirade, listing all his faults.

But William A. Wellman never filmed such a scene, since David O. Selznick cut what Parker and Campbell wrote.

Streisand made sure to put a very similar scene in her *A Star Is Born* but shortened it considerably. The fight scene features what became the most quoted line from the film, because it's so terrible. "You can trash your life, but you're not going to trash mine," Esther tells John Norman after one big fight.

Streisand, despite all her on-screen bravado with Kristofferson and talk of role reversal, continued to have difficulty confronting the man in her own life. After one especially difficult day on the set, Streisand did not drive herself home or hop a ride with Jon Peters in his red Ferrari or red Jeep or whatever else he was driving that day. Instead, she begged Pierson, "For God's sake, take me home! He gets so furious. I don't know what to do."

She knew firsthand her boyfriend's rage and self-admitted penchant for violence. Two years before they started filming *A Star Is Born*, Streisand and Peters had traveled to New York City to see Muhammad Ali fight Joe Frazier at Madison Square Garden. There at the stadium, a man broke through the security team to grab Streisand. Peters prided himself with his quick reaction. "Pow! I let him have it!" he recalled. "He made a motion like he's gonna touch, maybe he's gonna hit Barbra: He's gonna hit my woman! I go crazy! Bam! Pow! They're pullin' me off him. The cops come take him away. You can't go anywhere with her! That's the meaning of 'star'!" Peters took inspiration from the violent episode at Madison Square Garden. He even told the story to Pierson and insisted, "We gotta get that in the picture!"

Streisand pointed to another pre-Peters episode of violent that she wanted to get into the film. "I'll never forget going to the premiere of *Hello, Dolly!* with Marty [Erlichman], and it was like watching the film *The Ugly American* where they surrounded the car in the movie and they broke the windows, and the public started to do that. They were shaking the car, and we couldn't get out of the car. Marty grabbed a guy's camera, and the guy hit him with the camera. And I'm screaming, and it's not pleasant when you go through this and you have to escape."

Streisand didn't stop there. "I want to show in this movie what it's like to be a star—what the pressures are. The isolation. I wrote a lot of things into this movie that come from my own life. I will be revealed in this picture more than ever before. People watching will get to know Barbra Streisand a whole lot better."

Pierson got the picture. In the end, the second remake of *A Star Is Born* is replete with scenes of fans and reporters behaving abominably. None is worse than a radio DJ given the sacrilegious named Bebe Jesus, played by M. J. Kelly, who has a vendetta against John Norman Howard. Streisand could identify. "It was like living in a fishbowl," she said.

Defensiveness with her public often translated into defensiveness with everyone else, including her director. "I don't feel you really want to love me," Streisand told Pierson after a few weeks of filming. "All my directors have wanted to make me beautiful. But I feel you hold something back; there's something you don't tell me. You never talk to me."

Pierson lied and told her he loved her. "But I'm not the demonstrative type," he said.

Streisand appeared to have forgotten that she was codirector of *A Star Is Born*. She never spoke about the need for her to love Pierson. Then again, the pressure confronting her dwarfed anything she ever experienced on her other movies. She told Pierson, "If this film goes down the drain, it's all over for Jon and me. We'll never work again."

Pierson thought she was being overly dramatic. He told her, "All you have to do is offer to sing, and they'll fall all over you to do a picture. Why are you trying to panic yourself this way?"

Streisand basically agreed. "I know, but what will happen to Jon?" she asked.

The director-screenwriter knew how to play good cop/

bad cop, but most important, he knew how to play the punching bag, getting hit from all sides. At one point in the filming, Peters told Pierson, "I'm so sick of you. I'm waiting until the production is finished. Then I'm going to punch you out."

On other days, Peters was conciliatory to the point of warning Pierson about his temperamental girlfriend. "Frankee! Your turn," Peters whined. "The Jewish princess wants you! She doesn't think you like her, she's getting panicky, and when she's like that, she starts calling in her friends."

Each side won a few, lost a few. Streisand wanted to use a barn on her Malibu ranch for Esther and John Norman's retreat in New Mexico; Pierson insisted on and got a remote adobe-style abode, built on the Empire Ranch in Sonoita, Arizona. Pierson called her idea for a mud fight in front of that house "like an episode of *I Love Lucy*." Streisand adored Lucille Ball and made sure that Kristofferson wrestled her to the ground where mud would soon outline her "great ass." At least she thought it was mud. When instead she smelled excrement, the crew told the star it was a preservative. They lied.

Pierson had little control over a kissing scene that morphed into a spitting scene. The fiction being filmed again borrowed from reality even when it came to Streisand and Peters's hygiene. In one scene, set outside the Empire Ranch house, Esther and John Norman take kissing to a Niagara Falls level of wetness. "Jon and I had a spitting fight the other night," Streisand noted. "Well, not a fight, but we were in bed, and we were kind of drooling all over each other. And you know, when you're in love, that's a very intimate thing. That's in the movie too."

Otherwise, if the star and director disagreed, those disputes were resolved in front of the crew.

When Streisand didn't like where the director placed a

dozen extras, she asked, "Why are they here?" and went on to order, "They should be over there!" When Pierson tried to explain that the dozen extras start "here" and end up "there" later in the scene, she screamed, "I want it!"

At another point in the filming, she called his direction "shit!" Streisand delivered the expletive in front of the entire cast and crew.

Pierson asked to see her out of earshot. "You're red," he told Streisand privately. "There's no reason to talk that way to me, so don't do it anymore. You're in a rage. What's that about?"

She told him, "Because I should have codirector credit. I've directed at least half of this movie. I think I should have the credit for it, don't you?' "

Pierson said she could have half his credit if he could get half the credit for her on-screen performance. She looked at him, dumbfounded. "You mean costarring Barbra Streisand and Frank Pierson?" she wondered aloud.

He thought fast. "I'm not so sure about the order of billing." Pierson was a writer, after all. He asked, finally, why she hadn't directed the film herself from the very beginning.

"I couldn't just take over as director from Jon, could I?" Streisand explained. "But I couldn't let Jon direct; can you imagine Jon Peters directing? I wanted someone to be a buffer between Jon and me."

Pierson had no interest in being a human shield for his star. Regardless, Streisand wanted the codirector credit, and she wanted Pierson to give it to her. She couldn't demand it, because "people criticize me enough as it is. I think it's something you have to give of your own free will," she said.

He replied that he would think about it, which he didn't.

The nightly screening of rushes turned into yet another contest of ego and power. "I told you not to do that. Why did you do it? It's wrong!" Streisand told Pierson repeatedly. After a few such episodes, the rest of the cast and crew stop going to the dailies, leaving Streisand and Pierson alone together in the dark. Finally, Pierson also stopped watching the rushes.

Working on the film led Streisand to conjuring up weird images in her head. She recalled Edvard Munch's painting *The Scream*, with a man's hands covering his ears, his mouth wide open in pain. "You know, a scream with no sound," she said of her own anguish and frustration.

Shortly into the production of *A Star Is Born*, Pierson found himself nominated for an Oscar for his *Dog Day Afternoon* screenplay. He asked Streisand and Peters if he could attend the Academy Awards on March 29 in Los Angeles, and Streisand and Peters promptly said no. They didn't have it in the budget. Pierson would have to watch the ceremony from his hotel room. He chose instead a local bar, where he watched as Gore Vidal gave the names of the nominees for best original screenplay, and then announced, "And the winner is, Frank Pierson, *Dog Day Afternoon*." Pierson nearly fell off his barstool. Warren Beatty and Robert Towne were expected to win for their *Shampoo* screenplay.

The next day, almost everyone in the crew offered their congratulations to the surprise winner. Almost everyone. Not extending their congratulations were Streisand and Peters. Only later did Peters acknowledge the award, when, after a typical disagreement, he let his director know, "I'm not afraid of your Oscar."

Chapter 12

Frank Pierson held the right to first cut on *A Star Is Born*, which meant next to nothing, since Streisand had final cut. According to her, the executives at Warner Brothers didn't like Pierson's edit when he gave it to them. "But I had to work fast," Streisand recalled.

The studio executives were obligated to take what she gave them, not what Pierson gave them.

Peter Zinner received credit as the editor, but like everything else on this version of *A Star Is Born*, his work was subject to Streisand's approval and dictates. Also, she brought on lesser, uncredited editors who worked around the clock. Streisand had installed a state-of-the-art editing studio at her Malibu ranch, making it possible for her to keep an eye on the progress at any hour. Jon Peters warned Pierson that when his girlfriend became insecure about anything on the movie, she turned to her friends for advice. It had happened to the first director on the film, Jerry Schatzberg, and it would also happen to Zinner. On a typical Friday night, he and Streisand would agree on the cut of a scene. They shook hands on it. Then, over the weekend, she showed their work to her unofficial advisers, people like lyricists Alan and Marilyn Bergman, agent Sue Mengers, and close friend Cis Corman.

"Her friends influenced her, I think, quite a great deal," Zinner said. Every Monday morning like clockwork, she told him, "There's just one more thing I'd like to do."

And he would say, "But we discussed that."

And she would reply, "Well, I know, but . . ."

"Of course, I had to change it," Zinner said. He came to regard their Friday handshakes as "almost like a joke."

Regarding the edit of the film, Streisand's primary concern was that "her character needed more time on the screen," Zinner said. "She felt that some of the sequences were too heavy with Kristofferson. I would say that she made major changes, not so much with the storyline but as far as the characters were concerned. Her character became much more pertinent."

Despite all the editing disagreements, Zinner believed there existed one scene that would not be decided by Streisand and her gang of friends. The two of them agreed they would screen two different endings of *A Star Is Born* and let the preview audiences tell them which one to include, which to dump. In the film, when the widow Esther Hoffman takes the concert stage at the end, an announcer introduces her entrance to the concert stage, "Ladies and gentlemen, Esther Hoffman Howard." According to Streisand, that's "our modern way of doing Judy Garland's 'Mrs. Norman Maine' line . . . it's Esther's name plus his. She adds his name because she doesn't want people to forget him."

However, the moment has no punch, as it does in the first two *A Star Is Born* films. In the 1937 and 1954 versions, Janet Gaynor and Judy Garland's Vicki Lester delivers the line, "Hello, everybody! This is Mrs. Norman Maine." Pauline Kael in her pan review of Streisand's *A Star Is Born* points out that it was "actually worse" from a feminist perspective to have an off camera, anonymous male announcer say, "Ladies and gentlemen, Esther Hoffman Howard."

The self-aggrandizement didn't stop there. Rather than the finale being about the man, it is all about the woman. Streisand wanted the concert to begin with her backstage. "When I'm walking on to the stage for the last time, I described to Bob Surtees a painting by Erté," Streisand said, mentioning an Art Deco artist she greatly admired. "It is a little figure of a woman on stage and her shadow is very big on the curtains. The image, the shadow is much bigger than the person. [The public] reads things into their dreams about you."

Unlike the character's self-deprecating gesture in the first two *A Star Is Born* films, Streisand's Esther flexes her ego when she sings "With One More Look at You" and then follows it with her dead husband's signature song, "Watch Closely Now." The tour de force clocks in at seven and a half minutes.

The finale had been shot two different ways.

"It was her big number. There were seven or eight cameras on that goddamned thing," Zinner said. One version keeps a single camera in close-up on Streisand's face for all seven and a half minutes. Streisand preferred this version.

Zinner wanted to go with a second version that featured a variety of angles, as well as judicious editing, to connect the multiple shots.

Two previews of the film were held on the same day, each audience seeing a different version. "In the afternoon, we had the ending with multiple cuts, and in the evening, we had her ending, the one shot," the editor said. "I felt that the edited version was stronger. The other one was too long. It went overboard. Seven and a half minutes is too much of a load for one person, no matter how good you are."

George Cukor had also insisted on one shot with Garland singing "The Man That Got Away," but there the camera moves dramatically, and the song clocks in at four and a half minutes, a full three minutes shorter than the Streisand blowout.

After the two screenings of their *A Star Is Born*, Streisand and Zinner looked forward to analyzing the preview cards. "Everybody was kind of anxious to see which ending played better," Zinner recalled. "When it was all over, Barbra said, 'Well, Peter, I guess you won.'"

Until Zinner hadn't won.

A few days later—after getting feedback from her friends, Streisand decided her instinct was right, as usual. She picked the ending she always wanted: the one shot of her in close-up with plenty of backlighting of her frizzy hair for seven and a half minutes. "Once I saw it with an audience, I made up my mind," Streisand said. "It has to stay in one shot. The audience is held by it. When you do other shots, you lose concentration."

Streisand's first cut of *A Star Is Born* came in at three and a half hours, which she reduced to 140 minutes, forty-one fewer than the first remake of *A Star Is Born*.

Streisand relished pointing out all the role reversals in her *Star*. "It was the women's lib movement, and I was involved," she explained. The movie's poster, however, was quite another thing, if not downright retro. Photographing Streisand and Kristofferson, Francesco Scavullo simply updated the 1939 *Gone with the Wind* poster with a very macho and dominating Clark Gable embracing and looming over a very feminine and submissive Vivien Leigh. The only real difference, besides the use of black-and-white photography instead of color, is that both Streisand and Kristofferson are naked from the waist up.

Streisand had originally envisioned something less stereotypical—the woman on top. Photos were taken that put Streisand in a man's suit, as usual, and Kristofferson bare-chested, as usual. His performance remains one of the most topless ever committed to film by either a woman or a man.

The poster's original intent of role reversal would be splendidly achieved a few years later when a naked John Lennon and a fully clothed Yoko Ono posed for photographer Annie Leibowitz in 1980. It became one of the most famous covers ever for *Rolling Stone* magazine. Perhaps if Leibowitz had been hired by Warner Brothers, the iconic poster of the 1976 remake of *A Star Is Born* might have been a little more cutting edge. Instead, the man responsible for hundreds of cleavage-centric covers of Helen Gurley Brown's soft-core porn magazine *Cosmopolitan* delivered what he always delivered: human skin air-brushed to android perfection.

After taking a few shots of Streisand and Kristofferson for the poster, Scavullo started to shake his beret-topped head. Finally, he took Kristofferson aside to inform him, "Show her who the man is." Streisand wasn't within earshot but no matter. When the three of them regrouped in front of the white seamless backdrop, she let them know, "I heard everything you said—and may the best man win!"

The photograph they picked for the poster was so successful in its glossy depiction of traditional sex roles that Carol Burnett parodied it on her weekly eponymous TV comedy hour.

When Kristofferson saw a rough cut of the film, he stopped drinking cold turkey. "I realized it was my own life I was seein' on the screen," he said, then went on to refer to his wife. "It was like seeing myself through Rita [Coolidge]'s eyes—when I saw the corpse at the end [of the film], I had a weird feeling of sadness, like a character in *The Twilight Zone* who sees a coffin with his name on it. I feel so goddamn lucky to have gotten out in time—I'd been drinking for twenty years."

Joan Didion and John Gregory Dunne based their John Norman Howard on James Taylor. Frank Pierson mentioned Janis Joplin, and Peters talked about Elvis Presley. But most prominent were the comparisons to Jim Morrison, the enigmatic and dissolute lead singer of the Doors who died of a drug overdose only five years earlier.

Kristofferson didn't have to look even that far afield to bring his John Norman to the screen. "I don't think I ever met Morrison," he remarked. "A lot of people said we looked alike—shirts off, beards—but that washed-up rock star was more about me."

Streisand and Pierson argued over who got credit for his direction and who got credit for her performance, and the arguments didn't stop there when he left the film for her to edit it. When Sue Mengers saw the end credits scroll, she expressed extreme concern.

"I couldn't believe that you had taken both an editing and wardrobe credit," the agent told her client.

Streisand defended herself. "Why shouldn't I have those credits?" she wanted to know. "I picked out all my clothes. It's my taste that you see reflected on screen. And I have worked hard on the editing of the picture. I deserve the credits, and I'm taking both of them."

"You can't do a thing like that in Hollywood," Mengers reminded her. "There are unions. You'll have an ugly fight on your hands and you'll be the laughingstock of the town!"

Streisand didn't give up. "Well, I did the work, and I want the credit!"

In the end, Mengers's wisdom regarding the ways of Hollywood prevailed. Her client received no credit for either editing or wardrobe, except to say the clothes came "from her closet," leaving it to the public to decide whether it was Barbra Streisand or an assistant who carried the garments from her Malibu ranch to the movie studio.

Much of what Streisand wore in the film, indeed, looks like it came from her closet. Her Esther preens like a big diva, the kind of behavior that Gaynor, Garland, and Lady Gaga vigorously eschew in their respective *Star* vehicles. At one point, Streisand even dons a turban! She never looks like a novice singer on the verge of breaking into the business bigtime. Streisand defended her wardrobe choices, citing money over character. "I collect a lot of antique clothes," she said. "We were also trying to save money. We didn't want to have a big costume budget. I really didn't have the time to shop and see sketches and try on clothes, so I just used things that I thought were just very Esther-like," she said.

Beyond the turban, the most egregious of her many unfortunate costumes was Streisand's decision to wear a man's pale gray pinstriped suit designed by Ralph Lauren, which she topped off with a pastel shirt and bow tie. Esther wears it for her very first session in a recording studio. Blue jeans and a sweatshirt would have been more likely for a novice or even a veteran performer.

What Streisand did with her own clothes can be seen as the reverse of what Sid Luft and Judy Garland did on their remake of *A Star Is Born*. While the couple took costumes and decor from the production to fill their own closets and living room, Streisand brought her own stuff to the set, including a few pieces of furniture to dress the adobe house in Arizona.

Chapter 13

Warner Brothers pulled out all the stops to publicize the film. They scheduled their female star to put her hand- and footprints in cement in the courtyard at the Chinese Theater. Barbra Streisand would then walk a few feet in front of the historic theater at 6925 Hollywood Boulevard to see her bronze star placed into the sidewalk. It was prime real estate. It would be quite a night.

Streisand canceled both events.

Without having to ask her, Warner Brothers never even considered one publicity platform that all studios consider de rigueur for any actor with a major film about to be released. In 1975, Streisand had been scheduled to appear on *The Tonight Show* to publicize *Funny Lady*. It was going to be a reunion of sorts. When Jack Paar and Groucho Marx hosted the late-night talk show in the early 1960s, the teenage Streisand appeared to plug her Broadway show, *I Can Get It for You Wholesale*. Groucho even gave his full support for her being cast in *Funny Girl* when Anne Bancroft and Carol Burnett were the frontrunners to play Fanny Brice. When Johnny Carson made his debut appearance as host on October 1, 1962, Streisand appeared two nights later and six more times in the following five months.

Maybe Streisand never recovered from Carson initially mispronouncing her name on October 3 as "STREE-sand." Thirteen years later, she canceled her 1975 appearance on *The Tonight Show* the day before her expected grand return there. That kind of thing just didn't happen to the almighty king of late-night television, who immediately informed his viewers, "Streisand will not be here Wednesday night—nor will she be here in the future."

He remained so pissed that his nightclub act in Las Vegas soon featured a new quip, "I was out in the alley playing Frisbee . . . with Barbra Streisand records."

Barbara Walters might have felt that Carson got off easy after she conducted her interview with the star. Streisand hated TV shows that were taped live. They made her nervous. She wanted control, and she got it with Walters. Streisand's appearance marked the first of many Barbara Walters interview specials on the ABC network, and the star would share the night with Jimmy and Rosalynn Carter. Unlike the future president and first lady, Streisand demanded final cut of the interview, and she got it. Then, after viewing it, Streisand decided she had worn the wrong outfit (a pink sweater), and Walters needed to do the interview over again so she could change clothes.

"I nearly went out of my mind," Walters recalled. The two women engaged in trans-country phone calls nearly every day until December 14, when the "damned thing" finally aired, "because she's such a perfectionist. She will worry, literally, about whether these flowers should look like this or whether the buds should be opened," the TV journalist noted.

Streisand's micromanagement did not end there. At the premiere at the Westwood Village Theatre on December

18, Streisand somehow forgot that the only purpose for such an event is to generate publicity. That night, she chose to use a secret entrance to deprive her fans, reporters, and photographers of a glimpse of her on the red carpet. Weeks earlier, she had sent out invitations to a very select group of a few hundred friends, informing them to wear "all white." Of course, she showed up wearing all black. Her seventy-four-year-old *Funny Girl* director disobeyed the dictated color scheme for the fete by wearing a traditional black tuxedo. "I don't have a white suit," William Wyler apologized, "but my underwear is white."

Streisand had already categorized the experience of making *A Star Is Born* as a "long-running nightmare."

Which did not prepare her for the reviews.

After previews before journalists and private screenings with friends and movie executives, Streisand and Jon Peters had been told their film was great, if not a masterpiece. It was the best of all the movies titled *A Star Is Born*.

The critics saw another film. *Rolling Stone* titled its review, "A Star Is Born—Dead on Arrival." In his New York *Daily News* review, Rex Reed called it "a junk heap of boring ineptitude." Pauline Kael at *The New Yorker* wrote that the film was "not convincing—even for a minute." And *Newsweek* remarked that Streisand's "constant upstaging of Kristofferson goes beyond run-of-the-mill narcissism."

Streisand's fans, however, got what they wanted—her singing six songs—and flocked to the theaters presenting the newest *A Star Is Born*. Warner Brothers executives had been conservative in their estimate that her singing those half a dozen songs would bring in $60 million at the box office. The film grossed $80 million in North America. Only *Rocky* that year grossed more. And there were other rewards for all those songs Streisand sang. The soundtrack for *A Star Is Born* held the number one spot for six weeks,

"Evergreen" became Streisand's second number one song, after "The Way We Were," and it delivered an Oscar nomination for best song for her and Paul Williams.

Streisand made sure not to repeat her mistake at the 1974 Academy Awards with "The Way We Were," which she refused to sing live at the ceremony. When the show's producers asked Peggy Lee to do the honors and she accepted, Streisand changed her mind and decided she wanted to sing the movie's theme song—but that call came only days before the ceremony. The Academy refused to fire Lee, who ended up mangling the lyrics of "The Way We Were." Many pundits charged that Streisand not singing the title song on the telecast cost her the best actress Oscar that year, the award instead going to Glenda Jackson for her performance in the forgettable comedy *A Touch of Class*. Lucky Glenda, she did Streisand one better and stayed home in England.

On Oscar night March 28, 1977, Streisand jumped at the opportunity to sing "Evergreen" at the Dorothy Chandler Pavilion in downtown Los Angeles.

Neil Diamond, who graduated from high school with Streisand back at Erasmus Hall in Brooklyn, was picked to present the award. The Oscars too often indulged in these chummy handoffs, because Diamond had already told Streisand three weeks before that he was going to read her name regardless of whether she won. That unfortunate remark made several gossip columns before Oscar night, forcing Diamond to explain to Streisand from the Pavilion podium, "So, if I call your name out, you actually won it, and if I don't call your name out, you wrote a fantastic song first time out. We'll see." At this moment in time, one could only wonder how the other eight nominated composers and lyricists felt. The only real competition that year for best original song was Bill Conti's "Gonna Fly Now" from *Rocky*.

Then the man who wrote and sang "Sweet Caroline" a few thousand times made it known, to no one's surprise: "And the winner is, 'Evergreen.'"

For a moment, it had been forgotten that Streisand wrote the music for the song but not the lyrics. Paul Williams, after hearing Diamond's Streisand-centric comments, ran in the wake of his more famous collaborator to receive his Oscar too. He also ran a few acceptance lines through his head. He considered saying, "Isn't it nice they gave me one too."

Streisand gave him plenty of time to reconsider. She took the microphone first to say, "In my wildest dreams, I never thought I would win an Oscar for writing a song." Williams, finally given his moment to speak, decided at the last moment to play it cute. "I was going to thank all the little people," he said, "then I remembered I am the little people."

Streisand later called her Oscar for writing the "Evergreen" music "the biggest thrill of my career."

A Star Is Born led to Streisand directing three other movies and taking full credit for them: *Yentl, The Mirror Has Two Faces*, and *The Prince of Tides*. She resented not taking the reins sooner. "I never had the power," she remarked the year after the release of her *A Star Is Born*. "If I did, some of my movies would have been better. . . . But when I've made movies in the past, I haven't had the same freedom. The director would say one thing, and although I might disagree, I always gave in, you know, him being the director and all. And, of course, I had no say in the editing of anything like that. In this movie, I'm in control." It would take her another four years to be completely free, which happened when she broke up with Jon Peters in 1982.

Nearly fifty years later, Streisand was even more pointed in discussing the obstacles of being a woman in the film industry and how she overcame them. "It's kind of ironic," she said in a 2018 interview. "I wanted the character I played to be a liberated woman, and yet I stupidly gave away the title of producer and took a lesser one. I even cut certain scenes of mine so I would have less screen time, because I didn't want to attract more criticism. Happily, *A Star Is Born* turned out to be the second-highest-grossing film of [1976] after *Rocky*. Phew!"

The movie also turned out to be First Artists's most successful film by far. The actor-driven company enjoyed other hits during the 1970s. They included *The Main Event* starring Streisand, *The Getaway* starring Steve McQueen, and *The Life and Times of Judge Roy Bean* starring Paul Newman. But the company's box office flops dominated, and they included *Up the Sandbox* with Streisand, *Pocket Money* with Newman, *An Enemy of the People* with McQueen, and *A Warm December* with Sidney Poitier. First Artists shuttered in 1980.

Part Four

"I'm Ally Maine."

Chapter 14

Constance Bennett was not an immediate fan of the script titled *What Price Hollywood?*.

"Oh no—not again!" she complained to her director. "I am tired and weary of having an illegitimate baby in every picture I make."

George Cukor wasted no time correcting her. "Read the script again, Connie," he said, "This time it's different. You get married first." The director liked this spontaneous exchange so much he put it into the film, removing the forbidden word "illegitimate." It made the retort even funnier.

The blond kid named Jackie in *What Price Hollywood?* is just one of the characters dropped not only from the first *A Star Is Born* but also the three other versions that followed. The thought of even having children is never mentioned between the four couples in those four movies. Esther Hoffman has the best opportunity of these female characters to bring up the subject. It comes when Barbra Streisand sings Esther's second song in the 1976 remake. After Kris Kristofferson's John Norman Howard has so rudely interrupted her club performance of the song "Queen Bee," written by Rupert Holmes, Esther and John Norman come to a quick understanding. They flirt a little, and she sings "Everything," written by Holmes and Paul Williams. The second song mentions a lot of things Esther wants to accomplish in life. She sings, "I'd like to plan a city, play the cello / Play at Monte Carlo, play Othello / Move into the White House, paint it yellow / Speak Portuguese and Dutch."

Her desire to perform blackface aside, one might wonder why she doesn't instead want to speak Arabic or paint the president's residence a feminist pink. The big, unanswered question is why she doesn't have children on her nearly bottomless bucket list. Before production on the second *A Star Is Born* remake began, Jon Peters made a declaration about the film's central love story. He said, "The most important thing to both of them is communicating. Wanting to have children. Not the thousands of agents and press agents . . ."

Somehow the desire to have kids, much less the kids themselves, never made it into the final movie.

One reason for these childless marriages is that the movies' first three Esthers, as well as Lady Gaga's Ally, are deprived long marriages. That consideration aside, none of these women even brings up the subject of having a family. For a moment, it was going to happen in the 2018 version. The song "Is That Alright?" had been written to be performed during Ally and Jackson's wedding. The song is a series of vows, and one of them explains, "I dream of our story of our fairytale / Family dinners and family trees / Teachin' the kids to say thank you and please . . ."

In the editing process, the song "I Don't Know What Love Is" replaced "Is That Alright?," now relegated to the end credits.

In the final cut of this third remake of *A Star Is Born*, the newly married couple that is Ally and Jackson do what none of their predecessors on screen even think about. They do what a lot of couples in this millennium do. Instead of kids, they get a dog.

When Kristofferson's John Norman takes Streisand's Esther to his Beverly Hills manse for the first time, his vrooming red Ferrari is greeted by a couple of barking German shepherds that scare the hell out of her. The two hounds are clearly guard dogs, not pets, and they are never shown in the house. The dog in the fourth *A Star Is Born* film is without question a child substitute. Bradley Cooper cast his own rescue dog, Charlie, a crossbreed, and went on to win an award for that bit of nepotism. *Variety* reported, "If the pope wasn't happy, PETA gave Cooper an award for putting his own dog in the film and not using one of Hollywood's 'notorious' animal exhibitors."

The senior vice president of the animal rights organization praised the dog's performance. "It's clear that he loved being with his real-life 'dad,'" Lisa Lange announced.

Variety's 2018 reference to the pope was prescient. Pope Francis called out the "selfishness" of people having pets instead of children in 2022, one year after JD Vance's infamous "childless cat ladies" comment to Tucker Carlson on Fox News.

The word "authentic" became Cooper's mantra as the director of the third remake of *A Star Is Born*. Adding a child substitute to the plot was just one of the changes he made from the previous versions, most notably the 1976 remake, which is the most inauthentic of the four films and the one the 2018 version most resembles, much to Barbra Streisand's consternation—but more about that simmering spat later in this book.

The phenomenon of remaking *A Star Is Born* had been occurring at a regular interval of every two decades, with the fourth version needing double that time to arrive on-screen. It was not for lack of trying.

Mike Nichols toyed with remaking the film by putting it in the world of stand-up comedy clubs. The director of *The Graduate* and *Postcards from the Edge* even went so far as to hire playwright-director George C. Wolfe to do the script. "Whoopi Goldberg was going to be the rising comedian, and Richard Pryor was going to be the comedian on his way out," Wolfe recalled. "It fell apart before I ever wrote a script, and it was totally my fault because I got tied up writing other things."

Around this time, in the 1990s, Will Smith and director Carl Franklin were in talks to do a remake of *A Star Is Born* with Alicia Keys, who showed no interest in the project, and as a result, Smith went on to make the Muhammad Ali biopicture *Ali* instead.

A Star Is Born then caught the interest of Jamie Foxx and his *Any Given Sunday* director, Oliver Stone, with singers Lauryn Hill and Aaliyah seen as possible female costars. Aaliyah turned the offer down flat. Hill proved a bit more elusive. Curious reporters asked Foxx about the movie project. "Nobody can get in touch with Lauryn," he told them. The actor even resorted to attending Hill's concerts to make the necessary contact. "She thinks I'm a stalker," he added. "I was trying to get her interested in the thing, so I was going to her concerts. I saw her in Vegas. I saw her in Irvine, and after a while, she was like, 'You know, you're making me nervous.' "

A former manager and promoter of rock and roll performers sat in on some of those meetings when Smith and Franklin and then Foxx and Stone expressed interest in retelling the story of a fading star who marries too well only to commit suicide. Warner Brothers continued to hold the rights to *A Star Is Born*, and one of its executives, Bill Gerber, wondered aloud one day at the negotiating table, saying, "Hey, I'd like to take a shot at that."

He had grown up watching old movies and remembered with fondness, as a teenager, seeing the Streisand version of *A Star Is Born*. "I never doubted it was a good idea, even when I had nothing to do with it," Gerber said. "It wasn't like trying to remake *Casablanca* or *The Wizard of Oz*. There was a precedent here."

Eventually, he left Warner Brothers to start producing his own movies, including *American Outlaws* with Colin Farrell and *The In-Laws* with Michael Douglas. "In the beginning, I think it is 2007," Gerber recalled, "we get a first draft from [screenwriter] Pamela Gray of an interracial love story based on *A Star Is Born*. She pitched it. The Warner Brothers creative group got excited about it."

But how to cast *A Star Is Born* in the twenty-first century?

Gerber mentioned the name Beyoncé to a bunch of pertinent executives.

"Beyoncé?" someone at Warner Brothers asked. "Why?"

"Because she is Beyoncé!" Gerber exclaimed. The superstar had already given the world "Naughty Girl" and "If I Were a Boy," as well as dozens of other hit songs. By the time she left Destiny's Child in 2003, her voice graced more than 60 million records sold.

Somehow the Beyoncé brick wall would not go away. "Who is going to come see Beyoncé?" someone else at the table asked.

"If she is singing, *everybody*!" Gerber replied.

Eventually, the Beyoncé fan at the table won the argument that *A Star Is Born* starring the superstar, who had already appeared in the movie version of *Dreamgirls* in 2006, was a good and financially sound idea. "At this point, there were no other elements," Gerber recalled, except for Pamela Gray's script, "which went to Beyoncé's team."

The world-famous singer and *Dreamgirls* veteran read it. Better yet, she liked it. "We immediately started talking about directors," Gerber said, "and it was her idea to talk to Clint."

Serendipitously, Gerber happened to be producing Clint Eastwood's film *Gran Torino* at the time. "I was actually a bit nervous bringing it up to him, Clint," the producer recalled. Gerber thought to himself, "I'm going to go to this legendary filmmaker about a third remake of a kind of campy movie with a woman who is a singer, not necessarily an actress?"

Eastwood returned Gerber's phone call while the producer was on vacation in the Caribbean. The conversation started easily enough. "Hey, I read the script of *A Star Is Born*. What do you want to do?" the Oscar-winning director asked.

"We'd like you to direct it," Gerber said with trepidation.

"Okay," Eastwood said.

Gerber took a deep breath. "I literally looked up at the heavens. Thank you!"

At the glacial pace of today's Hollywood, Eastwood and Beyoncé would not actually meet face-to-face until 2010 or 2011, according to Gerber.

"To be sitting with those two was really epic," the producer recalled. "Clint was telling her about having seen Billie Holiday several times." Gerber thought to himself, "I'm watching something historic about to happen."

Until it didn't happen. When Eastwood went off to make another movie, Gerber wondered, "Do we wait?" He chose to remain philosophical: "It's just the movie business." Waiting was much better than quitting, because the film Eastwood went on to make, *American Sniper*, would bring Bradley Cooper to the project.

Meanwhile, because Beyoncé remained interested, Gerber kept the project alive. He even had lunch with Frank

Pierson, who, having written the 1976 version of *A Star Is Born*, regaled him with stories of working with Jon Peters and Barbra Streisand. The producer also read John Gregory Dunne and Joan Didion's *Rainbow Road* screenplay. "It is 160 pages," Gerber recalled, about twice the length of a normal screenplay. "It's basically what the TV series *Daisy Jones and the Six* ended up like. Fleetwood Mac, that story. Their screenplay is really good. It's a lot different. It is a band story."

Working on other film projects, Gerber met a young writer whose script *The Lucky One* was in development and would eventually star Zac Efron and Taylor Schilling in 2012. Another script by the same writer, *Crazy for the Storm*, impressed Gerber, and while the two of them tried to get that one made, Gerber mentioned the new but already long-gestating remake of *A Star Is Born*. Will Fetters had never seen any of the other versions of the movie, a minor liability that turned out to be quite commonplace with most of the major players on the fourth version of the story. One weekend, Fetters decided to watch all three films.

"My favorite is the Garland and Mason film," Fetters said. "A lot of things had changed since 1954, however. How do you modernize it? The gender politics are crazy. The male character can't get a job? That is supposed to be a tragedy?"

Fetters didn't think so. He called story and character "a chicken-and-egg question, but the story here was set, and so I had to figure out who the characters were, figure out how to make this movie work in the modern era." Unlike the previous versions of *A Star Is Born*, he felt that "fame and success could not be the destination for the female character. The pureness of the expression of her voice—that was the story."

And Fetters made it the central aspect of the story even

when writing for Beyoncé. "There were even other directors before Clint," he recalled. "I remember a few meetings with Nick Cassavetes."

Mentioned to star were the usual suspects, Brad Pitt and Leonardo DiCaprio.

"Bradley Cooper wasn't the first person we spoke about," Bill Gerber noted. "Clint hadn't done *American Sniper* with Bradley yet."

Now it was 2014, and Gerber and Fetters did not care that another remake of *A Star Is Born* had beaten them into the cineplexes, because those theaters were in India where *Aashiqui 2* offered moviegoers there a near beat-by-beat replay of the Streisand version but to a Bollywood pop sound. One of that film's major changes from the *Star* formula is the awards ceremony. In *Aashiqui 2*, Aditya Roy Kapur's pop star on the decline watches as his wife, played by Shraddha Kapoor, wins her music award on a TV screen in the venue's bar. Instead of his humiliating her with a drunken speech and a slap, he listens as two men at the bar praise his wife and trash him for being a complete has-been. *Aashiqui 2*, directed by Mohit Suri, also features the youngest couple ever to star in a reprise of the *A Star Is Born* story. At the time of the film's release, Kapur was twenty-eight, Kapoor only twenty-six.

Not deterred by any competition from a movie playing halfway around the world, Gerber visited the set of *American Sniper* to mention *A Star Is Born* to Cooper, who now joined the big league of Pitt and DiCaprio, thanks to *Silver Linings Playbook* and the *Hangover* franchise of films.

"I don't think I'm old enough to play the character," Cooper told Gerber. Besides, the actor was soon going off to Broadway to perform on stage in a revival of *The Elephant Man*. Sometime during that theatrical engagement, however, he began to have second thoughts about *A Star Is Born*.

"It kept haunting me, this broken love story," Cooper said. "Shots kept coming into my head. And I would dream about it. I had to purge it in a way. I knew that I had to do it."

Cooper also liked that it was a love story between two people "and there's no infidelity and still how hard it is," he said. In all the versions of *A Star Is Born*, Kris Kristofferson's John Norman is the only one who cheats on his wife, with a female reporter wanting an interview with Esther.

Before he became involved, Cooper had also not seen any of the films that carried the title *A Star Is Born*. Having watched them, finally, he called the Garland version a flat-out "masterpiece." He was much more circumspect regarding the Streisand film, saying, "I felt reverberations of the 1976 *A Star Is Born*, because it was so iconic for its time."

Translation: The movie had dated badly.

Cooper worshipped rock stars, and his becoming a movie star carried the major fringe benefit of meeting many of his idols, Neil Young and Willie Nelson among them. "I'd been playing air guitar since I was a kid," he claimed. The music, he felt, was key to keeping the film authentic. "You can't fake it when you sing," he said. "It's impossible, because your voice is the first thing that goes when you're not connected to yourself. So, I loved the idea that these two characters were expressing themselves through singing, that I would have a beeline right to their soul."

When Cooper mentioned doing a remake of *A Star Is Born* to a rock star friend, he got a surprising response but one that the actor believed kept him honest and "authentic" in his approach to the material. The rocker warned, "You better create a character that meets the standards of what it is to be a rock star because no one's ever gotten it right."

It forced Cooper to look at himself in the mirror. "Honestly," he said, "I could see it on my face. I just felt it." The movie star in him was now old enough to play the rock star. Considering how long it takes to get a movie made in Hollywood these days, the production process would only help make him look and feel older—forty-two years old, to be exact, when the cameras finally rolled. Plus, the studio sweetened the deal: Cooper could write the script and direct the movie.

"I have to give Warner Brothers credit for backing the idea of his directing the movie," Bill Gerber said. "They had no reservations whatsoever about giving Bradley that job."

With Cooper aboard, the theme of the new *A Star Is Born* became especially personal for his co-screenwriter. "In my career, when you first start out, I had so many things offered by people I idolized," Will Fetters said. "You consider ideas and to do them, are you doing them for the right reasons? The machinery of the music business and movie business—these are forces that act on you. We think we're going to do things differently, and then you get a big offer from a movie. 'Hey, I can do this Justin Timberlake movie!'"

Even better than Timberlake, Fetters was now doing this Bradley Cooper movie.

He refashioned the story of *A Star Is Born*, removing some of the male insecurity and humiliation that comes when the character's wife becomes the much bigger story. "Jackson has been through everything, and he sees what is happening to her. She has some insecurity," Fetters said. "I saw her getting caught up in the machinery of the business and his trying to get her to trust her voice was a big chunk of it. That core thing was always in the script."

Working on the script with Cooper, Fetters saw his journey being replicated by Ally's in their evolving screenplay.

Cooper had finished his run in *The Elephant Man* on Broadway and had taken the play, written by Bernard Pomerance in 1977, to the West End in London. "I was there for five or six weeks that summer," Fetters recalled. "Bradley would do the show, and then during the day, we hung out." The writer couldn't recall the name of his hotel in London but vividly remembered Cooper staying at the Chiltern Firehouse. "It is the hip spot for famous people. People like me couldn't get in. I was with fancy people for a few weeks."

Cooper and Fetters were writing the script specifically for Beyoncé. "I still have the voice mail, the text, after Bradley met her. We were both so excited," Fetters recalled.

Cooper liked the core element of Fetters's script, that the male rocker would want the female singer-songwriter he discovers "to trust her voice." He also wanted to incorporate his belief in the romantic power of song. "With music, it's impossible to hide," Cooper said. "Every fiber of your body becomes alive when you sing."

While Cooper felt he was now old enough to play the male lead, he didn't think his singing or speaking voice quite up to the task. For six months, he worked with a vocal coach to lower his speaking voice an octave. "Your voice is everything as an actor," he said. "It's everything. It's everything. And if you're not connected to your voice, it's over. It's impossible. It's like plugging in the electrical cord to truth."

That was his speaking voice. He next had to grapple with how he sang. In October 2016, Cooper traveled to Indio, California, to check out Desert Trip, a six-day musical festival that quickly got dubbed "Oldchella" due to the advanced ages of the legendary rockers performing there. They included Bob Dylan, the Rolling Stones, Paul McCartney, the Who, and Neil Young. Lukas Nelson and his band, Promise of the Real, were doing backup for

Young, and during that performance, Cooper's eye kept going to the twenty-eight-year-old son of Willie Nelson. He saw something in the young rocker that he wanted his Jackson Maine to be in *A Star Is Born*. He also thought Nelson could teach him how to play the guitar like one of his rock idols.

"I had the sound in my head what I wanted Jackson's guitar to sound like, and it was heavily influenced by Neil Young," Cooper said. "His guitar strumming never floated around the neck. It tapped the neck."

Lukas Nelson helped with that technique but soon found himself taking on more tasks. "I got those Magnatone amps and that 1956 Gibson Les Paul Jr., and that became Jackson's sound," he said.

Cooper gave his new music teacher even more credit, decreeing, "There is no Jackson Maine without Lukas Nelson." And Lukas Nelson was there ready to take that credit. "Definitely, he based a large part of it on me," he said.

Another part came from Sam Elliott. Cooper, working to lower his speaking voice to a bass-baritone, began to watch movies featuring the actor whose career went back to the 1970s with the TV series *Mission: Impossible*. Elliott typically played heavies, often in Westerns, due to his extraordinarily cavernous yet sonorous voice. Cooper set out to replicate that sound. In Cooper's *A Star Is Born*, Jackson Maine has an older half brother, Bobby, an erstwhile singer who accuses him, "You stole my voice." Cooper wanted Elliott to play Bobby.

Eventually, the two men met at Cooper's house. Cooper told Elliott, "I've got something I want you to listen to. You might think it's kind of weird."

He then played a tape of his reading a few of Jackson Maine's lines from the screenplay. "It sounded uncannily like me," Elliott said, and he thought, "What the fuck."

"We had never met, so I felt like I was taking a gamble," Cooper said.

Elliott saw it in more practical terms. "I figured if he committed to my voice, I had a good chance of getting the part," he noted. Nothing was agreed to on the spot. There were agents and managers to get involved, but before Elliott could drive away, Cooper told him in his driveway, "If you trust me, you'll be glad you did."

Indeed, "I'd have been fucked if Sam didn't do the part," Cooper said.

Then Beyoncé got pregnant with twins, and to further complicate matters, she asked for $8 million on a film budgeted at $37 million, with about $5 million of that already spent on false starts. The makers of the new *A Star Is Born* could have waited for the singer to deliver those two children, Rumi and Sir Carter, in June, but that $8 million fee slammed that door shut. It recalled Cary Grant's demand back in 1953 of $300,000 plus 10 percent of the gross to make the Garland version of *A Star Is Born*. Money killed the deal with Grant, and money would do the same with Beyoncé.

Enter Lady Gaga. Cooper thought of her immediately and went to see her perform as soon as possible. It happened to be a cancer fundraiser in Sean Penn's backyard in Los Angeles. When she sang "La Vie en Rose," Cooper fell in love, or something even more intense, if not downright injurious to his health. "It shot like a diamond through my brain," he said. "I loved the way she moved, the sound of her voice." Except for a couple of bars of "Over the Rainbow" during the opening title sequence, Édith Piaf's signature song would be the only standard song that Gaga performed in the movie. Even before filming began, Cooper set down the rule: "Let's not do any covers."

"La Vie en Rose" and "Over the Rainbow" also add an important beat to what would be Gaga's character: In the beginning, Ally writes songs but only sings covers. She feels "uncomfortable" performing her own material—until Jackson gives her the confidence and "the trust in her own voice."

After the Sean Penn fete, Cooper phoned Gaga's agent, and a meeting was set up for the two to meet later that day at her home in Malibu. When Bradley Cooper calls, things happen fast in Hollywood. As the two of them tell it, the meeting for her to star in *A Star Is Born* went so well that it could have been written by a not-very-original screenwriter.

Gaga recalled, "The second that I saw him, I was like, 'Have I known you my whole life?' It was an instant connection, instant understanding of one another."

Cooper recalled, "She came down the stairs, and we went out to her patio and I saw her eyes, and honestly, it clicked, and I went, 'Wow!'"

"Are you hungry?" she asked.

"I'm starving," he replied.

Cooper remembered her heating up some spaghetti and meatballs. Gaga remembered it being leftover lasagna. "We're both from the East Coast; we're both Italian," she explained.

He saw a white piano in her living room, and not holding that bit of questionable taste in interior decoration against her, Cooper asked if they could sing a song together. She laughed at him. Not taken aback, he explained, "The truth is, it's only going to work if we can sing together." They were both nervous. "You're a musician, and I'm an actor," he told her, "and we're going to make an exchange."

Suddenly, "For me there was not nervousness," Gaga noted.

"It was because I had that camaraderie on stage, I

Adela Rogers St. Johns, the "Mother Confessor of Hollywood," meets with Douglas Fairbanks Jr., whom she often interviewed. Her writings give birth to the *A Star Is Born* legend. *Photofest*.

The marriage of Colleen Moore and John McCormick inspires Rogers St. Johns to write stories about two Hollywood careers that move in opposite directions. *Photofest.*

Lowell Sherman's director (far left) makes Constance Bennett's ingenue a star in *What Price Hollywood?* (1932), but she falls in love with Neil Hamilton's polo-playing millionaire. *RKO/Photofest.*

The trio in the Pre-Code *What Price Hollywood?* pushes the boundaries of sexual resentment only hinted at in such later classics as *Laura* and *All About Eve*. *RKO/Everett Collection.*

Barbara Stanwyck becomes a movie star while actor-husband Frank Fay fails to score in Hollywood, providing even more fodder for the *A Star Is Born* scenario. *Photofest.*

Fredric March's Norman Maine and Janet Gaynor's Vicki Lester in *A Star Is Born* (1937) watch the preview of her first movie. Moments later, he proclaims, "A star is born." *United Artists/Photofest.*

Joseph Schildkraut's costume designer (center) contributes to Esther Blodgett's makeover in *A Star Is Born*, but the "pansy" character is deleted due to pressure from the Production Code. *United Artists/Photofest.*

Director William A. Wellman (far left) attends the Hollywood premiere of *A Star Is Born* with Gaynor and producer David O. Selznick, who also brought *What Price Hollywood?* to the screen. *United Artists/Everett Collection.*

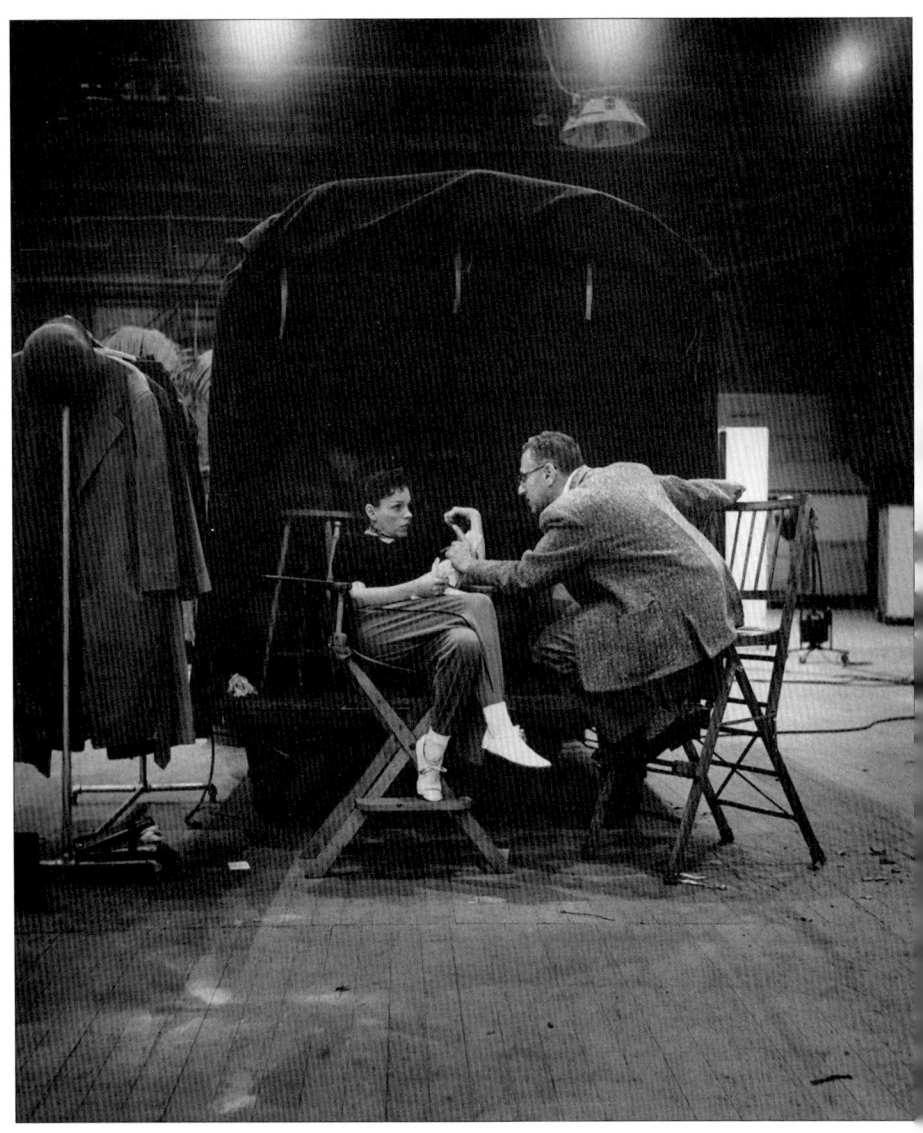

George Cukor, who also directed *What Price Hollywood?*, confers with Judy Garland between scenes. He admires her talent but chafes at her lack of discipline and professional courtesy. *Warner Bros./Photofest.*

James Mason's Norman Maine, shouting at children not to vandalize his car, reunites with Judy Garland's Esther Blodgett at her apartment building. This scene and many others are cut after the film's release. *Warner Bros./Photofest.*

Norman Maine accidentally slaps Vicki Lester in the first *A Star Is Born* remake (1954). All four versions of the film feature an awards-ceremony humiliation. *Warner Bros./Photofest.*

Sid Luft and Judy Garland attend the New York City premiere of *A Star Is Born*. It ends his career as a film producer. She does not appear in another movie until *Judgment at Nuremberg* (1961). *Warner Bros./Everett Collection.*

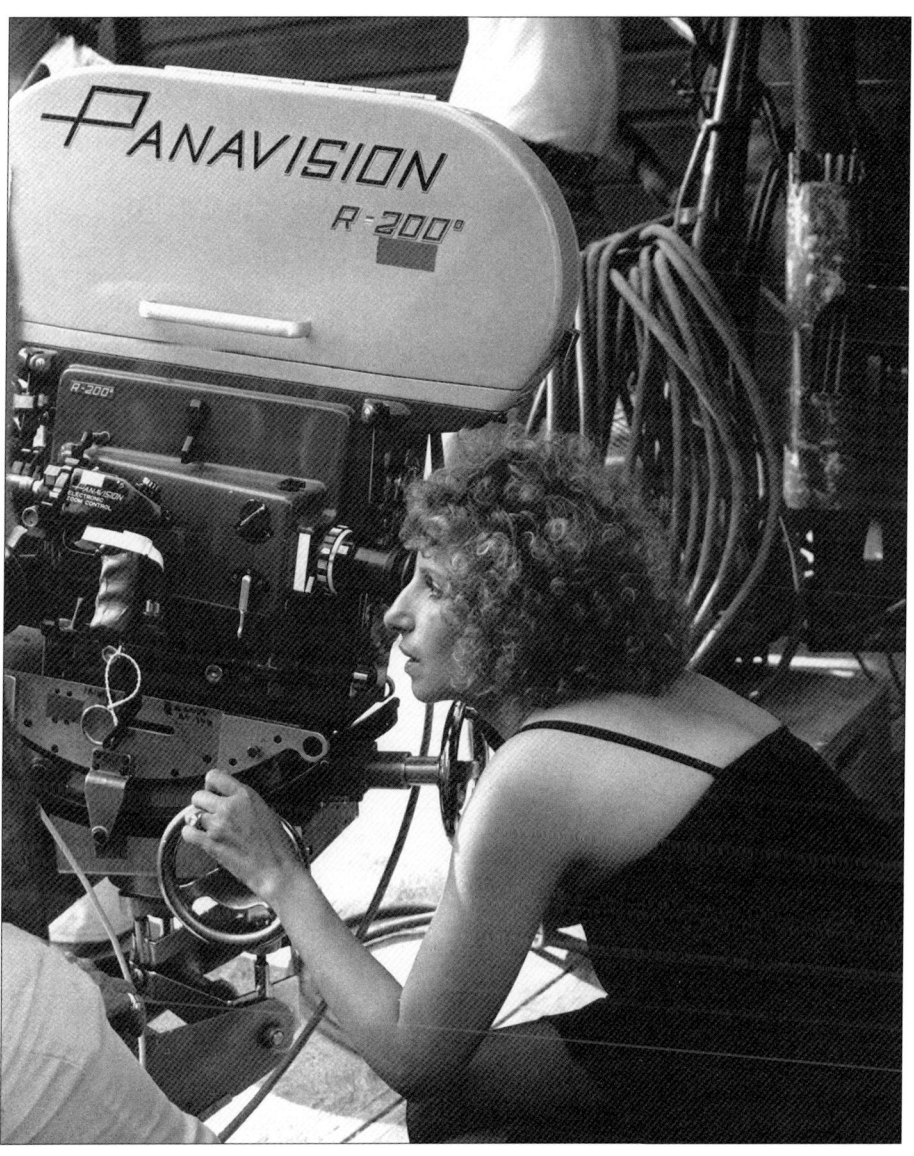

Barbra Streisand doesn't get all the credits she wants, but she ends up directing much of the second remake of *A Star Is Born* (1976). She also stars, edits, writes a song, and provides her own wardrobe.
Warner Bros./Photofest.

Streisand's Esther Hoffman and Kris Kristofferson's John Norman Howard enjoy a bath after making love in *A Star Is Born* (1976). Critics pan the film, which cleans up at the box office. *Warner Bros./Everett Collection.*

Streisand rehearses with backing vocalists Clydie King (far left) and Venetta Fields. Together, they are called the Oreos ("two chocolate girls and me") in the 1976 film. *Warner Bros./Photofest.*

Everyone looks in a different direction and agrees on almost nothing regarding their *A Star Is Born*: (clockwise from top) producer Jon Peters, director-screenwriter Frank Pierson, and stars Streisand and Kristofferson. *Warner Bros./Photofest.*

Kristofferson sits for interviews at the press junket during the film's shoot of the big concert scene at Sun Devil Stadium, Tempe, Arizona. *Warner Bros./Photofest.*

Variety columnist Army Archerd interviews Streisand and Peters at the Los Angeles premiere of *A Star Is Born*, with the Francesco Scavullo poster on vivid display. *Warner Bros./Photofest.*

Bradley Cooper directs his first film, the third remake (2018) of *A Star Is Born*.
He also stars, produces, screenwrites, and contributes to a few songs. *Warner Bros./Photofest.*

Cooper's Jackson Maine writes the song "I'll Never Love Again" in rehab
and then performs it for Lady Gaga's Ally Campana in *A Star Is Born* (2018).
Warner Bros./Photofest.

Cooper casts Charlie, his own crossbreed rescue dog, as Ally and Jackson's child substitute in the film.
PETA rewards Cooper with an Oscat for his animal-friendly gesture.
© *Warner Bros./courtesy Everett Collection.*

Lady Gaga attends the Venice premiere of *A Star Is Born*. Despite the rain, several umbrellas and canopies prevent the feathered Valentino gown from turning her into a wet Big Bird.
Matteo Chinellato/NurPhoto, Shutterstock.

Joanne Woodward and Paul Newman star in *The Long, Hot Summer* (1958):
What happens when the roles are reversed? *20th Century Fox/Photofest.*

thought, 'It's gonna be okay,'" Cooper said. "When she's looking at me and believes I'm a musician, well, then I must be a musician."

Sitting at the piano, she asked, "Well, what song?" and he suggested "The Midnight Special." She printed out the sheet music, and they read the lyrics from his iPhone. After a few bars of their singing together, Gaga stopped. "Oh my god, Bradley, you have a tremendous voice. Has anyone ever heard you sing before?" she asked.

He said no, even though he had been studying and preparing for months for just this moment.

"I took vocal, guitar, and piano lessons. I spent five days a week for six months," Cooper recalled. "I would get two verses that sounded good and then half of one that was off key."

Lukas Nelson had warned him, "You're going to have to sing a thousand times before you get in front of a live audience."

After their singing a few more bars of "The Midnight Special," Gaga said, "We should film this!" Cooper switched on his phone's camera so they could sing the song for posterity.

"He sings from his gut, from the nectar," Gaga said. "I knew instantly. This guy could play a rock star. And I don't think there are a lot of people in Hollywood who can. That was the moment I knew this film could be something truly special."

"And that video is one of the things I showed to Warner Brothers to get the movie green-lit," Cooper said. Actually, the movie had already been green-lit. Cooper needed the video of their singing together just to get Lady Gaga a screen test at Warner Brothers.

"The studio had doubts," Bill Gerber said, thinking back to "a former executive at Warner Brothers who wasn't convinced she should get the role. Bradley believed in her, and Warners was generous enough to budget a proper screen test.

"There were certain situations where I think it was a little overwhelming for Bradley before we got to the point of the screen test," the producer recalled.

In the beginning, that screen test was for Gaga, to convince wary executives that she could play the female lead. She had recently been nominated for a Golden Globe Award for her appearance on an episode of the Hulu TV series *American Horror Story*, but unlike all the other famous film actresses who had played the female lead in *A Star Is Born*, this remake would mark an actress's screen debut. The film would, or would not, give birth to a movie star.

"We watched a star being born with that screen test," Gerber said. In this instance, the producer wasn't talking about Lady Gaga the actress but rather Bradley Cooper the director. "The moment Bradley started directing Gaga, which was the first time he had directed anybody," Gerber noted, "it was crazy."

Cooper admitted he had more than one reason to make the screen test. And one of those had nothing to do with Gaga. "It was the first time I'd ever directed anything," he said. "It was selfish for me, a test run."

It may have been his first directing job, but Cooper held very definitive ideas about what he wanted to achieve. He took aside Gaga—a performer known as much for her hair, makeup, and outrageous costumes as her music—and told her, "Take it off."

For the screen test at her Malibu home, she had applied the works—concealer, mascara, rouge, lipstick. Cooper held a makeup wipe in his hand for her to remove what it had taken an hour to apply. "Completely open," he said. "No artifice."

Gaga didn't look aghast. She did as told. "I took off my makeup, and that allowed me to open up to be vulnerable to put my despair, my insecurities on film," she said.

Warner Brothers did not stint in giving Gerber, Cooper, and Gaga everything they wanted to make a successful screen test. No less a cinematographer than Janusz Kamiński, winner of Oscars for shooting *Schindler's List* and *Saving Private Ryan*, arrived to film Cooper and Gaga cavorting around in bed and dancing in front of wind-blown curtains. Sometime during the shoot, Kamiński turned to Gerber to remark about Cooper, "Did this guy make ten movies we don't know about?"

"Bradley had complete command," the producer said. "If there had been a second reservation about his directing, it evaporated instantly."

And along with them, concerns about Gaga as a screen actor. "It wasn't unanimous until we did the test, and when Warner Brothers saw it, it took them seconds to say yes to Lady Gaga," Gerber said.

Cooper sent that test, as well as the tape of his and Gaga's singing "The Midnight Special," to a British producer he admired. Lynette Howell Taylor had produced *The Place Beyond the Pines*, a film in which Cooper starred in 2012, and he saw there how closely she worked with director Derek Gianfrance on the casting and the script, among other aspects of the production. "I ended up being a partner with the filmmaker," said Howell Taylor. "Bradley wanted that. He brought me in to partner with Bill Gerber." Ravi Mehta, a twenty-year veteran at Warner Brothers, also came aboard as an executive producer.

Howell Taylor, born in Liverpool, England, had never seen any of the *A Star Is Born* films. She binged. She also read Cooper and Fetter's script. "Bradley wanted a significant rewrite on it," the producer recalled.

To facilitate that overhaul of the script, Fetters met with

Gaga at her Malibu home. He bought his tape recorder. "We had never met. She let me record her; she trusted me to do that," Fetters said. And yet, "She was so open about her own life. That was invaluable. *That* was the character."

Fetters found Ally "the toughest character to crack. I knew what it meant to be a young man in a cutthroat industry."

But a young woman in the music business? Not so much.

Fetters listened and recorded as Gaga filled him in on the discrimination she experienced being the young Stefani Germanotta and walking into a room of male executives who wanted to sign a more conventional beauty. "Ally in a lot of ways was me," she said. "I had brown hair and was behind a piano, writing songs, and they said they liked the way I sounded but didn't like the way that I looked. These are things that happened to me in real life."

In what can be read as an homage to Barbra Streisand, Ally in the 2018 film thinks her less-than-petite nose has prevented her from becoming a star. "Can I touch it?" Jackson asks her shortly after they first meet. She is aghast. "I've been looking at it all night," he says. In the finished film, he and Ally take turns outlining her nose with their fingers.

It was personal for Gaga. "It put me right in the place I needed to be. When my character talks about how ugly she feels—that was real," she said. "I'm so insecure. I like to preach, but I don't always practice what I preach."

And the abuse wasn't limited to her looks. At age nineteen, Stefani Germanotta was raped by a record producer. "It took years," Gaga said of dealing with that trauma. "No one else knew. It was almost like I tried to erase it from my brain. And when it finally came out, it was like a big, ugly monster. And you have to face the monster to heal."

The bright spot in her life, beyond having incredible talent, were her parents, Joe and Cynthia Germanotta. As Gaga told Fetters, both her mother and father supported her career from the beginning. While Cynthia escorted the young Stefani to clubs where she was underage. Joe emerged as the real force, both emotionally and financially. "He is my hero," Gaga said.

Joe Germanotta was an internet entrepreneur who founded Guest-WiFi, which provided wireless service to hotels. When asked about boyfriends in her teen years, the newly monikered Lady Gaga replied, "I'm married to my dad."

For Beyoncé, Fetters created an older sister with whom the female character bonded. To rewrite the screenplay for Gaga, Fetters turned the sister into the character's father. The writer took the burly Italian wealthy businessman dad Joe and turned him into the burly Italian limousine driver dad Lorenzo in *A Star Is Born*. He also gave the character a few other edges. Where Joe supported Stefani unconditionally, Lorenzo in the movie appreciates his daughter's enormous talent but doesn't quite think she has what it takes to be a star. He tells his limo-driver buddies, "With a voice, like, from heaven! But you know what? It's not always the best singer that makes it, you know? I know a couple of guys that could sing Sinatra under the table . . ." Ally walks away, shaking her head, more depressed than ever about her career.

Fetters also changed the venue where the female lead meets Jackson Maine. For Beyoncé, it had been a conventional bar and performance space. For Gaga, he turned it into a drag bar that just happens to share the same name as the after-hours club Bleu Bleu in the 1954 version of *A Star Is Born*.

"Anybody who knows Lady Gaga's mythology even a little bit, the drag club came out of that. It is woven into the fabric," Fetters said. Indeed, she had once said, "God put me on earth for three reasons: to make loud music, gay videos, and cause a damn ruckus."

Cooper agreed about making gay men central to Ally's story. "We talked a lot about where she started on the Lower East Side, and she told me about this drag bar where she used to hang, and I thought, 'Oh, this is just ripe for the story,'" he said.

In a 2009 interview, Gaga said, "When I play at gay clubs, it's like playing for my friends; they get it and understand what I'm trying to say."

However, like Ally who performs with "the gay girls," as she calls the drag performers, Gaga's sexual orientation was never in doubt. "That period of my life was about me trying to be cool, being the queen of a very small scene, getting my picture taken, dating the hottest bartender. Bartenders are like movie stars down there," Gaga said of the Lower East Side. "Being Queen of the Scene is like being the queen of two blocks. But it got me in magazines, and it got Interscope interested," she said, referring to her first record label.

If those music executives didn't like the way she looked, Gaga tore a page from Prince, Elton John, and David Bowie and started creating bizarre characters to play on stage, often obliterating her own physiognomy. In the beginning, she called it "rock 'n' roll burlesque," but with reservations. "I was never a stripper, never topless." She was soon calling herself a "Monster" and her fans "the Monsters."

Where the character of Ally would diverge from Gaga is the relatively young age at which Stefani Germanotta became a star, as well as the fierce determination and focus it took.

"I used to walk down the street like I was a fucking star," Gaga said. "I want people to walk around delusional about how great they can be—and then to fight so hard for it every day that the lie becomes the truth."

Cooper told his new leading lady, "This is a movie about what would have happened if you didn't make it until you were thirty-one instead of twenty-one."

Unlike all the other films titled *A Star Is Born*, the female singer in the 2018 version has given up on herself as a performer. She writes music but doesn't perform her own songs. The only venue in which she does perform is a drag bar, and even there, she sticks to the tried-and-true repertoire of piano bars, in this case, "La Vie en Rose."

Gaga and Ally would come to share a lot of traits, but the character's "vulnerability" is a notable departure. "She was nothing like I was when I started," Gaga said. "When I wanted to become a singer, I really believed in myself. I was banging down every door that I could and dragging my piano around New York, trying to get any gigs. This is not who she is at all."

Chapter 15

In this century, only Madonna rivals Lady Gaga in the gay pantheon of divas. In the previous century, it was Judy Garland and Barbra Streisand vying for that singular status. That three of these four women have starred in a movie called *A Star Is Born* automatically douses the title in a deep shade of lavender. And then there is the first Esther Blodgett.

Janet Gaynor enters that pantheon through a different door. Part of the attraction gay men have for stars like Gaga, Garland, and Streisand, as well as Bette Davis and Joan Crawford, is that they exude sexual aggression and, in their respective private lives, enjoyed sex with gorgeous straight men whom gay men can only fantasize about. Even Gaynor admitted that she lacked oomph. Her selling card in Hollywood was something far less intoxicating. She possessed "sweetness," she said. Unlike the other aforementioned female stars, however, Gaynor's sexual orientation has always been open to debate. Her surprise marriage to MGM costume designer and longtime bachelor Adrian provoked several one-liners, whether apocryphal or not.

"Adrian designs the trousers, and Gaynor wears them" is just one line that made the rounds of the Brown Derby after their marriage in 1939. When a child was born a year later and almost died, cruel wags heard Adrian moaning, "Oh no, I'm going to have to do *that* again!"

And it didn't stop there. Gossips speculated on why Gaynor purchased a ranch in Brazil right next door to land owned by Mary Martin of Broadway fame. Rumors of their years-long affair continued when a serious car crash involving the two women led to Gaynor's death two years later in 1984, at age eighty-one.

It's telling that in his early days of putting together the 2018 remake of *A Star Is Born*, Bill Gerber called it "campy"—code for gay—when he spoke of first broaching the subject with Clint Eastwood. Whether intended or not, a subtext has emerged in the *A Star Is Born* legend that says talent makes someone different, if not downright exotic. And a price will have to be paid. Female stars pay that price; gay men pay that price. With enormous success comes the epithets "difficult" and "temperamental." For too much of the twentieth century, it was better for homosexuals not to be famous, or their true identity would be revealed.

Considering her affinity for all things gay, it's no surprise that Lady Gaga was one of the few people working on the latest remake of *A Star Is Born* who had actually watched previous versions of the film, and she liked them all—with one major exception.

"Judy Garland is by far my favorite actress of all time," she said. "I used to watch her *A Star Is Born*, and it's devastating. She's so real, so right there. He eyes would get glassy, and you could just see the passion and the emotion and hear the grit in her voice."

Suddenly, Garland became a huge part of Fetters and Cooper's ever-evolving script. "Ally had this fixation with

Judy Garland, and Jackson used that," Lynette Howell Taylor recalled. A scene was written where Jackson, to impress Ally, takes her to the house where the teenage Garland lived while filming *The Wizard of Oz* in 1938. Ravi Mehta explained, "They show up at a strange family's house at midnight and because he's Jackson Maine . . ." The production company even found the real house in the Boyle Heights neighborhood of Los Angeles. The film's supervising art director was not impressed.

"The actual house is small and didn't feel right," Bradley Rubin said. "A bad renovation, bad stucco."

Mehta agreed. "It was renovated, just drywall," the producer said. "No fucking way."

There was only one problem. "I love it!" Cooper told Mehta.

In another scene that was written but not filmed, "Jackson even gives Ally a pair of the ruby red slippers," Howell Taylor recalled. Ultimately, wiser minds prevailed. "It all felt heavy-handed. I'm glad Bradley got rid of that," the producer added.

One thing that did remain is Gaga singing a few bars of "Over the Rainbow" when she walks out of the kitchen of the restaurant where she works as a server. The title *A Star Is Born*, emblazoned in red letters, slowly appears on the movie screen as she sings, walking down the alley. Gaga was going to sing the entire song or a good portion of it. Even that got cut back. "Let's just do the prelude," Cooper said. In the finished film, only "When all the world is a hopeless jumble . . ." is sung a cappella.

While Cooper and Fetters incorporated Gaga's history into Ally's story, Lukas Nelson also found his own life being used as source material. His gig as a vocal and guitar coach to Cooper continued to expand. The producers were relying on him to make sure the rock concerts looked accurate, and his band, Promise and the Real, was hired to back up Jackson Maine in the film. And there was more. "It was a natural process of evolution," Nelson said, "just the fact that I was there, and I do write. We were trying to find the character of who Jackson Maine was. The song-writing sort of helped shape that."

Nelson would cowrite eight of the songs in the film, including "Black Eyes," which Jackson sings in the film's first scene, shot at the Stagecoach music festival in Indio, California.

Nelson knew a lot about the pitfalls of fame, his father being a famous musician-singer. Once the young Lukas started performing professionally, his mother even gave him a refrigerator magnet and told him to put it on the fridge in his band's tour bus. "Fame is a vapor," it read. "Only one thing endures and that is character."

Nelson also collaborated with Gaga, writing "Music to My Eyes" and "I Don't Know What Love Is." He liked that she had a tattoo of David Bowie on her arm. "Bowie was my hero as well," he said. "We grew up listening to the same type of thing."

In total, eleven composers and lyricists would contribute to the film's original score. One thing gave them cohesion, held them all together: What the characters sing had to reflect what is happening in their respective lives. "There's no point where a lyric is sung that it isn't related directly to what their fear is, their hope, their dream," Cooper said.

In the end, Gaga's greatest contribution to the finished score would be the film's iconic love song, "Shallow," written with lyricist Mark Ronson.

It is the song Ally sings a cappella to Jackson in the parking lot of a supermarket where he wraps a bag of frozen peas around her swollen fingers after she has punched out a fan in a cop bar on the same night that they first meet at a drag bar. It is a tribute to Gaga and Cooper that their performances make dramatic sense of that bizarre confluence of events. Jackson has already heard her sing "La Vie en Rose" at the Bleu Bleu club, but it is Ally's singing of the incomplete and yet-untitled "Shallow" that causes him to exclaim not only "holy shit" but also to tell her, "I think you just might be a songwriter."

Cooper used the song in a way that its two songwriters did not intend. "What the movie turned the song into is just another level," Ronson said. "In the original script, Jackson was going to drown at the end. So Gaga comes in, sits down at the piano, and starts playing a few chords, and it just sounds big, right off the bat. And she comes up with the chorus, 'I'm off the deep end; watch as I dive in.'"

"We thought it might be the ending song," Gaga explained. "Then as the script changed, we made it a song about the two falling in love. I do feel it was more than the literal drowning element of the original script. It was much more about wanting a deep connection and love than it was about water."

"Shallow" functions in the film much the way "Lost Inside of You" does in the 1976 version of *A Star Is Born*. There, Barbra Streisand's Esther begins the song at a piano, and Kris Kristofferson's John Norman starts to sing a countermelody. Finished performing, the couple then consummates their love. In the 2018 remake, "Shallow" achieves much more than signaling Ally and Jackson's love affair. The song is the first real showcase for Ally's talent as a performer when Jackson later forces her to sing it as a duet with him on stage, a tape of which goes viral, much to Papa Lorenzo's pride. From her singing "Shallow" a cappella in the parking lot to their singing it together at a live concert in fewer than fifteen minutes of screen time is an economy of storytelling often missing in the other musical versions of *A Star Is Born*.

"It starts in the parking lot," Gaga said. "Then she arrives at the concert, and Jackson has had some time to think about it, and he has added his verse. ['Tell me somethin', girl.'] And she's so overwhelmed by what he's done for her and this arrangement. It gives her the courage to go out there and sing in front of his audience. It's a song that essentially inspires both of them to be fearless in different ways. For him, fearless in love; for her, fearless in not just one love but her ability to share that part of her that's a songwriter, the part of her that doesn't feel comfortable singing her song. I mean, this girl has completely given up. She's completely depressed. She doesn't think she has what it takes."

Despite his intensive work with Lukas Nelson and Will Fetters, Cooper felt the characters and the story needed to be taken to another level. Executives at Warner Brothers suggested he enlist the help of a veteran screenwriter, one who had four Oscar nominations to his credit and one win for his adapted screenplay *Forrest Gump*.

"This is the material we have," Cooper told Eric Roth. "What do you think?"

"Some was for me, some was not," Roth replied. "I'd like to see if we can rework it in some ways." He spent the next eight weeks on the screenplay. "Which is way shorter than anything I've ever done," Roth noted. He had already seen the Garland and Streisand remakes of *A Star Is Born*, but now took a first look at the original 1937 version.

"Really great writers were involved with all of them," he said. "Even though the tale is many times told, it resonated with me. I locked in on the love story. That gave me comfort because I think I've done a number of love stories, and I feel confident about the interrelationships with certain characters. Also, it had the built-in tragic ending, which is obviously a good thing for a love story. I don't think you can think of many great love stories that have generally a happy ending. . . . One of the foundations of a great love story is that the people just can't be together, whether it's by race or economics or class or anything. There's always some kind of an impediment, all the way back from *Romeo and Juliet*."

Not that the seventy-two-year-old screenwriter felt completely secure. "This had been done a lot of times, and I didn't know if I could crack the code to make it special and modern," Roth said. "The fear was trying to do it again, whether anyone was really interested anymore." His guiding principle has always been one of fear. "I was worried about ending up with egg on my face," the writer explained.

In addition to her long interview with Fetters, Gaga also spoke to Roth. She asked him, "What can I learn from?"

"Look at Cher in *Moonstruck*," he replied. "She's strong, so sure of herself, kind of tough-minded." The screenwriter went on to explain, "You had a vulnerable quality in that character. Very streetwise and sure of herself in certain areas and a little bit lost in others."

He and Cooper also decided to give Gaga a big entrance in the film, one worthy of any golden-age diva, except for the fact that they set it in a restroom. Cooper introduced Ally by putting her in a toilet stall where she's on a cellphone call with her soon-to-be ex-boyfriend, who wants to marry her. "Are you crazy?" Ally asks. She's not getting married! She's breaking up with him! Ally then walks out of the stall to scream into the overly lit ladies' room of the restaurant, where she works as a server.

Cooper said he learned something important from making *Silver Linings Playbook* with director David O. Russell: A major character needs a major entrance. He explained, "Ally isn't even aware of her power, and the camera is always looking at her right full on. At the beginning, she doesn't even know she's being watched, but the camera is us: We see you even if you don't.'" Then Ally walks out of the toilet stall. "And all of a sudden, the bathroom is a stage and the movie is telling you, 'She's the story.' "

Before filming could begin, one former major player had to be confronted and dealt with.

"Jon Peters attached himself to a lot of prize possessions he was producing," Ravi Mehta said. "He got the rights; he was a rights holder on *Superman* also and a handful of titles at Warner Brothers. Those would be crazy, nonexistent deals today. They don't exist anymore."

The studio's negotiations with Peters were tough. "Warner Brothers took a strong stance on the deal," Bill Gerber said, "and Jon had to make some adjustments."

Chapter 16

At last, filming on the fourth version of *A Star Is Born* began on April 17, 2017, at Coachella in Indio, California. That year, the headliners were to be Beyoncé, Radiohead, and Kendrick Lamar. Beyoncé's pregnancy with her twins, to be born that June, opened the way for Lady Gaga to be cast in *A Star Is Born*. It also led to her debut that year at the annual music and arts festival held at Indio's Empire Polo Club.

"Let's get some of the concert stuff at Coachella right out of the gate," Bill Gerber announced. "It's great energy for the crew. It sets the tone."

And the film's cinematographer explained other reasons to film there. "We were able to get the production values of their stages and their lighting," Matthew Libatique said. "It's a Warner Brothers movie, but it had that independent feel—there was not studio presence like you get on a normal film."

Gerber had been in talks with Coachella and the Anschutz Entertainment Group even before Beyoncé canceled. As a former rock promoter and manager, he was able "to contribute all my historic DNA into this film." As a result, *A Star Is Born* could use the stage and lighting on the four nights between the two weekends of the festival at next to no cost.

There was only one catch. "If Radiohead needed the stage to rehearse, we had to get the fuck out of there," the producer recalled. "We were literally holding our breath whether Radiohead is not going to decide to rehearse."

To everyone's relief, Radiohead decided to wing it. Fans working as extras were requested to be "decked out in your most comfortable denim and boots." That scrappy use of an existing concert venue put to rest one big concern. "Okay, Bradley Cooper's a rock star," Gerber thought after seeing him perform on stage. "We can get on with the story now."

Other rock venues would also be used to capture a real audience at a concert. While Gerber worked his old professional connections, Ravi Mehta went right to the top, phoning Goldenvoice Concerts, which operates several California festivals and venues, including Coachella and the Shrine Auditorium. "Bradley was obsessed with there being twelve performances," Mehta recalled. "But how do you pull off twelve performances with no money? He wanted live audiences; it was extremely difficult."

Cooper remained insistent, telling his producers, "Look at *Crazy Heart* with Jeff Bridges. That's a real audience. Ravi, how do we do that?"

With Coachella, the *A Star Is Born* production had the stage for four consistent days. Elsewhere, they would often get only a few minutes on stage. "With these live performances, there is a half-hour change over from artist to artist," Mehta explained. "If you can give up setup rehearsal time and you can jump on stage, it can be done."

On April 29, the company filmed at Stagecoach between sets performed by Willie Nelson and James Johnston. Mark Rothbaum managed Nelson, and when Gerber asked for permission, the rock manager emailed back in five minutes: "Our stage is your stage." It didn't hurt that Nelson's son's band just happened to be Jackson Maine's in the movie. The ten minutes they filmed on stage there led to Cooper scrapping a planned staged concert at the historic Biltmore Hotel in downtown Los Angeles. That decision saved them a lot of money.

Mehta recalled, "Bradley wanted to have this huge opening where you can see Jackson in all his glory in black tie at a full-orchestra performance. Jackson has his demons but performs in all his glory. The Biltmore Hotel, that was the opening, and Ally's working down in the kitchen."

Then Stagecoach happened. Jackson swallows a fistful of pills, gives the V-sign, and sings "Black Eyes." Cooper knew it immediately. "*That* should be the opening of the movie!" he told his producers. They were all relieved. "We cut three shooting days out of the schedule," Mehta said of the suddenly scrapped concert at the Biltmore. "Bradley foamed the runway. He set it up for the landing."

Even a televised concert used the real locale. When Ally appears on *Saturday Night Live* to sing her new hit single "Why'd You Do That?" Mehta told Cooper, "We can just re-create it."

"No, dude," said Cooper. "Everybody is going to know."

"Lorne Michaels welcomed us in there. We used all of his crew to shoot that scene, which was amazing," Gerber said. "Alec Baldwin did it as a favor for Bradley. We went in on the dark Monday after they did the show."

Cooper knew what he wanted to achieve with all the concert scenes, and again, it had everything to do with his deep admiration of rock stars. He remembered a concert he attended on September 14, 2011. "To shoot subjectively came out of the Metallica concert," he said, "and I was behind the drummer kit at Yankee Stadium, and I could see the sweat on the back of Lars Ulrich's neck while still getting the scope of the crowd, and that was the first time that I thought this composition in a film would be incredible. . . . I'm actually there with the artist and also seeing the breathtaking experience that it must be to be up there on the stage in front of that many people."

Matthew Libatique sometimes used only a single camera or two. "We didn't have much time," the cinematographer recalled. "I'd never experienced anything like that before. You get to feel what it's like to stand on a stage in front of all those people. You could feel the energy from the crowd, the frenzy of being at a live show."

"Bradley, early on, went for the point of view of the artist," Mehta explained. "We never have cheap crowd shots of the small stage. You are always backstage as an artist."

Those camera angles would create a problem in some concert scenes. "I told Bradley I needed enough extras to get a clean matte line to avoid having to Rotoscope around the performers on stage," Mehta said. In some situations, they had a hundred extras where they needed five hundred. "We don't have the money," the producer said.

Then someone mentioned Gaga's Monsters. "What is this?" Mehta asked.

"Her fan base," he learned. "They'll show up."

The Warner Brothers labor-relations lawyer immediately sent up a red flag: not paying her fans to be extras would subvert union rules. "What if they paid us?" Mehta asked.

"If they paid to come, you're golden," the lawyer said.

The producer noted, "We charged ten dollars, and the money went to Gaga's own charity, Born This Way," which supports mental health through acts of kindness.

In other circumstances, when the *A Star Is Born* players had only a few minutes on stage, the audience was reduced to a backdrop. "And they didn't even know what we were doing," Libatique recalled, "because they didn't want anyone to hear the music." Since Cooper worried about the songs being pirated, he and Gaga would sometimes sing "but only those movie technicians with an earpiece could hear them," the cinematographer noted.

It left the audience wondering, "Why does Bradley Cooper have a beard? Why is he wearing that hat?"

Cooper handled that situation by introducing himself from the stage, "I just wanted to say we're here filming a movie, and we came here for you. I'm Bradley Cooper, and we're making *A Star Is Born*."

One of those moments happened when the production shot its last few feet of film, on June 23, 2017. The Pyramid Stage at the Glastonbury Music Festival in Pilton, England, is one of the most iconic in the world; its forty tons of glittering steel replicate the Great Pyramid of Giza in Egypt. Again, it was rock manager Mark Rothbaum who helped give access to the filmmakers. And it was Rothbaum who introduced Cooper to the actor who preceded him as the male lead in the previous remake of *A Star Is Born*. Kris Kristofferson, no longer making movies, would be a headliner at Glastonbury, and he and his wife, Lisa, readily agreed to meet Cooper. "She and Kris showed up from Malibu at the [movie location], and, of course, we freaked. Bradley and Gaga freaked," Gerber recalled. That meeting led to their filming at Glastonbury.

"We had four minutes before Kristofferson went on," Libatique said. The cinematographer stood ready with the sound mixer Steve Morrow and camera operator Lars Arledge. "We had a second camera," Libatique noted, and he told Arledge, "Why don't you throw that camera over your shoulder and go out there?"

Those four minutes at Glastonbury appear as part of a montage, when, early in the film, Ally and Jackson perform together on stage at a variety of venues.

While the initial concert scenes with Gaga and Cooper at Coachella went well, concerns remained about her as an actor when it came to delivering pages of dialogue.

Eric Roth initially delivered a 180-page script "with lots of prose," as he put it. "No disrespect to Lady Gaga, but I'm not sure it's in her DNA to do big set pieces with monologues."

Cooper put it somewhat more diplomatically. "While a lot of it is written, we decided early on to do it as conversational as possible," he said. "Let's make this as first-person as possible, in all respects."

Early in the process, Libatique asked Cooper, "Is she going to be really good in take one, two, or three? Or is she going to be one of those actors who gets there between takes seven and ten?"

They didn't know.

Take one of the two stars' first "acting" scene together did not go well. Cooper and Gaga were seated at a real cantina outside Palm Springs. In the film, the restaurant is located near the Arizona ranch that Jackson bought for his brother, Bobby, and is where their father is buried. Jackson and Ally have taken to the road to perform together on stage, and he visits the grave, only to find the desert sand blowing across his boots, the tombstone long gone. It leads Jackson to punch out his brother, Bobby, for letting the ranch be turned into a wind farm. Regarding their father's grave, Bobby screams at Jackson, "He washed away in a fucking storm! But you were fucking drunk, you were fucking loaded, and already pissing yourself a swan song." Bobby finally levels with his brother about their father, "You idolized that piece of shit for no goddamned fucking reason. All Dad ever did for you was make you his fucking drinking buddy."

Jackson and Ally's scene in the diner sets up that brother-against-brother drama—the veritable calm before the storm—and Gaga had memorized her lines and how to deliver them. On his motorcycle, Jackson and Ally have just crossed the border of Arizona and California into his home state. Seated at a table in the diner, Jackson asks Ally, "What're you writing down in here?"

Ally says, "My songbook, but usually I use a typewriter. But I had this idea on the bike, and I don't want to forget it." They are the lyrics to "Look What I Found," a song written by Gaga, Aaron Raitiere, Lukas Nelson, Paul "DJWS" Blair, Nick Monson, and Mark Nilan Jr.

Gaga kept repeating the lines she had learned, and Cooper kept saying something other than Jackson's lines in the script. "What's going on?" she thought.

Cooper came up with a novel approach to being both actor and director: When he was also performing, he often began a scene without calling "action." He began in character, as Jackson, and started to carry on a conversation that diverged radically from the script. After a few false starts, Gaga finally realized Cooper's method. He was "just trying to have a conversation with me. I felt the first day I was wrapped up in a preconceived idea of how the lines should be read," she said.

He told her, "There was no rule except not to fake it."

Cooper taught Gaga how to let go of the written lines. "Just be there and be in the circumstances and the moment," she said.

Cooper learned from Clint Eastwood on *American Sniper* how to create an environment on the set and let the actors perform within that space to achieve spontaneity. "It's finding a way for the energy to come through to the camera," Cooper explained. As a director, he also used a couple of trick words to trigger reactions in Gaga. Knowing her deep affection for Tony Bennett, with whom she had performed on stage, he said the name "Tony" to get more warmth from her as a performer. He soon learned that saying "Ninja" or "assassin" made her act tougher.

The cinematographer's questions were also answered about what take would be Gaga's best. "She's more technical than a lot of other actors I've worked with who've been around for a long, long time," Libatique noted. "What I came to find out was that she could hit a mark. She knows exactly where the light is."

On May 5, the production filmed Ally and Jackson's parking lot scene where she first sings a few bars of "Shallow." It was Cinco de Mayo, and a mariachi band entertained and margaritas were served afterward. Days later, on May 23, Cooper filmed the lead up to that moment with an equally important song. At the Bleu Bleu club, Jackson hears Ally sing for the first time. There, the song is "La Vie en Rose."

Set designers had dressed The Virgil, a club in downtown Los Angeles, to look like a drag bar. To prime the assembled audience of extras, Cooper showed scenes from the movie already committed to film, including Ally's singing of "Shallow" in the parking lot. When the screening concluded, "There was complete silence," Willam Belli recalled. "Then everybody cheered." Belli, a female impersonator, had never heard the soon-to-be-famous song. Nor had any of the extras hired to play clubgoers that day.

How these assembled actors reacted to Gaga's singing replicated what happened in preproduction when the star broke into song at a meeting with Cooper and the producers. "The parking lot scene with the peas was inspired by what happens when you're in a room with Stefani when she sings," Lynette Howell Taylor recalled. "We went to her house in Malibu. Stefani wanted to brainstorm with a small group of us. She sat at one end of the table."

At one point, about twenty minutes into the confab, Gaga said, "I have this idea for a lyric, and I want to test it out on you guys." She sang a few bars of the song.

"And the entire table leans back; it is overwhelming the impact of her voice," the producer said. "You have an entire table of respected professionals, and they are all reduced to dust in front of her. There is something powerful about her voice in a space, and that inspired Bradley. He wanted to capture the rawness."

Belli, cast as the drag artist Emerald, wasn't part of the intended audience at the Bleu Bleu when Gaga sang the Édith Piaf classic. "But I wasn't going to miss that!" he said. "I was watching through a crack in the curtain in the back."

Belli knew the other actors playing female impersonators. They were all professionals. "We brought the drag," Bill Gerber recalled. "Gaga's manager had helped us in terms of casting and making sure that the audience also felt that it was credible and realistic."

One of those performers got a direct phone call from the film's director. Cooper and Derek Kevin Jones had attended college together, and Cooper remembered with fondness his friend's drag act in which he impersonated the late singer Etta James. In *A Star Is Born*, as soon as Jackson approaches the Bleu Bleu, the host-bouncer Ramon, played by Anthony Ramos, asks him, "Do you know what kind of bar this is?" Jackson asks, "Do you sell alcohol? It's my kind of bar." The film then cuts to Jones lip-synching "At Last" as sung by James. The inclusion of Jones's act was the last remnant of what had been planned to be a Dead Legends night at the Bleu Bleu. In other incarnations of the screenplay, it was going to be a *Wizard of Oz* theme-night there.

Originally, "Bradley wanted flying monkeys," Ravi Mehta recalled. "He was going further with *The Wizard of Oz*." It was another reference that played into Ally's love of Judy Garland. When a Dead Legends night had been planned, Belli auditioned twice: once as Marilyn Monroe and once as Barbra Streisand. Belli wanted the part so much that he didn't dare tell anyone that one of those female icons was very much alive. In the final film, the Dead Legends got "distilled down to the guy who plays Etta James," Mehta said.

For a few days, even the drag bar itself got the axe. Belli, famous for being rudely kicked off *RuPaul's Drag Race* in season four, auditioned and then got a phone call from his agent that there would be no female impersonators cast in *A Star Is Born*. No drag, no job. "You tell a gay guy you were in a Gaga movie and then you fire him?" Belli asked incredulously. "Worst day of my life! What did I do wrong?" His extreme disappointment echoed what actor John Carlyle said when his Chinese junk scene in the first remake of *A Star Is Born* ended up on the cutting room floor in 1954.

Belli, in the end, turned out to be far more fortunate than Judy Garland's ultimate fan. While he didn't get to do his Marilyn, Belli ended up playing another blonde buxom icon. His character is named Emerald, but nothing more had been revealed to him about the role. He asked for a script beforehand, but the producers refused that request.

When Belli walked into The Virgil, ready to play someone named Emerald, only then did he learn: "Bradley wants you to play Dolly Parton in white."

The actor's response was immediate: "I have the perfect dress at home!" He dispatched a messenger to get the dress from his closet. "And bring the fake boobs!"

Belli remained nonplussed. "But this information could have helped me an hour ago," he said.

The film's costume designer provided a whole rack of wild and oversized female clothes for the drag artists to wear that day. "They brought some stuff; I brought some stuff," Erin Benach said. "We riffed in the moment."

While the white dress and shoes were from his closet, Belli had to admit, "The belt was Erin's."

Over the next two days, the supervising set designer used mirrors and a fake wall to create the dressing room where Ally and Jackson meet. "We did squeeze in a dressing room in a hallway space of The Virgil," Bradley Rubin recalled. In the scene, Jackson removes one of Ally's plastic eyebrows. He also signs Emerald's fake breasts, which had arrived just in time from Belli's closet. One thing about Cooper immediately impressed Belli: The star was wearing almost as much makeup as the drag queens. "Bradley was really using the spray tan to give him that rugged look," he noted.

Belli memorized his lines, all two of them, but Cooper had other ideas, just as he had other ideas with Gaga when they performed their Arizona greasy-spoon scene. Surrounded by half a dozen drag queens, Cooper told them, "Act as you would in a dressing room." Belli noticed something different about Cooper from the previous day, when he directed Gaga singing "La Vie en Rose." There, he stood behind the camera at the monitor. Now, Cooper was already in character. He was Jackson Maine. Belli did as told. "I started doing my thing and asked him to sign my boobs," he recalled.

As often happens backstage at a drag bar, a tiff breaks out between two of the female impersonators. Playing the club emcee, D.J. "Shangela" Pierce got dishy with Emerald, saying, "Bitch, can you get off that stage and help me close this bar, please?" And Belli's Emerald shot back, "Don't talk to me like that in that bus driver wig, girl." These were things never written or even thought of by Cooper and his two screenwriters, Eric Roth and Will Fetters.

Ready to shoot the scene again, Gaga approached Belli to inform him, "It's perfect. Just switch the order of the jokes." In the second take, the "bus driver wig" joke followed the moment when Jackson signs the fake tits, and Emerald says, "I showed you mine, now you show me yours." Jackson has no choice but to accept Emerald's white guitar to perform a song.

"Bradley Cooper created a world for us, and he stayed in it," Belli said, who ended up improvising much of his role. One line was all Gaga, however. It's when Ally tells Jackson. "Yeah, it's BYOB around here. Bring Your Own Boobs."

"That was Gaga," Belli noted.

The scene in the dressing room with the drag queens highlights the beginning of Ally and Jackson's romance. Their heterosexuality is thrown into relief. It also achieves something more significant. Watching these male performers get out of their female clothes, Jackson looks around and says, "Wow." But he says "wow" without an exclamation point. He's surprised but not too surprised. He's comfortable but not too comfortable.

"It's where you first like Jackson," Bill Gerber noted. "Mainly we wanted the bar to be as out of the way as possible, to make it as awkward as possible. Jackson is so desperate to get a drink, he doesn't care. Jackson is talking to a man in drag, and he's happy to be talking. He is so nonjudgmental, and everyone is so nonjudgmental about him."

While Belli may have improvised his own lines—a few more than in the original script—the core exchange in the scene comes from that script: It arrives when Ally retires to get into her street clothes, and Emerald corners Jackson. The drag queen hands him her flashy guitar, and after

Emerald says, "I showed you mine, now you show me yours," Jackson is asked to sing.

"Jackson's likability was totally in Bradley's performance," Fetters said of the moment when Jackson sings "Maybe It's Time," a song written by Jason Isbell. "When he takes the bedazzled white guitar, he is so polite and respectful. Jackson asks, 'Does this mic work?'—then his voice gets caught and you hear 'oh yeah'—then quietly, to himself 'fuck, all right'—straightforward dialogue, but the way he says it tells you so much about who Jackson is and what he's about. Because the mic is on, he's gonna have to use it because he has a deep abiding respect for performance. You see his artistic integrity. His innate shyness. It's a little moment, and Bradley just gets so much out of it."

Like all the songs in the movie, "Maybe It's Time" relates to the emotional state of the characters. It's the first song that Ally hears Jackson sing, and the lyrics "It takes a lot to change a man / Hell, it takes a lot to try" signal that maybe it's time for him to fall in love.

On day three at The Virgil, Cooper also filmed the cellphone call that the drag queens make to Ally once she has become a star. Insecure, she lounges in a bathtub at the Chateau Marmont hotel in Hollywood when her gay friend Ramon comes to console her. He puts her on the phone with the "gay girls" back at the Bleu Bleu.

Cooper filmed much of the 2018 remake out of sequence, and the female impersonators wanted to put on different costumes to film a scene that actually takes place a few months into the future. "Can we change so it doesn't look like we shot it the same day?" Belli asked. "We should be wearing different outfits."

He was told there wasn't time, unfortunately.

Otherwise, Gaga knew how to treat her core fans. After Belli's first day on the film, Gaga left a white rose in his trailer. "What's this?" he wondered, then read the note: "Sorry I didn't get to play with you today. Look forward to tomorrow. Lady Gaga." When she finally did get a scene with Belli and the others, they asked why the drag bar scene had been cut only to be reinstated a week later. She let them know, "Yeah, I had to fight for that."

It had been and would be a film in constant flux.

Chapter 17

"You know when you have a first-time director who is also a first-time screenwriter that there are going to be a lot of changes when he's sitting behind the camera monitor." That was the opinion of one talent who worked behind the scenes with Bradley Cooper on *A Star Is Born.*

A producer on the film put it more diplomatically. "We changed so much," Lynette Howell Taylor explained. "It was almost happening in real time. Bradley knew the emotion he wanted to convey, but he was finding it by talking to actors and scouting locations."

One thing did not change. Twice, Jackson tells Ally, "I just want to take another look."

"That was Bradley's idea and that was in every version of the script," Will Fetters said. The line is repeated multiple times in every film titled *A Star Is Born.*

For Ravi Mehta, nothing beat the filming of the concert scenes for sheer excitement, especially the day at Glastonbury. When it came to pure acting and no music, he pointed to those moments between Ally and her father, Lorenzo, as being most special.

"Andrew Dice Clay had a joyous effect on the production," Mehta said. Gaga told the producer, "He reminds me of my dad. He is such an Italian dad."

Cooper agreed. "Wow, he's bringing it!"

When Clay was cast, it caused the film's production designer, Karen Murphy, to look for a certain kind of house. She didn't want the one Ally shares with Lorenzo to look too California or too modern. "We wanted to give it more of an East Coast vibe," Bradley Rubin said. The set design team found an older house in Angeleno Heights, a neighborhood near downtown Los Angeles that is replete with stately Victorian mansions. The house at 739 E. Kensington Road is traditional but less grand. However, a few years after the release of the 2018 film it sold for $1.33 million, a tad more than a limousine driver and his server daughter could probably afford. "It's near the famous *Fast & Furious* house," the supervising set designer said, referring to the one where Vin Diesel's Dominic Toretto hangs out in the action-movie franchise.

Where Erin Benach brought glitz to the outfits in the drag bar, the costume designer looked for something far simpler but equally effective to dress Ally and her father. "Their costumes were part of the story of telling the social hierarchies of their life and where they were at and how it evolves and changes," the costume designer said. When Lorenzo first appears, he and his chauffeur friends are all essentially wearing what Ally wears at work as a restaurant server: white shirt, black jacket, black tie. "I find the emotional connections of uniforms really interesting, because in every culture we do them differently," she explained. "In Europe it's more designed, it has more personality, and there is less class difference. In America, on the other hand, it's very stark. These uniforms are devoid of personality and are simplistic."

The costumes telegraph that Ally is a server who waits on wealthy people, and she is destined for the same fate as her father and his friends who transport wealthy people around Los Angeles in stretch limousines. Lorenzo is a crooner in the style of Tony Bennett and Frank Sinatra, except for the fact that he never made it. Fame is also Ally's escape, but time is running out for her.

In Fetters's original script with Cooper, Jackson's core crisis had been the character's problem with his hearing. "Bradley is a huge music fan, and he knows a lot of rock stars, like Eddie Vedder, who have struggled with tinnitus," Fetters said. "It was the kind of detail he got from friends of his who were famous rock stars who were aging in their business."

Included in those first drafts were Jackson's "strained childhood and a strained relation with his father," the writer recalled. "The mom was out of the picture in most drafts. The specificity of that detail came later." In a conversation with Ally, Jackson reveals that his father, already middle-aged, impregnated the underage daughter of his employer, a rancher, and she had died giving birth to their love child, Jackson Maine.

Much of Eric Roth's contribution to the script had to do with Jackson's backstory. Or as Ravi Mehta explained it, "The male suffering tone, the magic and nuance of character." Beyond those additions and changes, "The blueprint was set," Mehta added. "Those weren't Eric's changes."

Roth can be credited for being prescient. Just as he began work on rewriting Cooper and Fetters's screenplay, the most grievance-prone president in the history of the United States was sworn into office. The following year, when *A Star Is Born* went into theaters, Brett Kavanaugh gave an on-the-verge-of-tears defense on September 24,

2018, before the Senate Judiciary Committee. Had he raped Christine Blasey when they were both teenagers? Kavanaugh defended himself against those charges and went on to complain of being attacked by a "frenzy on the left." Days later, at Kavanaugh's swearing-in ceremony, President Donald J. Trump apologized "on the behalf of our nation" to the newest Supreme Court justice for what he and his family had "endured." The Me-Too movement had met its match in Trump and Kavanaugh.

Jackson Maine, as reenvisioned by Roth, also came down with a whole host of nasty male grievances. In addition to his mother dying in childbirth, the character idolizes his dead father but was raised by his much older brother, Bobby. Add to those injustices the character's original source of trouble—tinnitus—and suddenly Jackson became a character beset with problems. In the other versions of *A Star Is Born*, the male character is just a drunk. Now he is a rebel with too many causes. "The tinnitus evolved," Lynette Howell Taylor said. "It was going to be a big part of his downfall in his inability to keep his place at the top. That got scaled back a bit. It was no longer that driving force."

The final screenplay plays better than it reads, in part, because Cooper brings a dense, opaque quality to his portrayal of Jackson. With his newly honed gravel-filled baritone, the actor often emerges indecipherable in the finished film, and Cooper delivers much of Jackson's family history in lines that are barely intelligible, especially on a first viewing of the film. It is arguably the most mumbled performance since Heath Ledger played a conflicted and inarticulate gay cowboy in *Brokeback Mountain*.

While Jackson is angst ridden, drowning his problems in alcohol and drugs, he finds refuge in his growing love for Ally, and even more important for the dramatic effectiveness of the film, Jackson absolutely revels in their performing together on stage. "Jackson is at his happiest when he performs with Ally," Will Fetters said. Cooper's direction delivers those few upbeat moments in his life in a montage of rock concerts, filmed at a number of live concerts, including one at Glastonbury, England. "That was quite a day," Ravi Mehta recalled. "It's too bad that Glastonbury footage couldn't have been used for more than just a montage."

The costumes for Ally and Jackson carefully chart their very different journeys. In the early concert scenes, Erin Benach put Ally in clothes that "she would be able to find along her travels," the designer said. "Ally was inspired by the Southwest and some thrift stores she stopped at—a little bit of boho and Western wear. She didn't have a stylist yet; she didn't have these big outfits. She was still changing from her original Ally. It was the beginning of an evolution."

Jackson presented an entirely different set of challenges. "He's the nonmoving entity, and she was the moving entity," Benach noted. "He did not evolve. The character was at the point where he did not want to be involved in the business. He wasn't thinking about his clothes. You almost want to think he doesn't think about it. He had a uniform."

That simple outfit, however, featured a number of shirts that "were the exact same cut, and I had them made in different fabrics," the designer recalled. "But it still looks good and sexy and beautiful but very nonchalant."

She also found the leather hat Jackson wears in the movie's first scene at a rock concert, and he takes it off just before hanging himself in the garage. "I wouldn't say the hat had meaning," Benach mused. "I found it, a vintage piece, and thousands of people ask where to get that hat. I don't know."

Although Bradley Cooper wears a tuxedo very well at

various awards ceremonies, in real life, he is not known as a clothes horse. Lady Gaga, on the other hand, is one of this century's top fashion icons, and like all great models, she is forever evolving and changing her look.

"For me, fashion and art and music have always been a form of armor," Gaga said. "I just kept perfecting more and more fantasies to escape into, new skins to shed. And every time I shed a skin, it was like taking a shower when you're dirty: getting rid of, washing off, shedding all of the bad, and becoming something new. I just remember feeling so irritated at the thought that I had to conform to being normal or less of whatever I was already born as."

It's why she called herself a Monster and why her fans are known as the Monsters. If the film's costume designer anticipated any problems working with such a fashion-fixated celebrity, none emerged. "Stefani and Bradley leaned on me to take her out of what she knows," Benach said. That's most true in the movie's first half. "They wanted her to feel very real and antistyle." The costume designer took that ethos to the extreme when, for Ally and Jackson's impromptu wedding in the film, Benach lent her own white lace wedding dress to the production for Gaga to wear.

Of all the female characters in the four *A Star Is Born* films, Gaga's Ally evolves the most. Janet Gaynor's Esther remains sweet but determined throughout. Judy Garland's Esther develops some courage when she commits to having a career in film with or without Norman Maine. Both these Esthers are female characters without flaws. It's why everyone from James Mason to Arthur Laurents called Norman Maine the far more interesting role. Barbra Streisand's Esther is another creature entirely. With her, there's absolutely no learning curve. She dresses like a star throughout the film. She's a put-upon diva from the moment her Esther is introduced on-screen singing at a club. And when stardom comes overnight from singing "The Woman in the Moon," the character finds herself immediately at odds with the biggest villain of all famous people: the press. And she knows just how to treat them. "How many shots do you need?" this Esther screams at photographers. A star isn't born here so much as a diva is unleashed.

Ally, on the other hand, does as she is told—until gradually, she doesn't.

Unlike the other three films, the 2018 version does not hinge on the male lead character's demise in the movies or the music business. Jackson more than holds his own with Ally in a series of concerts. It is only when she meets the British manager Rez Gavron, played by Rafi Gavron, that she's given the dream to record a song and go solo.

"The difference between Jack and the other guys is he doesn't resent her success whatsoever," Bill Gerber said. "He's upset that she's not being true to her voice, and what he fell in love with, and the kind of music she wanted to create."

The 2018 remake dropped the scene where the unemployed husband fields phone calls for his famous wife. Nor is he ever addressed as "Mr." with her last name attached, as in the first two *A Star Is Born* films. While Jackson Maine is reduced to playing backup guitar to a singer at the Grammys, he is never *not* performing. He continues to rock. His emotional state, however, remains open to debate. Other major participants on the third remake found shades of resentment, if not humiliation, in his reactions to Ally's success.

"There is a selfishness [on Jackson's part] to be in his world," Will Fetters said of the moment when the Rez Gavron character appears.

Lynette Howell Taylor agreed. "There's no way you can watch and not think if you're Jack that you're not a little bit envious of the moment on stage that you had together previously," the producer said.

That evolution, or metamorphosis, is where Ally's costumes immediately become very flashy. Erin Benach picked a couple of outfits from other designers. Ally wears a golden Gucci gown at the Grammy Awards. YSL designed the striped electric blue, white, and black dress that Ally wears in the bathtub at the Chateau Marmont hotel in Hollywood when her drag queen friends from the Bleu Bleu cheer her up with a Zoom call.

Most outrageous is the skin-tight black lace catsuit that Benach designed for Ally's first solo performance. In the movie, Rez Gavron has arranged for Ally to perform with two dancers. At the last moment, Ally decides to perform alone, and as she comes off stage, the manager confronts her, "You can't go rogue on me!" Ally brushes off his concern; she wants to know why Jackson wasn't there to see her perform.

"I talked to Stefani about that catsuit," Benach recalled. "So much of this character she related to on so many levels. She had to fight for things she wanted. There's an element of Ally trying to hold on to her integrity and evolve as a star, but it was also a very fine line that the movie rode—we all rode, honestly—wanting her to feel she was going too far so fast, but at the same time, she was doing it with integrity. I think that ambiguity is what made the story more palatable at the end. You do think she contributed to his demise. She does feel guilt. It's not a one-sided, clear thing."

Fetters called it "her getting caught up in the machinery of the business and his trying to get her to trust her voice."

"It's her pop turn that starts the rift between them, not her success," Bill Gerber insisted.

To the movie's credit, it may be more complicated than

any of those assessments. Jackson wants to go back to singing on the stage with Ally, and she attempts to facilitate his wish by doing her first European tour with him. It is Rez Gavron who nixes that idea with a brutal tête-à-tête with Jackson.

"We're not friends," the manager tells Jackson. "If she stays with you, she looks like a joke."

Jackson's substance abuse drives him to insult her. After Ally receives her Grammy nominations, he begrudgingly congratulates her as she takes a bubble bath in a tub that is far less elegant than the one used by Esther and John Norman in the 1976 remake. Stoned, Jackson soon begins to trash her latest hit song, even mocking the lyrics by quoting them: "Why'd you come around me with an ass like that?" He tells her, "Maybe I fucking failed you . . . You're just fucking embarrassing."

The comment enrages Ally, whose hair is now dyed a fluorescent orange. She bursts into a tirade about Jackson's drinking and drug taking that is a vast improvement on Barbra Streisand's Esther telling her husband, "You can trash your life, but you can't trash mine." In fact, Ally's accusation is almost beat for beat what Dorothy Parker and Alan Campbell delivered for Vicki Lester and Norman Maine in the first *A Star Is Born*, a scene written but not filmed. In the 2018 version, Ally lets Jackson have it: "I'm embarrassing? I'm not fucking embarrassing. You're embarrassing, and you know what you're doing is you're so embarrassed of your fucking self that you gotta put me down . . . clean your shit up. You're fucking messy . . . Why don't you have another drink, and we can just get fucking drunk until we fucking disappear. Okay?"

That's when he tells her, "You're just fucking ugly."

Unlike what Parker and Campbell wrote for Vicki and Norman, Ally and Jackson do not immediately reconcile.

What inspires the fight in the 2018 film is Ally's first hit single, "Why Did You Do That?" The pop song also turned out to be the film's most controversial moment.

Wesley Morris in *The New York Times* wrote, "This song is delivered with such umbrage and so much alarm that you don't know whether to sing along or call Gloria Allred."

Zack Sharf in *IndieWire* called it "polarizing." The critic didn't know if the song was intentionally bad or just bad.

"Is it meant to be so glib?" Adam Chitwood wondered in *Collider*.

"Why Did You Do That?" quickly became known as "the butt song," and was written by Gaga with Mark Nilan Jr., Nick Monson, and Paul "DJWS" Blair. Diane Warren, the multi-Oscar-nominated songwriter, provided the lyrics, and she took full credit for the song's "ass" line. While Warren and Gaga were working on "Why Did You Do That?," the lyricist asked, "Can we say that?"

"Sure, why not?" Gaga replied.

"It surprised me when I saw it!" Warren said of seeing *A Star Is Born* for the first time. In the moment, when Jackson mocks the song's line "Why'd you come around me with an ass like that?," Warren grabbed a friend's arm to exclaim, "That's my line he's quoting!"

The lyricist liked that Ally "defended her music" in that scene. "It doesn't have to be what he thinks music should be—music can be everything. It can be a serious song; it can be pop song. It can be a song about an ass," Warren said.

Mark Nilan Jr. also experienced "a bit of a shock" to see the song "used in a sort of mocking type situation there." In fact, "Why Did You Do That?" was not written for *A Star Is Born*. "It was a Lady Gaga song," Nilan said, "and then a few months later, the movie process started, and that song was a good fit for the way the storyline played out. That's how the song found itself in the movie."

Nilan saw a more jaundiced side of Jackson Maine than others who worked on the film. "There's a similarity in real life with older musicians," he noted. "They feel their type of music is the only genre of music that should be considered worthwhile. Bradley's character has a lot of layers of jealousy."

In all the other films titled *A Star Is Born*, the male lead suffers far more humiliation than Cooper's Jackson Maine. The character is not, however, without his flaws.

"Bradley and I talked about this all the time," Howell Taylor said. "Jackson has a strong opinion about Ally's career. But it is only his opinion. We talked about the complications of the lead character and that his may not be the right point of view. A lot of people love that version of Ally. It is close to Lady Gaga. The movie works because you can interpret it so many ways: There is frustration and envy and his feeling that she's not what he wanted her to be. As a woman, you don't get to decide this. Bradley and I talked about what moments to keep in and not keep in. As an actor, Bradley played it with a certain intention, but his direction is open to other interpretations. His direction allowed for that."

Nilan, Warren, and Howell Taylor would find no disagreement from Gaga that only rock is great and that pop means you're selling out. Gaga takes that defense of pop one step further. "I've always hated the stigma around Las Vegas—that it's where you go when you're on the last leg of your career," Gaga said. "Being a Las Vegas girl is an absolute dream for me. It's really what I've always wanted to do."

The 1954 *A Star Is Born* credits four original songwriters; it would have been only two, Harold Arlen and Ira Gershwin, if the "Born in a Trunk" medley had not been added late in the production. The 1976 *Star* doubled that number of songwriters. It ballooned to eleven songwriters on *A Star Is Born* in 2018. Several original songs in the film feature no fewer than six composers and lyricists. At the Academy Awards in 1982, jokes abounded regarding how many people it took to screw together a song when Peter Allen, Burt Bacharach, Christopher Cross, and Carole Bayer Sager overpopulated the stage to accept their Oscars for "Arthur's Theme (Best That You Can Do)" from the film *Arthur* starring Dudley Moore and Liza Minnelli.

That kind of songwriting mob scene is no longer unusual. "It is standard now," said Nilan, who regularly works with Nick Monson and Paul "DJWS" Blair. Each specializes in a different instrument. Then there are the lyrics. The trio met for the first time with Lukas Nelson and Aaron Ratiere to write and produce "Look What I Found" and "Is That Alright?" for *A Star Is Born*. It took them one evening to get rough drafts of those two songs. The day did not begin auspiciously.

The trio thought they were supposed to meet at Gaga's home in Malibu. Upon arriving there, they learned the session was taking place in Hollywood, a two-and-a-half-hour drive in rush hour traffic. Regardless, or because of that misunderstanding, "The energy was high and creative ideas were flying," Nilan recalled. "Gaga was popping in and out, busy doing her thing. Once we had the starts of these songs, we presented them to her, and we expanded upon them from there."

Nilan also wrote "Hair Body Face" and "Heal Me" with Gaga, Monson, and Blair. Both songs appear after Ally has begun her solo recording career. While Nilan did get around to seeing the 2018 remake of *A Star Is Born*, he has never watched any of the other films with that title. "Which is maybe great," he explained. "Then you're not swayed when it comes to references and understanding the past."

Chapter 18

The most daring—and arguably, the best—departure in the 2018 remake from the other *A Star Is Born* films is the awards ceremony. In the first two versions, Norman Maine arrives drunk at the Oscars and stumbles onto the stage to interrupt Vicki Lester's Oscar acceptance speech and goes on to beg for a job from the podium. He begins to gesticulate wildly and accidentally slaps his wife, who stands behind him. In the 1976 version, the scene takes place at the Grammys, and again the male character embarrasses her by launching into a self-pitying speech. The slap, however, is dropped. Instead, Barbra Streisand's Esther takes Kris Kristofferson's John Norman into a restroom—men's or women's, we never learn—to chew him out. *A Star Is Born* in 2018 tops all those takes on professional humiliation. Here, Bradley Cooper's Jackson Maine is so under the influence of drugs that, standing next to Lady Gaga's Ally on the Grammy stage, he doesn't know where he is and begins to urinate in his trousers.

Ravi Mehta remembered when Bradley Cooper first told him about this new, very different interpretation of said. "Gaga can be glam, and a month later she will have pink hair or wearing a cowboy hat." The same is true of Ally. "Just because she is embraced as a pop star, at that moment with 'I'll Never Love Again,' she is taking on another chapter of her life after her husband's death. This scene is the end of the movie, but it is the beginning of her story."

Costumes played a big part in showing Ally's journey. Since his outfits don't change much, Jackson's relied more on the cinematography. "Jackson is someone who has lived an internal life being famous," Matthew Libatique said. "He's being looked at all the time, so he's kind of avoiding it, so we're often shooting the back of his neck or profile as he comes to terms with his past, his life, and the trauma of his life, so the camera leaves him no place to go. At the end, the camera when he's in bed and decided what he's going to do, the camera is right on his face, and there's no more hiding."

In the first two versions of *A Star Is Born*, the movie ends with the female character saying, "Hello, everybody! This is Mrs. Norman Maine." In the 1930s and 1950s, nothing was going to top a line like that, even in Garland's musical version of the story. After War World II, women were expected to subjugate themselves to the men they loved. Moss Hart tapped into that national mood and never wrote a place for a song to end the film, even though it is a musical. What movie musical doesn't end with a song? *A Star Is Born* in 1954 would be one of the very few. Equally important, unlike the "Born in the Trunk" medley, neither Garland nor Sid Luft ever questioned the screenwriter's decision to end the film without a song.

That was then. A female character calling herself "Esther Hoffman Howard" in 1976 and "Ally Maine" in 2018 is no big deal. The moment needs a song. The makers of the third remake learned from mistakes made in the

Streisand version and shortened the sung finale by two minutes. Ally's "I'll Never Love Again" clocks in at five and a half minutes. More significant, she does not carry the song alone. The 2018 remake cuts away from Ally at the very end to provide a flashback of Jackson singing the song's final lyrics to her at the piano in their home. He sings, "Don't want to give my heart away / To another stranger / Don't let another day begin / Won't let the sunlight in / Oh I'll never love again / Never love again / Never love again / Oh I'll never love again."

When he finishes, the film cuts back to Ally, in close-up, silent but looking directly into the camera for the first and only time.

Cooper and Fetters came up with the idea to have Jackson write the song while in rehab. At that time, the director told his screenwriter precisely how he wanted the final scene edited, with Jackson singing the last few lines of lyrics. "It is not a cut just for the sake of a cut," Fetters said. "It's a recontextualizing of the song. It was smart. It came from Bradley. Bradley would speak, thinking like a director in terms of shots. He was showing me some of the shots, where to put the camera. He saw that cut as the way to do that. These two characters have all these great but small little interactions. It is a beautiful moment." It gives Ally the chance to honor her husband without calling herself "Mrs."

The day before Sonia Durham's passing, another death took place that also had a profound effect on the making of *A Star Is Born*. On May 18, Chris Cornell committed suicide by hanging himself in a room at the MGM Grand in Detroit. Cornell, fifty-two years old, was an icon of the grunge scene and had performed that night with his band Soundgarden at the Fox Theatre.

The suicide was another example of the production being in a constant state of flux. "It was definitely open-ended," Ravi Mehta said of the suicide. "Was it an accident, or did he commit suicide? Jackson goes for a swim, he swims and swims, was he trying to kill himself or get lost at sea? That went away."

Cooper also decided against another kind of suicide for Jackson. "There are still remnants of it being a motorcycle accident," Mehta said. "It's seeded in the movie, with 'I'm going for a ride.' He picks up his helmet."

However, Cooper never felt satisfied with any of the suicide scenarios that he, Fetters, or Roth had devised.

Then Cornell hanged himself.

Cooper came to Mehta the next day. "Dude, I know the ending. He has to hang himself," he said.

Coincidentally, the switch to suicide by hanging did not require a change in the script where Jackson, in rehab, confesses to his therapist, played by Ron Rifkin, that he had attempted suicide at age thirteen. He tried to hang himself from an overhead fan. Instead of taking his life, the young Jackson only injured his forehead when the entire fan fell to the floor. Jackson and his therapist laugh ruefully over the anecdote.

Cooper explained, "I liked this idea of a guy who looks so much like a man—he's everything you would want to be as a man when you're young—but he's a child. He's thirteen years old. He's that moment that happened when his father died and his brother came back, and he had spent that year with his dad sick. That was the character I wanted to create. That character doesn't care about his fame dwindling, because that's not where he's found his sense of worth. Right away those aspects are gone, and it's much more about him trying to find a connection and being reinvigorated in his life and feeling things that maybe he hasn't been able to feel, finding a soulmate, and not having the tool to go on that journey with that person, because his journey is coming to an end."

Mehta found Cooper's performance grounded in reality. "Sobriety, Bradley knows that inside out. I don't think you can grab that realism unless you struggled yourself and been around it," the producer said.

Cooper's *A Star Is Born* is the only version of the story that explicitly identifies the lead male character's tragic flaw as his infantilism. He never really grows up, and his suicide stems from his seeing no other way out of his predicament.

Eric Roth's work on the film didn't end when production on the film began. It kicked into an even higher gear as constant rewrites were needed, the suicide being just one example. "I don't sleep much, and I guess [Cooper] doesn't either, so in the middle of the night, we'd text each other incarnations of stuff, and eventually it felt pretty good," the screenwriter recalled. "We had our moments [of disagreement], to be honest, we were both a little prickly about criticism, and this and that. But that is part of the process."

Will Fetters, on the other hand, wrote less after the film went into production. "Gerber asked me to do stuff. I sent a couple things to Bradley. I don't think it ended up in the movie," the screenwriter said. "Eric brought it home for him."

One of Roth's most important additions is the scene that foreshadows the suicide. It also helped deliver an Oscar nomination for best supporting actor to Sam Elliott. After the two brothers in the film have reconciled, Bobby drives Jackson to his house in the woods of Calabasas, and before Jackson gets out of the truck, he confesses to his brother that it is him, and not their father, whom he always idolized. Bobby tears up as he puts the truck in reverse and pulls away.

"I drive a truck. I've had a lot of experience with vehicles like that," Roth said. "That thing was a monstrosity, that truck in the scene. I had a little small window [of space] to put that truck in. When Jack reveals that he has always idolized Bobby, everything else floated on that beat. I just sustained it as he got out of the truck. I think [Bobby] wanted out of there. He didn't want to hang around anymore. I think he knew that Jack was going down, that he was on that collision course."

That modern house in the Calabasas woods where Ally and Jackson live and he commits suicide had been one of the tougher locations to find. Production designer Karen Murphy wanted it to look secluded, but the house could not be too far away from the production's home base, Warner Brothers across the Hollywood Hills in Burbank. "The owners of the house were moving," Bradley Rubin recalled. "They were about to sell it. We negotiated to keep some things, like books on the bookcases, some of the furniture. It was perfect timing."

Jackson's suicide by hanging in the garage of his home was filmed on June 15. It marked the last day of production except for the four minutes that Cooper and Matthew Libatique recorded at the rock concert in Glastonbury, England. On June 14, Gaga and Sam Elliott put in their last day, committing to film the scene where Ally and Bobby mourn Jackson's suicide. Gaga capped that emotional celluloid moment with a real-life one in which she expressed her deep gratitude to the crew and especially her director and costar.

She told the assembled crew, "Bradley, I really don't know what to say to you because you took a chance on me even in a very strange time in my life, and you brought me back to life, and you made a dream come true for me that I thought was lost. I am Ally. I was that girl that couldn't get the job, and you gave me the fucking job. Thank you."

Later that day, Gaga left a bouquet of roses for him on the seat of the truck in the garage where Jackson would take his life. "It's not romantic," Bill Gerber said of the suicide. Fredric March and James Mason walking off into the ocean at sunset is the essence of romance. Even Kris Kristofferson racing off over the hill in his red Ferrari as a dark cloud passes overhead and Streisand's singing voice blares on the radio can be thought of as a nice way to go. In the 2018 remake, only the leather belt is shown, after Jackson takes off his signature hat. It is the slamming shut of the garage door that delivers the final ominous jolt.

"I remember sitting with Bradley that night," Gerber said. "He is brilliant about compartmentalizing things. He is acting while he's directing while he's watching the light and everybody else in the scene. It was the only time I actually saw him sticking to the character after 'cut,' that night he dies."

The producer often found himself talking or kidding around with Cooper between scenes. That final shot was different. Afterward, Gerber did not approach the actor. The producer realized, "Oh, he's really Jack right now."

In the celebrity-driven world of Los Angeles real estate, having a movie, especially a successful movie, shot on the premises is what Realtors call a "fun factoid." It's a sales plus but not something that automatically sends the price soaring. The four-bedroom, three-bath house in *A Star Is Born* stands at 491 Cold Canyon Road in Calabasas. It was built in 1973 by architect Doug Rucker, most famous for his Pedestal House in nearby Malibu. Not for sale, it rented in 2024 for $12,000 a month. Its estimated value: $3 million.

What would adversely affect the selling price of any home is a suicide or other act of violence having taken place on the premises. Chris Cornell took his life in an anonymous hotel room. Although not ruled suicides, the early deaths of Janis Joplin and Jimi Hendrix also took place in hotel rooms. Unlike all the other films titled *A Star Is Born*, the male character in the 2018 version ends his life in a house he shares with his wife. Jackson's taking his life there harks back to *What Price Hollywood?* when director Max Carey shoots himself in the home of Mary Evans. In both cases, it removes much of the self-sacrifice that critic David Thomson found "phony" in the other films titled *A Star Is Born*. With the locale of his suicide, Cooper's Jackson Maine unquestionably emerges as the most tormented of all these male characters.

Chapter 19

A *Star Is Born* opened at the Venice Film Festival on August 31, 2018. A heavy rain did not prevent Lady Gaga from wearing a feathered Valentino gown, and the festival's organizers provided several umbrellas and canopies to prevent her from turning into a wet Big Bird. Other snafus could not be avoided. A projector mishap put a big dent in that glamorous world premiere, causing a twenty-minute blackout on the screen in the middle of the movie. Regardless, Lady Gaga and Bradley Cooper received an extended standing ovation. On September 10, the film crossed the Atlantic to play the Toronto Film Festival, where the projector worked without a hitch and the audience leaped to its feet at the end. Scott Feinberg in *The Hollywood Reporter* wrote, "It received the most enthusiastic response I have ever seen there. Concerns about whether Gaga could act or Cooper could direct and/or sing were unfounded—and the best picture Oscar race had a new frontrunner."

The film's early reception surprised Lynette Howell Taylor in one respect. "Lady Gaga is a real musician," the producer said. "I was surprised how many people didn't expect that. They saw her just as a pop star. They were surprised not only by her acting but her legitimate musical talent."

Eric Roth was less astonished. Just as he advised Gaga to watch Cher's performance in *Moonstruck*, he now noted a real similarity between the two actresses. "Working in front of those massive audiences allows [a pop star] to be just as comfortable in front of a camera," the screenwriter said. "Cher was that way. It was the same with Stefani. She was totally unflappable."

Someone who had been with the film from the beginning had the most to celebrate. "I was amazed, because there had been so many iterations and Bradley had so many ideas," Will Fetters commented. "When I saw the final cut, it was moving for me. I couldn't believe how much of the structure we had worked out together and was in my first draft. It was there on the screen."

To temper expectations about the Oscars, it would have been best for its makers to remember that only the 1937 version had been nominated for best picture by the Academy of Motion Picture Arts and Sciences. That version went on to win just one competitive Oscar, in the discontinued category of best original story, and an honorary award for its color cinematography, an unusual achievement in 1937. *A Star Is Born*, whether set in the world of Hollywood or rock music, is not a valentine to the entertainment business. It's an attack and just one of the reasons Academy voters have never fully embraced any version of the film. It being an indictment, however, is why the story still resonates with audiences.

"People are hungrier for fame than ever before," film critic Leonard Maltin said. "Who couldn't relate to the desire and the desperation and at the same time the utter sadness of someone who has it all and is losing it?"

The publicity that Gaga and Cooper did during the crowded awards season proved controversial, if not downright counterproductive. She changed her tune on how closely she resembled Ally. In the beginning, Gaga told reporters that she and Ally were practically one and the same person. Later, realizing that she was nominated for an acting award, Gaga wanted to prove she was not just playing herself. Speaking in a roundtable interview with other nominated actresses that year, she told the moderator from *The Hollywood Reporter*, "I wanted Ally to be nothing like me. This was very important to me because the truth is, I am nothing like Ally."

The other star (and director) of the new *A Star Is Born* saved his one big print solo sit-down interview for the august *New York Times*. It didn't go well. The title of the article by Taffy Brodesser-Akner set the tone for what was to come in the following 1,500-word profile: "Bradley Cooper Is Not Really into This Interview."

Back on December 17, 2015, in an ABC-TV interview with Barbara Walters, Cooper had shared personal details about his own substance abuse and the death of his father. When Walters referred to his success with *The Hangover*, she opined without much nuance, "The title of the movie was dripping with irony." She asked Cooper if it had been hard to stop drinking in his late twenties.

"Difficult, no. Beautiful. Unbelievable," he replied without hesitation. "I'd never be sitting here with you. No way. No chance. Because I wouldn't have been able to have access to myself or other people or even take in other people if I hadn't changed my life. No way. I would never have been able to have relationships that I do or take care of my father the way I did when he was sick, so many things."

In the interview, Walters pointed to a gold ring on the movie star's finger. Cooper told her it was the wedding ring worn by his father, the person who "introduced me to the movies."

These were the kinds of topics the *Times* reporter had every reason to believe Cooper would discuss with her, because Jackson Maine is also a substance abuser whose father had an enormous impact on his life. More recently, Cooper was open about his past in a brief interview with a *Variety* reporter at the Toronto Film Festival. He revealed there, "Anytime you're trying to tell the truth, you need to go to places and use things that have happened to you or you've read about or experienced."

A few days later, Cooper presented a quite different interview subject. He didn't respond kindly to questions of a personal nature or any other kind. When Brodesser-Akner asked a few softball questions, Cooper balked at each and every one. "I won't have any control, and it really isn't a collaboration," he said of the article this reporter had been assigned to write. When he saw Brodesser-Akner's dismay, Cooper tried to sympathize. "It's wonderful that people want to ask me questions," he began. "I just find that no matter how much time we spend together, it's only by spending time and doing something with somebody that you start to get to see how they work and how they interact with other people and who they are, you know? You couldn't get to know me in this scenario, just as much as I don't know who you are."

This is publicity?

Unlike Robert Redford (*Ordinary People*), Mel Gibson (*Braveheart*), and Kevin Costner (*Dances with Wolves*)—major movie stars who received Oscars for their directorial debuts—there would be no Oscar or Directors Guild nomination for Cooper, much less the prize itself. His film, however, did receive eight nominations, more than any other incarnation of *A Star Is Born*. He and Gaga were honored for their acting, and she received another nomination for the song "Shallow." Most important, the film was nominated for best picture, unlike the 1954 and 1976 remakes.

The producers at the Academy Awards asked Gaga and Cooper to sing the song at the Oscars on February 24, 2019. Gaga said yes. Cooper wasn't so sure. She gave him a push. When he showed up at her concert in Las Vegas the previous month, Gaga invited Cooper onstage to sing the duet. "It was as if the roles were reversed from the movie," Lynette Howell Taylor recalled. "She was all glammed up; he was wearing jeans." After the success of that performance, Cooper said yes to the Oscars—and the song "Shallow" would go on to receive the film's one and only Oscar.

Four days before the Academy Awards, on February 20, the list of presenters were released to the press. Barbra Streisand, for the first time in her long career, would be introducing one of the eight films nominated for best picture. Her appearance was a big deal. *The Hollywood Reporter* article on the subject announced the news and even went so far as to title its article "Barbra Streisand Among Presenters." It was already known that tennis star Serena Williams would be introducing *A Star Is Born*. Even so, *The Hollywood Reporter* writer felt the need to speculate, "It is unclear if Streisand will be part of that film's presentation, but seems like a very real possibility, given her starring role in the 1976 version of the film."

Streisand visited the set of *A Star Is Born* in Calabasas during the production's last two weeks of filming there, her Malibu ranch nearby. Cooper invited her. "It was a big thrill," Bill Gerber recalled. "Gaga got to hang out with Barbra."

Indeed, the star of the latest *A Star Is Born* was psyched by the appearance of her idol. "It was a magical moment.

She really made me feel like she passed the torch," Gaga said.

According to Gerber, Streisand "stayed in touch" with him almost from the beginning, ever since Beyoncé and Clint Eastwood had been involved. "She had been very supportive," he added. Later, Streisand and her husband, James Brolin, attended a screening of the latest *A Star Is Born*. "And then we had dinner," Gerber said. Streisand remained upbeat. She kept her opinion of the film to herself—for a few years, at least.

On February 24 at the Dolby Theatre in Hollywood, Streisand took the stage to introduce Spike Lee's film, not *A Star Is Born*. Perhaps she had read the infamous *New York Times* profile of Bradley Cooper in which he revealed that a rock star friend had told him, "You better create a character that meets the standards of what it is to be a rock star because no one's ever gotten it right." Or maybe she had read the *Variety* article that quoted Cooper as saying his favorite *A Star Is Born* was the Garland version and that the Streisand movie was "so iconic for its time."

Regarding Streisand's embrace of Lee's *BlacKkKlansman*, Page Six of the *New York Post* did not mince words. Its headline said it all: BABS SNUBS "STAR" AT OSCARS.

At the awards, Streisand's speech began, "When I first saw *BlacKkKlansman*, I was stunned. I was very excited, and I was very moved. It had everything a great film should have. It was so real, so funny and yet so horrifying because it was based on the truth. And truth is especially precious these days." She went on to call it "Spike Lee's masterpiece."

Earlier in the evening, Lee had won the Oscar for best adapted screenplay. *Green Book* would go on to win for best picture.

The makers and cast of *A Star Is Born* had won a prize better than the Oscar, however. Among the nominated best pictures that year, only *Black Panther* and *Bohemian Rhapsody* grossed more than *Star* took in at the box office worldwide.

It also didn't hurt that the film cost a mere $37 million and grossed $432 million at the box office. Even adjusted for inflation, that sum was more than what the other three *A Star Is Born* films had taken in combined. The original soundtrack sold more than 1.2 million copies worldwide, and globally, it turned into the fourth best-selling album of 2019.

"We had a very ambition budget target, especially for a first-time director," Ravi Mehta said. "That movie is proof that having budget constraints does not result in an inferior product. The push-and-pull and the vibrations that result from figuring out the parameters can help you; it can make magic."

Epilogue

"I'm Mr. Esther Blodgett?"

The once-close connection between the 1976 and the 2018 remakes of *A Star Is Born* continued to fray even after the Oscars. Negotiations with Jon Peters to secure underlying rights weren't easy for the producers of the new version. On that controversy, Bradley Cooper got the last word.

Finished with *A Star Is Born*, Cooper chose a most unusual follow-up acting assignment for a movie star of his expanding magnitude. He chose to play a small uncredited role in Quentin Tarantino's *Once Upon a Time . . . In Hollywood*. His impersonation of Peters in the 2019 film about the Charles Manson/Sharon Tate murders went right for the crotch. Cooper, in only a few minutes of screen time, portrayed an egotistical movie producer who kept touting his professional and romantic connection to a famous actress. "Her name is pronounced Barbra Strei-SAND! Strei-SAND!" Cooper's Jon Peters repeated to devastating comic effect.

While Streisand honored *BlacKkKlansman* at the Oscars, she held off on giving her real opinion of one of Spike

Lee's competitors for the top award. She spoke very positively about any new remake of *A Star Is Born*. "The story always works. It's like *Romeo and Juliet*," she said. "It's just a good story that can be told over and over again in different ways. You just change the music."

In 2021, the star of the second remake of *A Star Is Born* revealed what she really thought of the 2018 remake. Maybe Streisand also thought no one would be paying attention since she delivered her remarks Down Under on an Australian talk show. Somehow, no sooner did the words slip from her mouth on *The Sunday Project* than the news traveled all around the world.

"At first, when I heard it was going to be done again, it was supposed to be Will Smith and Beyoncé, and I thought, that's interesting," Streisand told the TV interviewer. "Really make it different again, different kind of music, integrated actors, I thought that was a great idea. So, I was surprised when I saw how alike it was to the version that I did in 1976." She went on to call it "the wrong idea," but that she "couldn't argue with success."

As *Variety* reported her critique, the article's title made it clear: "Barbra Streisand Says Lady Gaga and Bradley Cooper's 'A Star Is Born' was 'The Wrong Idea.' "

Regarding how much the two films were "alike," there was one other aspect of *A Star Is Born* that Cooper also did not mess with. Streisand, however, considered it.

"When we were first fooling around with the story, Jon and I were fooling around with the idea to reverse roles, and I'm the big star going downhill and the guy is coming up and what would that do to the story," Streisand recalled.

Will Fetters toyed briefly with reversing the sexes in the 2018 version, but that idea came to him even before Beyoncé and Clint Eastwood were involved, much less Lady Gaga and Bradley Cooper. "Those were very early conversations," Fetters said, "but it was more like, 'How could we get this movie made?' "

Upon the release of the 2018 remake, Todd McCarthy in *The Hollywood Reporter* put in a good word for making the switch. The critic wrote: "What if, for a change, the sexes were reversed and the career of a female, rather than male, star went into eclipse, accompanied by a relationship with a younger man? In the past, an uncomfortable sort of *Sunset Boulevard*–like desperation might have hung over such an approach. But at least since the Madonna era we've probably seen enough instances in show business of older women taking on younger lovers and husbands that it would not only add novelty but also fresh dramatic and psychological angles."

One condition left out of McCarthy's analysis is that Norma Desmond doesn't commit suicide. She does what women do in the movies. They go crazy instead.

I read McCarthy's take on *A Star Is Born* as seen through the lens of *Sunset Boulevard* with great interest. His essay took me back to the 1990s when I used to enjoy occasional dinners with my friend Roddy McDowall. His acting career went back to 1941 when he was only thirteen years old and the adolescent actor made a spectacular Hollywood screen debut in the John Ford classic *How Green Was My Valley*. McDowall knew the town and its major players, past and present, better than anyone else on the planet. I knew him well enough not to ask about his good friend Elizabeth Taylor, still living, but another friend of McDowall's had been dead for over thirty years. He and I enjoyed what we began to call our "Monty Clift moments" at Orso restaurant in Beverly Hills.

At one of these dinners, I asked, "Why did Clift pull out of Billy Wilder's *Sunset Boulevard* only weeks before shooting began?"

In 1950, Montgomery Clift was the hottest new actor in

Hollywood, having just come off *The Search*, *Red River*, and *The Heiress*. "We talked a lot about his decision," McDowall began. "Billy was very upset, but Monty thought he was wrong for the part of Joe Gillis. The role required an animalistic actor. Bill Holden was perfect. Monty thought he was more of a lyrical actor."

I mentioned something about Clift's relationship with Libby Holman, a singer who was sixteen years older than the actor. People speculated that Clift pulled out of *Sunset Boulevard* because Joe Gillis's affair with Norma Desmond replicated the real one between Clift and Holman.

"Monty didn't care about gossip like that," McDowall said. "And he and Holman did have a physical relationship. Monty rejected the role because he knew he was wrong for it. Nobody would have said it at the time, but if Monty had played Joe Gillis, Norma Desmond would have come off as a fag hag."

I often thought that Streisand should have made the switch in her *A Star Is Born*. She needed to play a heavy. In the 1970s, Jane Fonda and Faye Dunaway were the screen's two other reigning female stars. Fonda didn't shy away from edgy roles like the ones she brought to the screen in *They Shoot Horses, Don't They?* and *Klute*, two films offered to Streisand that she rejected. Dunaway won her Oscar playing a certifiable bad guy in *Network*. A darker role on her résumé would have enhanced Streisand's career, but *A Star Is Born* was probably not the right project to achieve that makeover.

After spending years at Warner Brothers and being one of the producers on the 2018 *A Star Is Born*, Ravi Mehta became head of production, post and Vfx at 20th Century Studios, and four years on his new job, he often heard things like, "We got a new *Die Hard*!"

"What's the take on it?" he would ask.

"It's going to be female."

"You think that's novel?"

Mehta also received a lot of pitches that "it's going to be a Black person." Again, he replied, "Come up with something a little more original than that."

For Mehta, there is another problem with switching the sexes in *A Star Is Born*. "Testosterone after our preteen years doesn't help us," he said. "It just accentuates. You can see a woman becoming more maternal. With men, you just become a bigger jackass."

One movie released in 2020 made the switch, and it is a textbook on why having a female star on the decline while the man's career takes off fails to create the same dramatic sparks.

During the 2020 COVID-19 pandemic, actor Ethan Hawke was presented with interview transcripts of a planned book on Paul Newman and Joanne Woodward that never materialized. Newman had burned the recordings but not the printed transcripts. It was those pages that the two actors' children gave to Hawke. "Was there a movie here?" the Newman children wanted to know.

Hawke thought yes. He took those transcripts and gave them life by having some of his actor friends read the quotes for an HBO Max documentary. George Clooney read Newman's lines, Laura Linney read Woodward's, and other actors played the couple's friends, directors, and co-workers. Existing filmed interviews with Newman and Woodward are also used in *The Last Movie Stars: Paul Newman and Joanne Woodward*.

Hawke points out in the film, "When they were first married, she had just won the Oscar. She was the star. And then the trajectory just changed."

In 1957, when Woodward appeared in *The Three Faces of Eve*, which brought her that Academy Award for Best

Actress, Newman's greatest success on screen to that date had been playing Rocky Graziano in the modest bio-pic *Somebody Up There Likes Me*.

In *The Last Movie Stars*, Brooks Ashmanskas voices the role of the couple's close friend Gore Vidal. The author of *Myra Breckinridge* and *The Best Man* speaks about what the movie star himself called "Newman's luck." Ashmanskas's Vidal reveals, "Mr. [Donald] Turnupseed who was driving the car that got in front of Jimmy Dean's Porsche. We always had sort of a joke that had it not been for Mr. Turnupseed, Paul never would have taken over Jimmy Dean's part in *Somebody* and if that had not happened dot dot dot, which is known in the trade as an ellipsis."

Prior to playing a real-life boxer in *Somebody Up There Likes Me*, Newman bombed spectacularly in a 1954 swords-and-sandals dud called *The Silver Chalice*, his film career essentially over before it began. He famously auditioned for twenty-six movie roles and been rejected just as many times. Even his early career on Broadway lacked remarkable success. When cast in the supporting role of Alan Seymour in the original 1955 production of William Inge's *Picnic*, Newman also understudied the lead role of the roustabout stud Hal Carter, played by Ralph Meeker. Joshua Logan, the show's director, suggested that Newman start exercising and lifting weights, so that he didn't appear such "a nice guy." Logan feared what would happen if, by chance, the understudy ever had to go on for an indisposed Meeker. Newman recalled Logan's suggestion about working out, saying, "The way I translated that was six hours in the gym every day." When Meeker left the production, the newly buff Newman thought he would finally get to be the male lead. "I don't think so," Logan told him, "because you don't carry any sexual threat."

Vidal in *The Last Movie Stars* comments, "Things happened quickly for Joanne. Not so quickly for Paul. Of course, he only got the part in *Our Town* [on TV] because Jimmy Dean was cast in *Rebel*. Every part he did get was a lesser role that someone better had passed on."

Martin Ritt directed Newman and Woodward in *The Long, Hot Summer*, the film that finally made the male side of that duo a bona fide movie star. Ritt, voiced by actor Jonathan Marc Sherman in the documentary, says, "You always had this image of Joanne being this great actress and Paul being this unworthy second banana who became a star. She was becoming a big star then, and we were casting *The Long, Hot Summer* and she introduced me to Paul."

Woodward opened the door which led to Newman becoming a star, just as all the characters named Norman Maine or John Howard Norman or Jackson Maine open doors for all the characters named Esther Blodgett or Esther Hoffman or Ally Campana.

Newman may not have been sexually threatening on stage, but the theater is not the movies. In *The Long, Hot Summer*, Newman knew how to lower his head and raise his eyes so their crystal blue shot straight into the hearts and libidos of moviegoers everywhere. And he did something else. The actor made sure, even if his "six hours in the gym every day" was hyperbole, to keep his pecs and abs in superb condition. On screen over the next decade, only Brigitte Bardot took off her top more often than Paul Newman. He never forgot Logan's "sexual threat" critique. "I've been chewing on that one for almost thirty years," he often remarked.

The formula for *A Star Is Born* doesn't fit perfectly with the lives and careers of Newman and Woodward. One important difference: He was the drunk, not her. Newman's alcoholism got so bad that at one point in the marriage, Woodward and their children rented a house in Malibu and refused to let him visit, much less live there, until he quit drinking. Since he didn't want to stay at the Hotel

Bel-Air, Newman slept in the car in the driveway of the beach house to be as near as possible to his family without seeing them. Finally, Woodward allowed that he could continue drinking a few Coors every day.

As his career went into superorbit and hers cratered—Woodward wondered why she wasn't getting any of the roles offered to Shirley MacLaine—their marriage created many other scenes that rival the theatricality of *A Star Is Born*.

"Paul and I were walking down the street one day," Woodward recalls in *The Last Movie Stars*, "and we passed these two girls, both of whom gave Paul the usual response, and then one looked at me and said, 'Is *that* her?' I just felt like running down the street shouting, 'Yes, it's me. It's me! I don't know what my name is, but it's me!' "

There's also the story of her wanting to costar with him in *A New Kind of Love*. The 1963 movie wouldn't get made without the star power of Newman, who had just come off such hits as *The Hustler*, *Sweet Bird of Youth*, and *Hud*. Meanwhile, a pregnancy prevented Woodward from making movies before she starred in *The Stripper*, a box office failure that got butchered in the editing process by Darryl F. Zanuck at 20th Century Fox. Newman considered the script for *A New Kind of Love* beneath him. When he delivered his opinion to Woodward, she freaked out, telling her husband, "I raised our children. I helped raise your children. I've done all these things for you, and now you don't want to do this movie where I get to do beautiful costumes changes and hair and makeup, and you don't want to do it!"

"I take it back!" Newman replied. "It's the best script I've ever read, and I can't wait to start."

Just as Lady Gaga's Ally wants to give her husband a job by making him part of an upcoming European tour,

Newman made a vapid softball comedy to keep his wife happy and give her a job. Unfortunately, Newman didn't have a manager like Ally's Rez Gavron in *A Star Is Born* to talk him out of making *A New Kind of Love*. It turned out to be one of the worst films of 1963, if not the entire decade.

In his documentary, Hawke comments on the divergent paths of Newman and Woodward. "Many of us lose our dreams, but most of us don't have a partner who has the exact same dream and his come true over and over," Hawke says. "When they married, she was the star. Slowly she found herself changing diapers, making baby food. Not getting what you want is hard, but getting what you want and slowly having it taken away from you, that's a different problem."

Woodward didn't go crazy like Norma Desmond nor did she kill herself like the male character in all the *A Star Is Born* films. She did what a lot of famous women do when their careers begin to evaporate. She had children, but with an important caveat. She reveals in the documentary, "When I was young, I wanted to act, and I didn't let anything stand in my way until I had children. I hope the children understand that each and every one of them is adored. If I had it all to do over all, I might not have had children. Actors don't make good parents."

Woodward explains, "You were guilty if you were on the set, because you should be home with the children. If you were home with the children, you thought, 'Why am I not on the set?' "

Her words hark back decades. Long after the whole *A Star Is Born* legend was but a twinkle in her eye, Adela Rogers St. Johns said, "I love my children, but I wish I hadn't any."

One of the Newman children describes her mother's

predicament. "She put everything on hold for him," Melissa Newman says in the documentary. "Her career would have been really, really different."

Another daughter gives an especially poignant interpretation of the marriage. "She knew that her husband, who was really famous, deeply believed that she was a way better actor than he was," Lissy Newman says. "And he worshipped her as an artist."

Woodward also did something else besides defining herself as a wife and mother. She mentored young actors like Laura Linney and Allison Janney. She became artistic director of the Westport Country Playhouse. She made a few movies, most of them for television. No doubt, Woodward would have preferred to have her husband's career. But she was not a thirteen-year-old like Bradley Cooper's Jackson Maine trapped in an adult body. She did not commit suicide. That's what men do, and it's why no one has ever switched the sexes in *A Star Is Born*.

In recent years, the real lives of movie stars finally provided an awards ceremony moment that matched, maybe even topped, the fictional one in all the films titled *A Star Is Born*. On March 28, 2022, at the Academy Awards in Hollywood, Chris Rock told a joke from the stage of the Dolby Theatre that referenced the shaved head of actress Jada Pinkett Smith. While Will Smith laughed out loud at Rock's crack, his wife looked very pissed at the comment about her lack of hair due to alopecia. Tellingly, Pinkett Smith did not get up and slap the comedian across the face. She left that duty to her husband, who, a few minutes later, went on to win the Oscar for best actor for his performance in *King Richard*. Imagine Pinkett Smith or any of the lead female characters in any of the *A Star Is Born* movies switching places with their respective husbands on the stage of the Oscars or the Grammys, and it's clear why the "jackass," as Ravi Mehta put it, always has to be male.

Movie aficionados may have to wait the usual twenty years, or even forty, before another version of the show business legend is made. Theatergoers are luckier. Warner Theatricals, a subsidiary of the fabled movie studio founded by four Jewish emigré brothers in 1923, is at work on *A Star Is Born* musical for the Broadway stage.

A great star is always reborn.

Acknowledgments

The film producers Bill Gerber, Lynette Howell Taylor, and Ravi Mehta brought the third remake of *A Star Is Born* to the screen, and their interviews were essential to tell the story of that movie. Interviews with Willam Belli, Erin Benach, Will Fetters, Mark Nilan Jr., and Bradley Rubin are also deeply appreciated.

My friends Gay Haubner and Howard Mandelbaum read an early draft of this book and offered great suggestions. Lisa Arden and Frank Rich made essential research materials available to me.

I am indebted to the researchers Ann Gaines Rodriguez and Lauren Cahoone, who performed some last-minute fact-checking at libraries in, respectively, Austin, Texas, and Beverly Hills, California.

Nonfictions books like mine don't get written without the enormous help of librarians, and fortunately for me, all the films titled *A Star Is Born*, as well as *What Price Hollywood?* and *The Last Movie Stars*, have generated an enormous video and paper trail. I relied mightily on those librarians at the Harry Ransom Center at the University of Texas, the New York Public Library for the Performing Arts at Lincoln Center, the Margaret Herrick Library, the New York Public Library's Stephen A. Schwarzman Building, and the USC School of Cinematic Arts.

Last and foremost, I thank my photographer friend Jill Krementz, my agent Lee Sobel, and all the talented people at Kensington Publishing, including designers Kristine Mills and Tom Lewis, copy editor Michelle Horn, and, of course, my editor John Scognamiglio.

Bibliography

Andersen, Christopher. *Barbra: The Way She Is*. New York: William Morrow, 2006.

Bacall, Lauren. *Lauren Bacall by Myself*. New York: Knopf, 1978.

Bach, Steven. *Dazzler: The Life and Times of Moss Hart*. New York: Knopf, 2001.

Bankhead, Tallulah. *Tallulah: An Autobiography*. New York: Harper and Bros., 1952.

Bennett, Joan, and Louis Kibbe. *The Bennett Playbill: Five Generations of the Famous Theater Family*. New York: Holt, Rinehart, and Winston, 1970.

Bosworth, Patricia. *Montgomery Clift: A Biography*. New York: Harcourt Brace Jovanovich, 1978.

Brown, Jared. *Moss Hart: A Prince of the Theatre: A Biography in Three Acts*. New York: Back Stage Books, 2006.

Callahan, Dan. *Barbara Stanwyck: The Miracle Woman*. Jackson: University Press of Mississippi, 2012.

Callahan, Maureen. *Poker Face: The Rise and Rise of Lady Gaga*. New York: Hyperion, 2010.

Carey, Gary. *Cukor & Co.: The Films of George Cukor and His Collaborators*. New York: The Museum of Modern Art, 1971.

Carlyle, John. *Under the Rainbow*. New York: Carroll and Graf, 2006.

Clarke, Gerald. *Get Happy: The Life of Judy Garland*. New York: Random House, 2000.

Codori, Jeff. *Colleen Moore: A Biography of the Silent*

Film Star. Jefferson, N.C.: McFarland and Company, 2012.

De Rosso, Diana. *James Mason: A Personal Biography*. New York: Lennard Publishing, 1989.

Edwards, Anne. *Streisand: A Biography*. New York: Little, Brown and Company, 1996.

Finch, Christopher. *Rainbow: The Stormy Life of Judy Garland*. New York: Grosset and Dunlap, 1975.

Frank, Gerald. *Judy*. New York: Harper Collins, 1975.

Furia, Philip. *Ira Gershwin: The Art of the Lyricist*. New York: Oxford University Press, 1996.

Gershwin, Ira. *Lyrics on Several Occasions*. New York: Knopf, 1959.

Griffin, Nancy, and Kim Masters. *Hit and Run: How Jon Peters and Peter Guber Took Sony for a Ride in Hollywood*. New York: Simon and Schuster, 1996.

Harris, Mark. *Mike Nichols: A Life*. New York: Penguin Books, 2021.

Haver, Ronald. *A Star Is Born: The Making of the 1954 and Its 1983 Restoration*. New York: Applause Books, 2002.

Hofler, Robert. *Money, Murder, and Dominick Dunne: A Life in Several Acts*. Madison: University of Wisconsin Press, 2017.

Hofler, Robert. *The Way They Were: How Epic Battles and Bruised Egos Brought a Classic Hollywood Love Story to the Screen*. New York: Citadel, 2023.

Jablonski, Edward. *Harold Arlen: Rhythm, Rainbows, and Blues*. Boston: Northeastern University Press, 1996.

Lambert, Gavin. *Norma Shearer: A Biography*. New York: Knopf, 1990.

Lambert, Gavin. *On Cukor*. New York: Rizzoli, 2000.

Levy, Emanuel. *George Cukor, Master of Elegance: Hollywood's Legendary Director and His Stars*. New York: William Morrow and Company, 1994.

Levy, Emanuel. *Vincente Minnelli: Hollywood's Dark Dreamer*. New York: St. Martin's Press, 2009.

Long, Robert Emmet (editor). *George Cukor: Interviews*. Jackson: University Press of Mississippi, 2001

Lorna, Luft. *Me and My Shadows: A Family Memoir*. New York: Atria, 1998.

Luft, Lorna, and Jeffrey Vance. *A Star Is Born: Judy Garland and the Film That Got Away*. Philadelphia: Running Press, 2018.

Luft, Sid. *Judy and I: My Life with Judy Garland*. Chicago: Chicago Review Press, 2017.

McBride, Joseph. *Frank Capra: The Catastrophe of Success*. New York: Simon and Schuster, 1992.

McGilligan, Patrick. *George Cukor: A Double Life: A Biography of the Gentleman Director*. New York: St. Martin's Press, 1991.

Mann, William. *Behind the Screen: How Gays and Lesbians Shaped Hollywood, 1910–1969*. New York: Viking, 2001.

Martin, Hugh. *Hugh Martin. The Boy Next Door*. New York: Trolley Press, 2010.

Marx, Samuel, and Joyce Vanderveen. *Deadly Illusions: Jean Harlow and the Murder of Paul Bern*. New York: Random House, 1990.

Mason, James. *Before I Forget: Autobiography and Drawings*. London: Hamish Hamilton, 1981.

Moore, Colleen. *Silent Star*. New York: Doubleday and Co., 1968.

Morella, Joe, and Edward Z. Epstein. *Paul and Joanne: A Biography of Paul Newman and Joanne Woodward*. New York: Delacorte Press, 1988.

Morley, Sheridan. *James Mason: Odd Man Out*. New York: Harper and Row, 1989.

Oumano, Elena. *Paul Newman*. New York: St. Martin's Press, 1989.

Owen, Michael. *Ira Gershwin: A Life in Words*. New York: Boni and Liveright, 2024.

Parker, Dorothy, and Stuart Y. Silverstein. *Not Much Fun: The Lost Poems of Dorothy Parker*. New York: Scribner, 1996.

Riese, Randall. *Her Name is Barbra: An Intimate Portrait of the Real Barbra Streisand*. New York: Birch Lane, 1993.

Rogers St. Johns, Adela. *Love, Laughter, and Tears: My Hollywood Story*. New York: Doubleday, 1978.

Schechter, Scott. *Judy Garland: The Day-by-Day Chronicle of a Legend*. New York: Taylor Trade Publishing, 2006.

Schickel, Richard. *The Men Who Made the Movies: Interviews with Frank Capra, George Cukor, Howard Hawks, Alfred Hitchcock, Vincente Minnelli, King Vidor, Raoul Walsh, and William A. Wellman*. New York: Atheneum, 1975.

Schmidt, Randy L. (editor). *Judy Garland on Judy Garland: Interviews and Encounters*. Chicago: Chicago Review Press, 2014.

Schulberg, Budd. *Moving Pictures: Memories of a Hollywood Prince*. Chicago: Souvenir Press, 1982.

Shipman, David. *Judy Garland: The Secret Life of an American Legend*. New York: Hyperion, 1993.

Spada, James. *Streisand: Her Life*. New York: Crown Publishers, 1995.

Streisand, Barbra. *My Name Is Barbra*. New York: Viking, 2023.

Thompson, Frank T. *William A. Wellman*. Metuchen, N.J.: The Scarecrow Press, 1983.

Thomson, David. *Showman: The Life of David O. Selznick*. New York: Knopf, 1992.

Wallace, David. *Capital of the World: A Portrait of New*

York City in the Roaring Twenties. New York: Lyons Press, 2012.

Warner, Jack L., with Dean Jennings. *My First Hundred Years in Hollywood: An Autobiography.* New York: Random House, 1965.

Wellman, William A. *A Short Time for Insanity: An Autobiography.* New York: Hawthorne Books, 1974.

Wellman Jr., William. *Wild Bill Wellman: Hollywood Rebel.* New York: Pantheon, 2015.

Wilson, Victoria. *A Life of Barbara Stanwyck: Steel-True 1907–1940.* New York: Simon and Schuster, 2013.

Notes

Introduction

2 **"a kind of romantic"**: Bennett and Kibbe, *The Bennett Playbill*, 252.

2 **"She was like some"**: Ibid., 252.

3 **a pay upgrade to $30,000**: Fredrick Santon, "What Price Hollywood," *Movie Collector's World*, Dec. 22, 2000.

3 **"the best femme poker player"**: Bennett and Kibbe, *The Bennett Playbill*, 252.

3 **"I couldn't spend that kind"**: Gene Ringgold, "Constance Bennett," *Films in Review*, Oct. 1965.

4 **"Connie Bennett was intelligent"**: Long, *George Cukor: Interviews*, 84.

5 **number one box office attraction**: Moore, *Silent Star*, 176.

5 **"This is Mrs. John McCormick"**: Ibid., 132.

5 **"It's our wedding night"**: Ibid.

6 **"You take up the option"**: Wilson, *A Life of Barbara Stanwyck*, 251.

7 **"This slapdash disregard"**: Arthur Knight, "Sex in the Cinema,"*Playboy*, Dec. 1970.

7 **"When she turns it on"**: TCM Barbara Stanwyck profile.

8 **"failed to put in an appearance"**: *Hollywood Reporter*, "Barbara Stanwyck Walks," July 17, 1931.

8 "This town of supreme sophistication": Louella Parsons, "Tell It to Louella," *Los Angeles Examiner*, July 27, 1931.

9 "a very unpopular guy": Callahan, *Barbara Stanwyck*, 27.

9 "dismissive and unpleasant": American Vaudeville Museum, "Frank Fay," Nov. 20, 2021.

9 "Everything I know of etiquette": Wilson, *A Life of Barbara Stanwyck*, 189.

9 "I am Mrs. Frank Fay": McBride, *Frank Capra*, 230.

10 "playing Ray Stark's mother-in-law": Marie Brenner, "Collision on 'Rainbow Road,' " *New Times*, Jan. 24, 1975.

10 suicide, endured electroshock treatments: Luft, *Judy and I*, 273.

Part One

Except as indicated below, quotes and facts in Part One came from the David O. Selznick Archives, Ransom Center, University of Texas at Austin.

Chapter 1

13 "the toughest, the funniest": Thomson, *Showman*, 135.

13 "Largely through David's influence": Ibid.

14 "my friend and mentor": Moore, *Silent Star*, dedication page.

16 "she had been raised": Schulberg, *Moving Pictures*, 311.

18 "From the time they met": Rogers St. Johns, *Love, Laughter, and Tears*, 217.

18 "Get that part for me": Moore, *Silent Star*, 129.

18 "The Modern Girl as we know her": Rogers St. Johns, *Love, Laughter, and Tears*, 218–19.

19 Maude Adams in *Peter Pan*: Ibid., 209.

19 "Any plain Jane": Moore, *Silent Star*, 135.

19 "Never had I been so happy": Ibid., 129

19 accepted her fans' adulation: Codori, *Colleen Moore*, 217.

20 "It was Colleen who was the big shot": Ibid., 188.

21 rejected the deal: Moore, *Silent Star*, 218.

21 "He ran my films": Ibid., 171.

22 "He pulled a gun out": Ibid., 134.

22 William Desmond Taylor case: Marx and Vanderveen, *Deadly Illusions*, 116.

23 Dorothy Millette case: Ibid.; 63, 82–83, 220, 227, 230–31.

23 Bern suicide note: Ibid., 153.

23 "To damn the radiant Jean": Tallulah, *Bankhead*, 31.

Chapter 2

25 "had a bad voice, a John Gilbert–bad voice": Schickel, *The Men Who Made the Movies*, 218.

26 "sail into the setting sun": Wilson, *A Life of Barbara Stanwyck*, 606.

26 "They didn't like it at all": Schickel, *The Men Who Made the Movies*, 218.

26 "He was the greatest agent": Ibid.

26 "No, Bill, I don't like it": Ibid.

26 "never told me a story": Thomson, *Showman*, 217.

27 "*A Star Is Born* is much more my story": Thompson, *William A. Wellman*, 163.

28 "word for word": Schickel, *The Men Who Made the Movies*, 219.

28 Academy also failed to invite him: Wellman Jr., *Wild Bill Wellman*, 331.

30 "They liked the scene so much": Lambert, *On Cukor*, 53.

30 "Then, years later, I found myself": Thompson, *William A. Wellman*, 164–65.

31 "Call me up in the cold gray dawn": Rogers St. Johns, *Love, Laughter, and Tears*, 216.

32 "Let me go with my granddaughter": Rogers St. Johns, Ibid., 208.

32 "You'll not be a bathing beauty": Ibid., 213.

32 "The device is one that Wellman": Thompson, *William A. Wellman*, 105.

34 "The love of Norma Shearer": Lambert, *Norma Shearer*, 239.

Chapter 3

38 "she earned $1,000": Parker and Silverstein, *Not Much Fun*, 40.

38 "queer as a billy goat": Wallace, *Capital of the World*, 184.

40 "I hate you, you weak": Moore, *Silent Star*, 175.

40 "racially insensitive": Luft, *A Star Is Born*, 53.

41 "throwing away $22,000": Schulberg, *Moving Pictures*, 260.

43 "I heard Mother saying": Ibid., 446.

43 "I always think of New Year's Day": "Budd Schulberg Remembers," *People*, Sept. 22, 1981.

43 "She was really Hollywood's first lady": Schulberg, *Moving Images*, 464.

43 "Nothing fails in America": Dave Kehr, "Hollywood, Back When . . . ," *New York Times*, Apr. 7, 2000.

44 Many of them took their own lives: Schulberg, *Moving Pictures*, 223–24.

44 "one of the hundreds of marquee names": Ibid., 123.

44 "Suddenly he wasn't a five-thousand-dollar-a week": Ibid.

44 "one of Father's favorite directors": Ibid., 224.

44 "That Sunday at Malibu": Ibid.

45 "Daisy Buchanan's East Egg home": "Swope's Mansion at Lands End," *Port Washington News*, May 9, 2008.

45 "involved reading one novel": Robert Van Gelder, "An Interview with Budd Schulberg," *New York Times Book Review*, Aug. 10, 1941.

45 "Moscow State University"/"won over"; Richard Severo, Ring Lardner Jr. obit, *New York Times*, Nov. 2, 2000; and "Lardner, Ring, Jr.," *Current Biography*, July 1987.

46 "an undercover chance to work": Schulberg, *Moving Images*, 268.

46 "a shoot-up-the-town fellow": Thomson, *Showman*, 217.

46 "slightly crazed as a result": Schulberg, *Moving Images*, 269.

46 "laying linoleum, different people": Robert Van Gelder, "An Interview with Budd Schulberg," *New York Times Book Review*, Aug. 10, 1941.

50 "credits the famous line to John Lee Mahin": Haver, *A Star Is Born*, 43.

50 "Adela Rogers St. Johns was with me": Moore, *Silent Star*, 177.

Chapter 4

51 "troubleshooter" and "tough Irish Catholic": Thomas S. Pryors, "Breen Is Retired as Movie Censor," *New York Times*, Oct. 15, 1954.

51 "They are, probably, the scum": "Hitler in Hollywood," *New Yorker*, Sept. 9, 2013.

54 "Virginia Rappe case": "Lowell Sherman Bankruptcy," New York *Daily News*, Feb. 18, 1922.

57 "You're nothing without me": Moore, *Silent Star*, 215.

58 "evidently in love with Esther": Haver, *A Star Is Born*, 55.

59 "I didn't make pictures for him": Wellman, *A Short Time for Insanity*, 107.

60 "I had been working steadily": David Bird, Janet Gaynor obit, *New York Times*, Sept. 15, 1984.

Part Two

Except as indicated below, quotes and facts in Part Two came from the Warner Brothers Archives, Film Department, University of California at Los Angeles, and the George Cukor Archives, Margaret Herrick Library, Beverly Hills.

Chapter 5

65 "Our daily life became": Luft, *Judy and I*, 198.

65 "When I left that business": Janet Maslin, "Street Smarts," *New York Times*, Jan. 29, 1978.

65 "One-Punch Luft": Luft, *Judy and I*, caption.

66 "a kid with dirty underwear": Marie Brenner, "Collision on 'Rainbow Road,' " *New Times*, Jan. 24, 1975.

66 "The prostitutes had red hair": Tatiana Siegel, "I'm the Trump of Hollywood," *Hollywood Reporter*, Jan. 20, 2017.

66 "whose motion picture experience": Frank Pierson, "My Battles with Barbra and Jon," *New York*, Nov. 15, 1976.

66 "A charming fellow, Sid": Warner, *My First Hundred Years in Hollywood*, 316.

67 "Don't ever do that to me": Streisand, *My Name Is Barbra*, 407.

67 she rejected him as the director: Luft, *Judy and I*, 164.

67 "Here come Lester and Lester": Levy, *Vincente Minnelli*, 12.

67 "He could poontang": TCM Vincente Minnelli feature.

68 "secluded himself and wouldn't explain": Luft, *Judy and I*, 198.

68 "Judy and Vincent's marriage": Ibid., 161.

68 "They were all gentlemen": Luft, *Me and My Shadows*, 49.

68 "so unlike the refined men": Ibid., 70.

68 "Sid kept telling me": "Happy Judy Stay Happy," *Screen Life*, Jan. 1954.

68 "Sid was a wheeler-dealer": Bacall, *Lauren Bacall by Myself*, 219.

68 "[M]y father saw her": Luft, *A Star Is Born*, 72.

68 "[Jack Warner] wanted to show": Luft, *Judy and I*, 242.

69 "[I]t was virtually impossible": Ibid., 277.

69 "I discovered this project": Marie Brenner, "Collision on 'Rainbow Road,' " *New Times*, Jan. 24, 1975.

69 "I wanted to do that picture": Frank, *Judy*, 332.

70 "Go to England": Luft, *Judy and I*, 171.

70 "the boonies": Ibid., 186

70 "important contribution to the revival": Tony Awards website.

70 "The atmosphere was explosive": Luft, *Judy and I*, 203.

71 "George Bernard Shaw's *Pygmalion*": Schechter, *Judy Garland*, 176.

71 "How Sid went about it": Sidney Skolsky, "Hollywood Is My Beat," *Citizen-News*, undated clip.

72 "Of course I want your baby": Luft, *Judy and I*, 199.

72 "I can't believe those two": Ibid., 243.

72 "I wanted George": Sidney Skolsky, "Hollywood Is My Beat," *Citizen-News*, undated clip.

73 "She did it with such feeling": Haver, *A Star Is Born*, 39.

73 "There has to be some compelling": Long, *George Cukor*, 171.

74 "she was sad": "The Film, Life and Times of George Cukor," *Point of View*, 1969.

74 lunch at Romanoff's: McGilligan, *George Cukor*, 27.

74 "I'd very much like to write": Ed Sullivan, "Toast of the Town," New York *Daily News*, Oct. 13, 1954.

75 "It was a difficult story": Ibid.

78 "I brought up the name Bogart": Haver, *A Star Is Born*, 68.

78 "Sid Luft rejected Humphrey Bogart": Warner, *My First Hundred Years in Hollywood*, 316.

78 every Christmas at his home: Clarke, *Get Happy*, 315.

79 "It just makes me cry": Hedda Hopper, "Hedda Hopper's Hollywood," *Los Angeles Times*, May 19, 1952.

79 "How about me doing the Norman Maine": Frank, *Judy*, 371.

79 "I'd rather work for a crude son": Luft, *Judy and I*, 279.

80 "[A]t its basic level, it examines": Luft, *A Star Is Born*, 14.

80 "I got more fucking class": Luft, *Judy and I*, 279.

81 Garland's "preferred costar": Ibid., 262.

81 "Everybody wanted Cary to play": Haver, *A Star Is Born*, 68.

81 "Can there be any doubt": McGilligan, *George Cukor*, 218.

82 "Judy was a drug addict": TCM Cary Grant feature.

82 "God, I wish I could": Luft, *A Star Is Born*, 110.

83 "I got to know her very well": Haver, *A Star Is Born*, 71.

83 "In fact, this was the best": Mason, *Before I Forget*, 340.

84 "A Chinese junk, surrounded by seventy-five": Carlyle, *Under the Rainbow*, 122.

84 "the worst thing that ever happened": Carlyle to author.

85 "There were no great expressions": Mason, *Before I Forget*, 33.

Chapter 6

86 this one was her favorite: Luft, *A Star Is Born*, 96.

87 "They went wild with joy": Jablonski, *Harold Arlen*, 238.

87 "I Can't Believe My Eyes": Owen, *Ira Gershwin*, 236.

88 "The title is as a paraphrase": Gershwin, *Lyrics on Several Occasions*, 242.

88–89 Garland/Martin contretemps: Martin, *The Boy Next Door*, 305–10.

89 "If she does a tour de force": Ibid., 308.

89 "company man": Luft, *Judy and I*, 164.

90 "You have to be strong": Haver, *A Star Is Born*, 125.

90 "In making a movie, there's no audience": Furia, *Ira Gershwin*, 220.

90 "I want to see her": Haver, *A Star Is Born*, 129.

93 "The higher-ups tended to forget": Mason, *Before I Forget*, 339.

94 "Cukor wanted to go away": Haver, *A Star Is Born*, 145.

95 "I had not learned of this": Mason, *Before I Forget*, 335.

96 "As soon as Mason reported": Warner, *My First Hundred Years in Hollywood*, 316–17; and Luft, *A Star Is Born*, 128.

98 "Judy was very out of control": Morley, *James Mason*, 105.

98 "My mother was used to having everyone": Luft, *Me and My Shadows*, 51.

98 "Judy, you've given us a lot of trouble": Clarke, *Get Happy*, 318.

98 "To get something as unique": Mason, *Before I Forget*, 339.

100 "She works intensely": Haver, *A Star Is Born*, 172.

100 "Someone told me I work": Sidney Skolsky, "Hollywood Is My Beat," *Citizen-News*, undated clip.

100 **"I'd be the last to deny"**: "The Real Me," *McCall's,* Apr. 1957.

102 **"Dr. Fred Pobirs, the same doctor"**: Luft, *Judy and I,* 273.

102 **"I never really liked myself"**: Bob Thomas, "Judy Garland," Associated Press, Nov. 1, 1953.

Chapter 7

104 **"I discovered a big hole"**: Luft, *Judy and I,* 284–85.

104 **"Our picture will show why"**: Bob Thomas, "Judy Garland," Associated Press, Nov. 1, 1953.

104 **"Mama's ambition for her picture"**: Luft, *A Star Is Born,* 134.

106 **"Don't know what to do"**: Owen, *Ira Gershwin,* 245.

106 **"It was, in fact, the story"**: Luft, *Judy and I,* 284–85.

106 **"messy situation"**: Owen, *Ira Gershwin,* 245.

107 **"original trainer and overseer"**: Luft, *Me and My Shadows,* 206.

109 **"When I asked why Warners"**: Hedda Hopper, "Curtain Going Up," *Los Angeles Times,* July 12, 1954.

109 **"big hit"**: Owen, *Ira Gershwin,* 245.

109 **"That huge fifteen-minute 'Born in a Trunk' number"**: Long, *George Cukor,* 61.

110 **"liability . . . all the film needed"**: Mason, *Before I Forget,* 336–37.

Chapter 8

114 "**The largest turnout of stars**": Roby Heard, "Filmdom Hails Judy's Comeback," *The Mirror*, Sept. 30, 1954.

114 "**overstressed**" **and** "**potentially a target**": Edwin Schallet, "'Star Is Born' Hit at Lavish Premiere," *Los Angeles Times*, Sept. 30, 1954.

114 "**Judy Garland arrived at Grand Central**": "Millions Miss Judy's Arrival," *New York World-Telegram*, Oct. 8, 1954.

114 "**I saw *A Star Is Born* opening night**": Arthur Bell, "Bell Tells," *Village Voice*, July 19, 1983.

115 "**showing a little short of phenomenal**": "A Star Is Born," *Variety*, Oct. 5, 1954.

116 "**It would have been much more palatable**": Ed Sullivan, "Toast of the Town," New York *Daily News*, Dec. 31, 1954.

116 "**The film's grosses fell off**": Luft, *Judy and I*, 299.

117 "**The story of what happened**": Long, *George Cukor*, 60.

117 "**We did too much of everything**": Clarke, *Get Happy*, 327.

118 "**letting me make a pitch for [Norman] Maine**": Harold Heffernan, "Jack Carson to Portray P.A. with Heart of Gold," North American Newspaper Alliance, Dec. 9, 1954.

119 "**she had aged Jack Warner ten years**": Martin Franks, "Has Success Washed up Judy Garland," *Uncensored*, Dec. 1957.

119 "**She knew it was then or never**": Bacall, *Lauren Bacall by Myself*, 220.

119 **Newspaper reports**: "Son Born to Judy Garland," *New*

York Times, Mar. 30, 1955; "Judy Garland Has 5½ Lb. Boy," *New York Herald Tribune*, Mar. 30, 1955.

121 **Bacall remembered it:** Bacall, *Lauren Bacall by Myself*, 220.

121 **There I was, weak and exhausted":** Joe Hyams, "The Real Me," *McCall's*, Apr. 1957.

121 **"I held Judy's hand":** Luft, *Judy and I*, 301.

122 **"She did everything to get rid":** Ibid., 232.

122 **"Garland brought to the role":** Carey, *Cukor & Co.*, 130.

123 **"Moss Hart understood when he wrote":** Luft, *A Star Is Born*, 98.

123 **"Wasn't Judy magnificent":** Bosworth, *Montgomery Clift*, 360.

Part Three

Chapter 9

129 **"Congratulations –Jon Peters":** advertisement, *Variety*, Apr. 21, 1976.

130 **"We had to stick":** *A Star Is Born* 1976, DVD special features.

130 **"The women in the previous films":** Streisand, *My Name Is Barbra*, 445.

130 **"Barbra had no compunction":** Hofler, *The Way They Were*, 9.

131 **"Don't let them do":** Ben Brantley, "The Divas," *New York Times*, Dec. 6, 2020.

132 **"woman who had the most influence":** William

Stadiem, "The Greatest Story Never Sold," *Vanity Fair*, Mar. 2010.

132 **"on this very attractive woman"**: Streisand, *My Name Is Barbra*," 407.

132 **"No, you're not my type"**: Ibid., 408.

133 **"He said I reminded him"**: Ibid., 411.

133 **"[H]aving a man in my life"**: Ibid., 414.

133 **"Peters taught her to have fun"**: Edwards, *Streisand*, 369.

134 **"Ray Stark's mother-in-law"**: Marie Brenner, "Collision on 'Rainbow Road,' " *New Times*, Jan. 24, 1975.

134 **"a discovery period for her"**: Edwards, *Streisand*, 386.

134 **"Jon is so strong"**: Frank Pierson, "My Battles with Barbra and Jon," *New York*, Nov. 15, 1976.

134 **"I'm a fella who"**: Marie Brenner, "Collision on 'Rainbow Road,' " *New Times*, Jan. 24, 1975.

134 **"The lead characters didn't even"**: Streisand, *My Name Is Barbra*, 444.

134 **"I don't particularly like doing"**: *A Star Is Born* 1976, DVD special features.

134 **"You idiot! That's been made"**: Spada, *Streisand*, 338.

135 **"Warners wanted us to see"**: Marie Brenner, "Collision on 'Rainbow Road,' " *New Times*, Jan. 24, 1975.

135 **"James Taylor and Carly Simon"**: Riese, *Her Name Is Barbra*, 359.

135 **"They went to Abercrombie"**: Hofler, *Money, Murder, and Dominick Dunne*, 53.

136 **"a savage look at the rock"**: Riese, *Her Name Is Barbra*, 360.

136 "I thought it was awful": Marie Brenner, "Collision on 'Rainbow Road,' " *New Times*, Jan. 24, 1975.

136 "It really didn't catch the contemporary": Ibid.

136 "It's the innocence or the lack": *A Star Is Born* 1976, DVD special features.

137 Ehrlichman didn't think: Griffin and Masters, *Hit and Run*, 44.

137 "Barbra Streisand and Jon Peters just walked": Andersen, *Barbra*, 244.

137 "It doesn't matter if": Spada, *Streisand*, 347.

137 "And it was so important for his ego": Streisand, *My Name Is Barbra*, 418.

138 "was a novice with no experience": Ibid., 445.

Chapter 10

139 "His influence over her": Spada, *Streisand*, 347.

140 "a man I identify with really": Riese, *Her Name Is Barbra*, 364.

140 "I did have this dream": *A Star Is Born* 1976, DVD special features.

140 "I don't think she was attracted": Ibid.

140 "Hey, I can do this part": Spada, *Streisand*, 347.

141 "He drove a red Ferrari": Andersen, *Barbra*, 244.

141 "The whole world is waiting": Marie Brenner, "Collision on 'Rainbow Road,' " *New Times*, Jan. 24, 1975.

141 "I don't want to shoot a documentary": Spada, *Streisand*, 348.

141 "I'm a very bad lip syncher": *A Star Is Born* 1976, DVD special features.

142 "shoot around me": Marie Brenner, "Collision on 'Rainbow Road,' " *New Times*, Jan. 24, 1975.

142 "I like to make it on my brain": Andersen, *Barbra*, 246.

142 "Can you believe Jon Peters": Streisand, *My Name Is Barbra*, 445.

142 "Forget about whether the screenplay": Frank Pierson, "My Battles with Barbra and Jon," *New York*, Nov. 15, 1976.

143 "I told Jerry [Schatzberg] to stay loose": Marie Brenner, "Collision on 'Rainbow Road,' " *New Times*, Jan. 24, 1975.

143 The president of Creative Management: Ibid.

143 "In 1976, people in Hollywood": Holly Millea, "Women and Power: Barbra Streisand," *New York*, Oct. 15, 2018.

144 "You have to understand the way": Edwards, *Streisand*, 386.

144 "Barbra and Jon saw the picture": Griffin and Masters, *Hit and Run*, 39.

144 "10 percent of the gross": Riese, *Her Name Is Barbra*, 225.

144 "We came out smelling like a rose": Marie Brenner, "Collision on 'Rainbow Road,' " *New Times*, Jan. 24, 1975.

145 "We should have someone young": Frank Pierson, "My Battles with Barbra and Jon," *New York*, Nov. 15, 1976.

145 "My original idea was to reverse": Marie Brenner, "Collision on 'Rainbow Road,' " *New Times*, Jan. 24, 1975.

145 "Axelrod was the right person": Ibid.

145 "I told her she should play": Edwards, *Streisand*, 369.

146 "The woman in our story": Frank Pierson, "My Battles with Barbra and Jon," *New York*, Nov. 15, 1976.

147 "I had actors act it out": William Stadiem, "The Greatest Story Never Sold," *Vanity Fair*, Mar. 2010.

147 "trapped by their money": Marie Brenner, "Collision on 'Rainbow Road,' " *New Times*, Jan. 24, 1975.

147 "I could tell you what to write": Andersen, *Barbra*, 247.

147 "Well, he doesn't make some dumb": Frank Pierson, "My Battles with Barbra and Jon," *New York*, Nov. 15, 1976.

148 "There's a lot of jealousy": *A Star Is Born* 1976, DVD special features.

149 "her own clear force and direction": Frank Pierson, "My Battles with Barbra and Jon," *New York*, Nov. 15, 1976.

150 "I saved him then": Streisand, *My Name Is Barbra*, 417.

150 "Ray Stark always used to bully": Frank Pierson, "My Battles with Barbra and Jon," *New York*, Nov. 15, 1976.

151 "It's like there's a theatrical aura": *A Star Is Born* 1976, DVD special features.

151 "It was real life": Ibid.

152 "He was going through hard times": "Barbra Streisand," *Daily Mail*, Sept. 20, 2014.

152 "he looked almost pregnant": Spada, *Streisand*, 350.

152 "I think Elvis Presley really wanted": *A Star Is Born* 1976, DVD special features.

154 "He's an actor": Spada, *Streisand*, 352.

154 "great teeth": *A Star Is Born* 1976, DVD special features.

154 "All my men are really attractive": "Barbra Streisand," *Daily Mail*, Sept. 20, 2014.

155 "I think he was a bit overwhelmed": *A Star Is Born* 1976, DVD special features.

156 "How can I write when": Frank Pierson, "My Battles with Barbra and Jon," *New York,* Nov. 15, 1976

156 "We didn't write rock and roll": Andersen, *Barbra*, 386.

157 "Barbra Streisand's hairdresser": Frank Pierson, "My Battles with Barbra and Jon," *New York*, Nov. 15, 1976.

Chapter 11

158 "Two chocolate girls and me": *A Star Is Born* 1976, DVD special features.

158 "They're stuffed in this little room": Spada, *Streisand*, 360.

159 "Let's get stock footage of Woodstock": *A Star Is Born* 1976, DVD special features.

159 March of Dimes: Streisand, *My Name Is Barbra*, 453.

159 "No more filming": Frank Pierson, "My Battles with Barbra and Jon," *New York*, Nov. 15, 1976.

160 "I'm always insecure": *A Star Is Born* 1976, DVD special features.

160 "Do you really like it": Spada, *Streisand*, 361.

161 "wanted to hire Evel Knievel": Frank Pierson, "My Battles with Barbra and Jon," *New York,* Nov. 15, 1976.

161 "What you hear in that stadium": Spada, *Streisand*, 338.

161 "You can't look at me": *A Star Is Born* 1976, DVD special features.

162 "You're not doing what I tell you": Andersen, *Barbra*, 242–43.

163 "I'm all for women's liberation"/"Shit": Arthur Bell, "Bell Tells," *Village Voice*, Mar. 15, 1976.

163 "I knew Barbra was writing": Spada, *Streisand*, 338.

164 "Did you hear what he said": Frank Pierson, "My Battles with Barbra and Jon," *New York*, Nov. 15, 1976.

164 "I was out of control": Andersen, *Barbra*, 250.

166 "This is how the two characters": *A Star Is Born* 1976, DVD special features.

166 "There's a moment in the love scene": Streisand, *My Name Is Barbra*, 416.

167 "We took that from real life": Spada, *Streisand*, 358–59.

167 "You think it's easy": Frank Pierson, "My Battles with Barbra and Jon," *New York*, Nov. 15, 1976.

167 "Jon insisted he put on some trunks": Streisand, *My Name Is Barbra*, 460.

168 "What the hell are they afraid": Edwards, *Streisand*, 378.

168 "When someone is truly masculine": *A Star Is Born* 1976, DVD special features.

168 "Esther is really the driving force": Streisand, *My Name Is Barbra*, 461.

169 "For God's sake, take me home": Frank Pierson, "My Battles with Barbra and Jon," *New York*, Nov. 15, 1976.

169 "I'll never forget going to the premiere": *A Star Is Born* 1976, DVD special features.

170 "I want to show in this movie": James Spada, "On Location: Streisand and Kristofferson Stage a Freak-Out in Phoenix," *In the Know*, July 1976.

170 "It was like living in a fish bowl": *A Star Is Born* 1976, DVD special features.

171 **"Jon and I had a spitting fight"**: Riese, *Her Name Is Barbra*, 375.

172 **"Why are they here"**: Frank Pierson, "My Battles with Barbra and Jon," *New York*, Nov. 15, 1976.

173 **"You know, a scream"**: Andersen, *Barbra*, 253.

173 **"I'm not afraid of your Oscar"**: Frank Pierson, "My Battles with Barbra and Jon," *New York*, Nov. 15, 1976.

Chapter 12

174 **"But I had to work fast"**: Streisand, *My Name Is Barbra*, 466.

175 **"Her friends influenced her"**: Riese, *Her Name Is Barbra*, 381.

175 **"her character needed more time"**: Edwards, *Streisand*, 381.

175 **"our modern way of doing Judy"**: Streisand, *My Name Is Barbra*, 462.

176 **"When I'm walking on to the stage"**: *A Star Is Born* 1976, DVD special features.

177 **"Everybody was kind of anxious"**: Riese, *Her Name Is Barbra*, 382.

177 **"Once I saw it with an audience"**: *A Star Is Born* 1976, DVD special features.

177 **"It was the women's lib movement"**: Ibid.

178 **"Show her who the man"**: Riese, *Her Name Is Barbra*, 385.

178 **"I realized it was my own life"**: Spada, *Streisand*, 368.

179 **"I don't think I ever met Morrison"**: Max Bell, "Q&A: Kris Kristofferson," *Classic Rock*, Aug. 2010.

179 "I couldn't believe that you": Edwards, *Streisand*, 384–85.

180 "I collect a lot of antique clothes": *A Star Is Born* 1976, DVD special features.

Chapter 13

182 Carson initially mispronouncing her name: Hofler, *The Way They Were*, 146.

182 "I was out in the alley": Riese, *Her Name Is Barbra*, 367.

182 "I nearly went out of my mind": Ibid., 384.

183 "I don't have a white suit": Ibid., 385.

183 "long-running nightmare": Andersen, *Barbra*, 253.

185 "Isn't it nice they gave me": Riese, *Her Name Is Barbra*, 387.

185 "biggest thrill of my career": *A Star Is Born* 1976, DVD special features.

185 "I never had the power": Lawrence Eisenberg, "Barbra Streisand," *Cosmopolitan*, Mar. 1977.

186 "It's kind of ironic": Holly Millea, "Women and Power: Barbra Streisand," *New York*, Oct. 15, 2018.

Part Four

Chapter 14

189 "Oh no—not again": Fredrick Santon, "What Price Hollywood," *Movie Collector's World*, Dec. 22, 2000.

191 "If the pope wasn't happy": Dave McNary, "PETA Honors Bradley Cooper," *Variety*, Oct. 4, 2018.

191 **"childless cat ladies"**: "The Pope Says Choosing Pets Over Kids Is Selfish," BBC, Jan. 2, 2022.

192 **"Whoopi Goldberg was going to"**: Harris, *Mike Nichols*, 424.

192 **Will Smith and director Carl Franklin**: "A Star Is Born," *Jam! Showbiz*, Mar. 9, 2000.

192 **"Nobody can get in touch with Lauryn"**: Sandra P. Angelo, "Jamie Foxx Is Planning to Remake 'A Star Is Born,' " *Entertainment Weekly*, Sept. 15, 2000.

193 **"Hey, I'd like to take a shot"**: Bill Gerber to author, June 20, 2024.

193 **60 million records:** Rebecca Aizin, "Beyoncé Is One of the Richest Women in the World," *People*, Oct. 24, 2024.

194 **"Do we wait"**: Ciara McVey, " 'Star Is Born' Producer," *Hollywood Reporter*, Nov. 4, 2018.

195 **"It is 160 pages"**: Gerber to author.

195 **"My favorite is the Garland"**: Will Fetters to author, Sept. 5, 2024.

196 **"Bradley Cooper wasn't the first"**: Gerber to author.

196 **"I don't think I'm old enough"**: Ibid.

197 **"It kept haunting me"**: Hilary Lewis, "Bradley Cooper Talks Lady Gaga," *Hollywood Reporter*, Apr. 22, 2018.

197 **"and there's no infidelity"**: Ramin Setoodeh, "Why Bradley Cooper was 'Terrified,' " *Variety*, Nov. 2, 2018.

197 **"I'd been playing air guitar"**: Baz Bamigboye, "Bradley Cooper's 'Maestro,' " *Deadline*, Dec. 6, 2023.

197 **"You can't fake it when"**: Kristopher Tapley, "Bradley Cooper Explains," *Variety*, Nov. 29, 2018.

197–98 **"You better create"/"Honestly . . . I could see it":**

Taffy Brodesser-Akner, "Bradley Cooper Is Not Really Into This Interview," *New York Times*, Sept. 27, 2018.

198 **"I have to give Warner Brothers":** Gerber to author.

198 **"In my career, when":** Fetters to author.

198 **"to trust her voice":** Jonathan Van Meter, "Boss Lady," *Vogue*, Oct. 2018.

199 **"Your voice is everything":** Taffy Brodesser-Akner, "Bradley Cooper Is Not Really into This Interview," *New York Times*, Sept. 27, 2018.

200 **"I had the sound in my head":** Tina Benitez-Eves, "How Lukas Nelson Inspired Bradley Cooper's 'A Star Is Born,' " *American Songwriter*, Feb. 21, 2024.

200 **"I got those Magnatone amps":** Ibid.

200 **"I've got something I want you":** Margy Rochlin, "Wrangling Emotions," *Los Angeles Times*, Nov. 8, 2018.

200 **"It sounded uncannily like me":** *A Star Is Born* 2018, DVD special features.

201 **"We had never met":** Ibid.

201 **"I figured if he committed to":** Jenelle Riley, "Sam Elliott Reflects on His Career," *Variety*, Jan. 7, 2019.

201 **"If you trust me, you'll be glad":** Margaux Sippell, "Sam Elliott Dishes," *Variety*, Dec. 8, 2018.

201 **"I'd have been fucked":** Margy Rochlin, "Wrangling Emotions," *Los Angeles Times*, Nov. 8, 2018.

201 **about $5 million of that:** Ravi Mehta to author, Sept. 20, 2024.

201 **"It shot like a diamond":** Jonathan Van Meter, "Boss Lady," *Vogue*, Oct. 2018.

202 **"The second that I saw him":** Ibid.

202 "We're both from the East Coast": Jess Cagle, "Bradley Cooper and Lady Gaga," *People*, Oct. 15, 2018.

202 "The truth is, it's only going to work": *A Star Is Born* 2018, DVD special features.

202 "For me there was not nervousness": Ibid.

203 "You're going to have to sing": Ibid.

203 "He sings from his gut": Jonathan Van Meter, "Boss Lady," *Vogue*, Oct. 2018.

203 "And that video is one of the things": Ibid.

203 "The studio had doubts": Gerber to author.

204 "It was the first time I'd ever directed": *A Star Is Born* 2018, DVD special features.

204 "Take it off": Amy Kaufman, "Lady Gaga Learns to Let Go," *Los Angeles Times*, Sept. 2, 2018.

205 "I took off my makeup": *A Star Is Born* 2018, DVD special features.

205 "Did this guy make ten movies": Gerber to author.

205 "Bradley had complete command": Ibid.

205 "I ended up being a partner": Lynette Howell Taylor to author, July 17, 2024.

206 "We had never met": Fetters to author.

206 "Ally in a lot of ways was me": *A Star Is Born* 2018, DVD special features.

206 "It put me right in the place": Amy Kaufman, "Lady Gaga Learns to Let Go," *Los Angeles Times*, Sept. 2, 2018.

206 "It took years": "Gaga Says She was Psychotic after Being Raped," CNN, May 21, 2021.

207 "He is my hero": Touré, "Lady Gaga Interview," *Fuse*, Apr. 2009.

207 "I'm married to my dad": Miranda Purves, "Lady Gaga," *Elle*, Jan. 2010.

207 "Anybody who knows Lady Gaga's mythology": Fetters to author.

207–8 "God put me on earth": Rob Sheffield, "Lady Gaga's Second Act," *Rolling Stone*, Dec. 17, 2018.

208 "We talked a lot about where": Jonathan Van Meter, "Boss Lady," *Vogue*, Oct. 2018.

208 "When I play at gay clubs": Callahan, *Poker Face*, 40.

208 "That period of my life": Ibid., 41–42.

208 "rock 'n' roll burlesque": Ibid., 51.

208 "I used to walk down the street": Ibid., 52.

209 "This is a movie about what": Jonathan Van Meter, "Boss Lady," *Vogue*, Oct. 2018.

209 "vulnerability . . . She was nothing like": Jess Cagle, "Bradley Cooper and Lady Gaga," *People*, Oct. 15, 2018.

Chapter 15

210 Hollywood was her "sweetness": David Bird, Janet Gaynor obit, *New York Times*, Sept. 15, 1984.

211 "Oh no, I'm going to have to": Mann, *Behind the Screen*, 234.

211 "Judy Garland is by far": *A Star Is Born* 2018, DVD special features.

211–12 "Ally had this fixation": Howell Taylor to author.

212 "The actual house was small": Bradley Rubin to author, Sept. 16, 2024.

212 "It was renovated": Mehta to author.

212 "I love it": Ibid.

212 "They show up at a strange family's house": Ibid.

212 "Jackson even gives her a pair": Howell Taylor to author.

212 "Let's just do the prelude": Pete Hammond, "Eric Roth on Life as a Top Screenwriter," *Deadline*, Apr. 16, 2021.

213 "It was a natural process": Ellen Gamerman, "Boosted by 'Star Is Born,'" *Wall Street Journal*, Oct. 4, 2018.

213 "Fame is a vapor": Ibid.

213 "Bowie was my hero": Jonathan Van Meter, "Boss Lady," *Vogue*, Oct. 2018.

213 "We grew up listening": Chuck Arnold, "Rising Star," *New York Post*, Oct. 15. 2018.

213 "There's no point where a lyric": *A Star Is Born* 2018, DVD special features.

214 "What the movie turned the song": Glenn Whipp, "Lady Gaga and Mark Ronson Take a Deep Dive," *Los Angeles Times*, Dec. 27, 2018.

214 "We thought it might be": Ibid.

215 "This is the material we have": Pete Hammond, "Eric Roth on Life as a Top Screenwriter," *Deadline*, Apr. 16, 2021.

215 "Some was for me": Ibid.

216 "This had been done a lot": Matt Grobal, "Eric Roth Discusses 'Dune' and 'A Star Is Born,'" *Deadline*, Feb. 13, 2019.

216 "What can I learn from": Dave McNary, "'A Star Is Born' Co-Writer Eric Roth," *Variety*, Feb. 8, 2019.

216 "Look at Cher": Ibid.

216 "You had a vulnerable quality": Pete Hammond, "Eric

Roth on Life as a Top Screenwriter," *Deadline*, Apr. 16, 2021.

216 **"Ally isn't even aware"**: *A Star Is Born* 2018, DVD special features.

217 **"Jon Peters attached himself"**: Mehta to author.

217 **"Warner Brothers took a strong stance"**: Gerber to author.

Chapter 16

218 **"Let's get some of the concert stuff"**: Melinda Newman, "How Lady Gaga and Bradley Cooper Shot at Coachella," *Billboard*, Oct. 15, 2018.

218 **It's a Warner Brothers movie"**: Will Tizard, "DP Matthew Libatique on Lensing with Bradley Cooper," *Variety*, Nov. 13, 2018.

218–19 **"to contribute all my historic DNA"**: Gerber to author.

219 **"decked out in your most comfortable denim"**: Melinda Newman, "How Lady Gaga and Bradley Cooper Shot at Coachella," *Billboard*, Oct. 15, 2018.

219 **"Bradley was obsessed"**: Mehta to author.

219 **"Look at *Crazy Heart*"**: Ibid.

219 **"With these live performances"**: Ibid.

220 **"Our stage is your stage"**: Gerber to author.

220 **"Bradley wanted to have this huge opening"**: Mehta to author.

220 **"*That* should be the opening"**: Ibid.

220 **"To shoot subjectively came out of"**: Ibid.

220 **"we can just re-create it"**: Mehta to author.

220 **"No, dude"**: Ibid.

220 **"Lorne Michaels welcomed us"**: Melinda Newman, "How Lady Gaga and Bradley Cooper Shot at Coachella," *Billboard*, Oct. 15, 2018.

221 **"We didn't have much time"**: Will Tizard, "DP Matthew Libatique on Lensing with Bradley Cooper," *Variety*, Nov. 13, 2018.

221 **"Bradley, early on, went for"**: Mehta to author.

221 **"If they paid to come, you're golden"**: Ibid.

222 **"And they didn't even know what"**: Will Tizard, "DP Matthew Libatique on Lensing with Bradley Cooper," *Variety*, Nov. 13, 2018.

222 **"Why does Bradley Cooper have a beard?"**: Margy Rochlin, "A 'Star' on the Stage," *Los Angeles Times*, Feb. 14, 2019.

222 **"I just wanted to say we're here"**: Ibid.

222 **"She and Kris showed up from Malibu"**: Gerber to author.

222 **"We had four minutes before"**: *A Star Is Born* 2018, DVD special features.

223 **"No disrespect to Lady Gaga"**: David McNary, "'A Star Is Born' Co-writer Eric Roth," *Variety*, Feb. 8, 2019.

223 **"While a lot of it is written"**: Pete Hammond, "Eric Roth on Life as a Top Screenwriter," *Deadline*, Apr. 16, 2021.

223 **"Is she going to be really good"**: Will Tizard, "DP Matthew Libatique on Lensing with Bradley Cooper," *Variety*, Nov. 13, 2018.

224 **"What's going on"**: *A Star Is Born* 2018, DVD special features.

224 **"There was no rule except"**: Ibid.

224–25 **"It's finding a way for the energy"**: Amy Kaufman,

"Lady Gaga Learns to Let Go," *Los Angeles Times*, Sept. 2, 2018.

225 **"Tony" and "Ninja"**: Ibid.

225 **"She's more technical than a lot"**: Will Tizard, "DP Matthew Libatique on Lensing with Bradley Cooper," *Variety*, Nov. 13, 2018.

225 **"The parking lot scene with the peas"**: Howell Taylor to author.

226 **"I have this idea for a lyric"**: Ibid.

226 **"But I wasn't going to miss"**: Willam Belli to author, Sept. 19, 2024.

226 **"We brought the drag"**: Gerber to author.

226 **"Gaga's manager had helped us"**: Melinda Newman, "How Lady Gaga and Bradley Cooper Shot at Coachella," *Billboard*, Oct. 15, 2018.

227 **"Bradley wanted flying monkeys"**: Mehta to author.

227 **"You tell a gay guy"**: Belli to author.

227 **"Bradley wants you to play"**: Ibid.

227 **"I have the perfect dress"**: Ibid.

228 **"They brought some stuff"**: Erin Benach to author, Aug. 15, 2024.

228 **"The belt was Erin's"**: Belli to author.

228 **"We did squeeze in a dressing room"**: Rubin to author.

228 **"Bradley was really using the spray tan"**: Belli to author.

229 **"It's where you first like Jackson"**: Gerber to author.

230 **"Jackson's likability was totally"**: Fetters to author.

230 **"Can we change so it doesn't"**: Belli to author.

231 **"Sorry I didn't get to play"**: Ibid.

Chapter 17

232 **"You know when you have a first time"**: Anonymous source to author.

232 **"We changed so much"**: Howell Taylor to author.

232 **"That was Bradley's idea"**: Fetters to author.

233 **"Andrew Dice Clay had a joyous effect"**: Mehta to author.

233 **"Wow, he's bringing it"**: Ibid.

233 **"We wanted to give it more"**: Rubin to author.

233 **$1.33 million**: Zillow.

233 **"Their costumes were part"**: Benach to author.

234 **"Bradley is a huge music fan"**: Fetters to author.

234 **"The male suffering tone"**: Mehta to author.

235 **"The tinnitis evolved"**: Howell Taylor to author.

236 **"Jackson is at his happiest"**: Fetters to author.

236 **"That was quite a day"**: Mehta to author.

236 **"she would be able to find"**: Benach to author.

237 **"For me, fashion and art"**: Jonathan Van Meter, "Boss Lady," *Vogue*, Oct. 2018.

237 **"Stefani and Bradley leaned on me"**: Benach to author.

238 **"There is a selfishness [on Jackson's part] to be"**: Fetters to author.

238–39 **"There's no way you can watch"**: Howell Taylor to author.

239 **"The difference between Jack"**: Rebecca Keegan, "Birth, Life, Birth," *Vanity Fair*, Oct. 2018.

239 **"I talked to Stefani about that cat suit"**: Benach to author.

239 **"her getting caught up in the machinery"**: Fetters to author.

239 **"It's her pop turn that starts"**: Rebecca Keegan, "Birth, Life, Birth," *Vanity Fair*, Oct. 2018.

241 **"This song is delivered with such umbrage"**: Wesley Morris, "That Song in 'A Star Is Born,' " *New York Times*, Oct. 25, 2018.

241 **"polarizing"**: Zack Sharf, "Lady Gaga's Polarizing Song," *IndieWire*, Oct. 19, 2018.

241 **"Is it meant to be so glib"**: Adam Chitwood, "Why Did You Do That," *Collider*, Oct. 19, 2018.

241 **"It surprised me when I saw it"**: Kyle Buchanan, "Is This 'A Star Is Born' Song Supposed to Be Bad or Glorious," *New York Times*, Oct. 19, 2018.

241 **"It was a Lady Gaga song"**: Mark Nilan Jr. to author, Oct. 29, 2024.

242 **"Bradley and I talked about this"**: Howell Taylor to author.

242 **"I've always hated the stigma"**: Jonathan Van Meter, "Boss Lady," *Vogue*, Oct. 2018.

243 **"The energy was high"**: Nilan Jr. to author.

Chapter 18

245 **"A little urine"/"No, a lot"**: Mehta to author.

245 **"We were prepared not to shoot"**: *A Star Is Born* 2018, DVD special features.

245 **"It means a lot because"**: Ibid.

246 **"Stefani's friend had died"**: Mehta to author.

246 **"It was a Grace Kelly image"**: Benach to author.

246 **"They are always trying to put Gaga"**: Howell Taylor to author.

248–49 **"It was definitely open-ended"**: Mehta to author.

249 **"Dude, I know the ending"**: Ibid.

249 **"I liked this idea of a guy"**: Kristopher Tapley, "Listen: Bradley Cooper Explains," *Variety*, Nov. 29, 2018.

250 **"Sobriety, Bradley knows that"**: Mehta to author.

250 **"I don't sleep much"**: Pete Hammond, "Eric Roth on Life as a Top Screenwriter," *Deadline*, Apr. 16, 2021.

250 **"We had our moments [of disagreement]"**: Matt Grobal, "Eric Roth Discusses 'Dune' and 'A Star Is Born,'" *Deadline*, Feb. 13, 2019.

250 **"Gerber asked me to do stuff"**: Fetters to author.

250 **"I drive a truck"**: Dave McNary, "'A Star Is Born' Co-writer Eric Roth," *Variety*, Feb. 8, 2019.

251 **"They were about to sell"**: Rubin to author.

251 **"Bradley, I really don't know what to say"**: *A Star Is Born* 2018, DVD special features.

252 **"It's not romantic"**: Gerber to author.

252 **"$3 million"**: Zillow.

252 **"fun factoid"**: Realtor Lisa Arden to author, Oct. 30, 2024.

Chapter 19

254 **"It received the most enthusiastic"**: Scott Feinberg, "A Star Loses Its Twinkle," *Hollywood Reporter*, Feb. 2019.

254–55 **"Lady Gaga is a real musician"**: Howell Taylor to author.

255 "Working in front of those massive": Pete Hammond, "Eric Roth on Life as a Top Screenwriter," *Deadline*, Apr. 16, 2021.

255 "I was amazed, because": Fetters to author.

255 "People are hungrier for fame": Todd McCarthy, "A Star That Never Sets," *Hollywood Reporter*, Nov. 2018.

256 "I wanted Ally to be nothing": Matthew Belloni, "The Actress Roundtable," *Hollywood Reporter*, Nov. 28, 2018.

257 "Anytime you're trying to tell": Meredith Woerner, "Bradley Cooper: Tapping into Painful Past," *Variety*, Sept. 9, 2018.

257 "I won't have any control": Taffy Brodesser-Akner, "Bradley Cooper Is Not Really Into This Interview," *New York Times*, Sept. 27, 2018.

258 "It was as if the roles": Howell Taylor to author.

258 "It is unclear if Streisand": Kimberly Nordyke, "Barbra Streisand Among Presenters," *Hollywood Reporter*, Feb. 20, 2019.

258 "It was a big thrill": Gerber to author.

258–59 "It was a magical moment": *A Star Is Born* 2018, DVD special features.

259 "stayed in touch": Gerber to author.

259 "You better create a character": Taffy Brodesser-Akner, "Bradley Cooper Is Not Really Into This Interview," *New York Times*, Sept. 27, 2018.

259 "Babs Snubs 'Star' at Oscars": "Babs Snubs 'Star' at Oscars," *New York Post*, Feb. 28, 2019.

260 "$432 million dollars": Financial Report, *The Numbers* website, 2018.

260 "fourth best-selling album of 2019": "Arashi Best-Of

Tops Taylor Swift for IFPI's Best-Selling Album of 2019," *Billboard*, Mar. 19, 2020.

Epilogue

Except as indicated below, quotes in the Epilogue came from the documentary *The Last Movie Stars: Paul Newman and Joanne Woodward*.

262 **"The story always works"**: *A Star Is Born* 1976, DVD special features.

262 **"At first, when I heard it"**: Ethan Shanfield, "Barbra Streisand Says Lady Gaga and Bradley Cooper's 'A Star Is Born' Was 'The Wrong Idea,' " *Variety*, Aug. 16, 2021.

262–63 **"Those were very early conversations"**: Fetters to author.

263 **"What if, for a change, the sexes"**: Todd McCarthy, "A Star That Never Sets," *Hollywood Reporter*, Nov. 2018.

264 **"We talked a lot about it"**: Roddy McDowall to author.

264–65 **"What's the take on it"**: Mehta to author.

266 **"The way I translated that"**: Morella and Epstein, *Paul and Joanne*, 23.

266 **"I don't think so"**: Oumano, *Paul Newman*, 43.

267 **"I've been chewing on that"**: Morella and Epstein, *Paul and Joanne*, 23.

Index